THE JEWS OF SOUTH WALES

THE JEWS OF SOUTH WALES

Edited by
URSULA R. Q. HENRIQUES

CARDIFF
UNIVERSITY OF WALES PRESS

© The Contributors, 2013

Reprinted 2022

British Library Cataloguing-in-Publication Data
A catalogue record for this book is available from the British Library.

ISBN 978-0-7083-2671-8

All rights reserved. No part of this book may be reproduced, stored in a retrieval system, or transmitted, in amy form or by any means, electronic, mechanical, photocopying, recording or otherwise, without clearance from the University of Wales Press, University Registry, King Edward VII Avenue, Cardiff CF10 3NS

The University of Wales Press wishes to make clear that the Joseph Cohen mentioned in chapter 7, 'The Tredegar Riots of August 1911', is not a relation of Anne Denham, David Landau and Anthony Hyatt.

Typeset by Hewer Text UK Ltd, Edinburgh
Printed by CPI Antony Rowe, Chippenham, Wiltshire

Contents

	Page
Preface	vii
Foreword to the New Edition: Conflict and Co-operation: *The Jews of South Wales* and the Study of Welsh Jewry *Paul O'Leary*	xii
Introduction *Ursula R. Q. Henriques*	1
1 The Jewish Community of Cardiff, 1813–1914 *Ursula R. Q. Henriques*	9
2 The Valleys Communities *Anthony Glaser and Ursula R. Q. Henriques*	45
3 The Jews and Crime in South Wales before the First World War *Ursula R. Q. Henriques*	69
4 The Conduct of a Synagogue: Swansea Hebrew Congregation, 1895–1914 *Ursula R. Q. Henriques*	85
5 The Ministry of the Reverend Simon Fyne in Swansea, 1899–1906 *Leonard Mars*	111

6 Lyons versus Thomas: The Jewess Abduction Case, 1867–8   131
   Ursula R. Q. Henriques

7 The Tredegar Riots of August 1911   151
   Anthony Glaser

8 Jewish Refugees and Jewish Refugee Industries   177
   Anthony Glaser

Epilogue   205
   Ursula R. Q. Henriques

List of Jewish Festivals   217

Glossary of Hebrew Words   219

Select Bibliography   221

Index   227

Maps

Jewish Settlement in Cardiff in the 1850s   10
Jewish Communities in Industrial South Wales   46

Preface

This book is about the Jews of South Wales. It is not a comprehensive history, and for this there are several reasons. One is the incomplete and sketchy nature of the available sources. Of the synagogue minute books, an almost indispensable source of information about the communities concerned, Cardiff's great minute book was lost as a result of the floods of 1981. Minutes, rule book and correspondence covering a comparatively short period for Swansea and one of Merthyr Tydfil's minute books are all that have been traced at present. It would have been most helpful to have consulted case records of the local Jewish charitable associations and Boards of Guardians, but few remain. Most of the business records of the truly remarkable group, the Jewish pawnbrokers, have disappeared. Most (although not all) of the families of the original Jewish immigrants have dispersed, taking their memories with them. Here and there a *cause célèbre* such as the Jewess Abduction Case of 1867 or the Tredegar riots of 1911 produced a hoard of official papers or newspaper reports which have survived, or a family business is fresh in the memory. Some of the studies are concentrated on these. Elsewhere, apart from the invaluable reports and correspondence in the *Jewish Chronicle*, we have had to rely on such general sources for the area as trade directories and census reports to help us to arrive indirectly at the history of the Jewish communities within the larger Welsh ones.

Another difficulty in writing the history of the Jews of south Wales — or indeed of any of the provincial Jewries — is the uncertainty as to who were Jews and who were not. We can be certain of those whose names appear on synagogue membership lists, in marriage registers, burial books and on tombstones in Jewish cemeteries. But there were always people of Jewish origin who for one reason or another, perhaps because they had drifted away from the synagogue, or had married a non-Jewish spouse, did not appear on any record. International trading ports and shipping centres such as those on the south Welsh coast attracted foreign residents, many with central European names. Lucovitch, well-known in the port of Cardiff, was an Austrian Roman Catholic count, while the Bruckewiches were probably Jewish.[1] Jewish immigrants, however orthodox or even shy of contacts outside their own community, have a strong propensity to anglicize, or render Welsh their names. Thus Schwarz became Black, Moses became Moss or Morris; in Wales many a Levy turned Lewis. Some names were quite common in both communities, e.g. Harris, Marks, Phillips and Lyons. In the religious climate of the early nineteenth century many Welsh families adopted Old Testament names; Abraham, Isaac, Jacob, Moses, Samuel and Emanuel are as likely to be Welsh as Jewish, although for some reason an 's' on the end, such as Abrahams, Isaacs or Samuels, entails a likelihood of Jewish origin. It follows that all statistical studies of local Jewish populations have to be provisional.

The difficulty of identification contributes to the unsolved problems of population numbers. While it may not have been too difficult to count the numbers of Jews in the smaller valley communities at any one time, we really do not know with any certainty the total number of Jewish immigrants who settled in south Wales, or even Cardiff. Maurice Dennis in 1951 gave the number of Jews resident in Cardiff at the turn of the century as 1,250, a number taken from the Jewish Year Books, which were certainly unreliable, and the total in south Wales as 6,000.[2] Geoffrey Alderman estimates a total in 1900 of 1,500 Jews in Cardiff, in 1914 of 2,000 Jews in Cardiff and altogether 4,500 to 5,000 in south Wales.[3] Henry Samuel, Cardiff correspondent to the *Jewish Chronicle* in the 1930s, thought there were 3,000 in Cardiff in 1904, almost certainly an overestimate. These estimates do not harmonize with the synagogue numbers — usually reckoned in families rather than individuals — which can indicate population trends although not population totals. This problem, as the research unit of the Jewish Board of Deputies agrees, has yet to be solved.[4]

There was not one Jewish community in south Wales, but dozens of them, located in and reflecting the dispersed nature of Welsh urban industrialized society. The consequence of this is not infinite variety but unavoidable repetition. While the historical details of each little community differed the outline was much the same. Each exhibited a roughly similar pattern of economic and social structure but in different stages of development, more advanced in the larger centres of Swansea, Cardiff and to some extent Merthyr Tydfil, less developed in the small towns and villages of the Welsh valleys. Each of these communities displayed similar characteristics, being self-reliant and mutually helpful while fissiparous and quarrelsome internally. But they were also, to a considerable degree, solid in the face of an indifferent and sometimes hostile world.

There is more to be discovered yet of the life of these people, especially during the period of the long decline. There are certainly further sources to be tapped. Meantime we hope that these studies will at least reveal something of the special character of the south Wales Jewish communities.

Among university historians, the pioneer of the study of the Welsh Jewish communities was Dr Geoffrey Alderman with three essays written in the 1970s.[5] If on the basis of further research and consideration we have not always agreed with Dr Alderman's conclusions, this is part of the process by which history advances. We owe much to local historians, notably the writers of historical articles in CAJEX, and especially the late Maurice Dennis.[6] Much help was derived from the fund of local information possessed by the late Mr L. M. Hamburg. The very detailed information available on the Tredegar riots is largely due to the remarkable work of the miner Mr Fred Hopkins, an eyewitness and a natural born historian who, regrettably, died before his long article could be put in shape for publication.[7] We owe much to Mrs Dorene Jacobs, collector and lender of historical material, and to Mr Alan Liss who, in addition to lending his thesis on the history of the Reform Synagogue in Cardiff, has collected and placed many family records in the Glamorgan County Record Office. We acknowledge much help and assistance from the staff of that office, from the staff of the Gwent County Record Office at Cwmbran, from Dr E. G. Cowley and Mr L. Holland of the University College Library, Swansea, and from Mr Brian James, lately of the University College Library, Cardiff. We should like to add the names of Mrs Trudi Levi of the Macotta Library (now the Library of Jewish Studies), University College, London, and Mr Charles Tucker, archivist to the Chief Rabbinate, London, One of the pleasant features of what can sometimes be the hard labour of research is the almost invariable co-operation and friendliness of university librarians and archivists.

The study on the ministry of Revd Simon Fyne is based on a research project on Swansea's Jewish community funded by the Memorial Foundation for Jewish Culture, New York, while the original impetus to write about the minister came from the late Mr Oscar Benjamin, formerly Hon. Solicitor to the Swansea Hebrew Congregation of which he was a member. His keen interest in Jewish history preserved the text of Fyne's lecture and other documents pertaining to Swansea's Jewish community.

We are particularly grateful to the trainee archivists, Helen Redmond-Cooper and Kevin Murphy for their work on both studies of Swansea, as well as Susan Black and Katherine Doyle who assisted in the early stages of the work on Cardiff. A grant from the Manpower Services Commission enabled much source material to be assembled and catalogued with their help.

We wish to thank the authors of a number of then unpublished theses who lent us their work; in particular Herbert Loebl, Paul Brendan O'Leary and Albert Colin Hughes. The titles of these and other dissertations of value will be found in Section III of the bibliography.

We also wish to thank the editor of *Morgannwg* for allowing the essay on 'The Jews and Crime in South Wales before World War I', the editor of the *Welsh History Review* for allowing 'The Jewish Community of Cardiff, 1913–1914', and the editor of the *Transactions of the Jewish Historical Society of England* for allowing 'Lyons versus Thomas: The Jewess Abduction Case' to be reproduced, with minor alterations, in this book.[8] In addition, the editor of *Jewish Social Studies* has permitted the inclusion of a version of Dr Mars's article on the ministry of Revd Simon Fyne in Swansea, which originally appeared in *Jewish Social Studies*, Vol. L, Nos. 1–2 (1988/1992), pp. 83–98.

We greatly appreciate a considerable grant from the Marc Fitch Fund of Oxford towards the cost of publication of this work.

Professor Aubrey Newman of Leicester University lent his microfilm of all the back numbers of the *Jewish Chronicle*, without which it would have been impossible to complete this work. In addition he gave much help and encouragement. Miss Jeane Cunningham undertook the onerous task of reading the proofs.

The history of the provincial Jewish communities, once somewhat neglected, has begun to flourish since the publication in 1976 of Bill Williams's *The Making of Manchester Jewry*.[9] We hope the present book will make a contribution to the revival.

Notes to the Preface

1. See p. 14.
2. Maurice Dennis, 'The Cardiff Jewish Community, part I. The Earliest days', CAJEX, I No. 3 (April 1951). See n.6 below.
3. G. Alderman, 'Into the Vortex: South Wales Jewry before 1914', *Report of the Jewish Historical Society of England*. Conference on 'Provincial Jewry in Victorian England', 6 July 1975, ed. Aubrey Newman.
4. Stanley Waterman and Barry Cosmin, *British Jewry in the Eighties. A Statistical and Geographical guide*, Research Unit, Board of Deputies of British Jews, 1986, 21, Table 9. This has been the subject of further discussion.
5. Geoffrey Alderman, (1) 'Jews and the Host Community. A Study of the Anti-Jewish Riots of August 1911 at Tredegar and adjacent Towns', *Welsh History Review*, 6 (1972), 190–200. (2) 'Into the Vortex. South Wales Jewry before 1914', *Report of the Jewish Historical Society of England*. Conference on 'Provincial Jewry in Victorian England', 6 July 1975. (3) 'The Jew of Scapegoat? The Settlement and Reception of the Jews in South Wales before 1914', *Transactions of the Jewish Historical Society of England*, XXVI (1974–8), 62–70.
6. CAJEX is the magazine of the Cardiff Association of Jewish Ex-servicemen, which serves the community of Cardiff.
7. Some of the footnotes have had to be made from a defective copy.
8. a. 'The Jews and Crime in South Wales before World War I', *Morgannwg*, XXIX (1985), 59–71.
   b. 'The Jewish Community of Cardiff', *The Welsh History Review*, 14 No. 2 (1988–9), 269–300.
   c. 'Lyons versus Thomas: The Jewess Abduction Case', *Transactions of the Jewish Historical Society of England*, XXIX (1982–86), 267–80).
9. Bill Williams, *The Making of Manchester Jewry* (Manchester University Press, 1976).

Foreword to the New Edition

Conflict and Co-operation:
The Jews of South Wales
and the Study of Welsh Jewry

PAUL O'LEARY

When this book was first published in 1993 it represented an important stage in the development of our understanding of the country's Jewish history. It also marked an important point in the development of studies of ethnic minorities in Wales in general.[1] Our understanding of the ethnic diversity of the country is now deeper and more thoroughly researched than it was at that time, and twenty years later it is time to assess the book's significance and to ask how we should locate it in the field of Jewish studies in Wales.

A number of historians had written articles about the history of Welsh Jewry before this book appeared, but the book provided an opportunity for taking stock of the field. Geoffrey Alderman, a distinguished historian of British Jewry, pointed out that these essays exemplified the 'rise, growth and ultimate decline of Jewish communities in provincial Britain', but that there was an unique dimension to the story of the Jews in Wales in the shape of the Tredegar riots of 1911.[2] One context for assessing the book's contribution, therefore, was in the light of other studies of Jewish communities in Britain outside London. Here the yardstick was a pioneering book about Manchester by Bill Williams, *The Making of Manchester Jewry, 1740–1875* (1976). Another distinguished historian of British Jewry, Tony Kushner, compared the two studies and thought that *The Jews of South Wales* suffered from the comparison.[3] In some ways, it was an unfair judgement. A group of essays by different hands was bound to be less compelling than a systematic study by one author, but Kushner did accept that one problem facing historians of Welsh Jewry was the fact that the sources for Jewish communities in Wales were patchy.

Outside academia, the controversial Labour politician Leo Abse launched an uncompromising attack on the book, sometimes accusing it of deficiencies it did not possess, but occasionally pointing out additional dimensions to the story that *The Jews of South Wales* had not covered. To this heady mix he added some compelling family history.[4] Abse bemoaned what he saw as the emphasis in these essays on the 'small-minded, inward-looking synagogal Jew' and he argued that non-religious Jews had been ignored.[5] For Abse, the really significant relationships between Jewish immigrants and the host community lay beyond what he described as the 'ghettos' of the synagogue and the pawnshop. He drew attention to the experiences of individuals such as the assimilated German Jew Ludwig Mond of Clydach (1839–1909) — chemist, founder of ICI and the only Jew to be memorialized in Wales with a public statue. He also mentioned neglected women, such as the novelist Lily Tobias and the Communist Dora Cox.[6] Abse also described links between anarchist Jews from the East End of London and syndicalists in south Wales, as well as pointing to the role of Jewish promoters of cinema in the industrial valleys. Ursula Henriques responded to these criticisms in an admirably restrained letter pointing out that Abse had attacked her for something she had never claimed: *The Jews of South Wales* had never set itself up to be a comprehensive history of all aspects of Welsh Jewry.[7]

One crucial area where Abse and Henriques disagreed was in their emphases on the balance between integration and conflict. Abse confidently asserted: 'Happily, the story of the Jews in south Wales is more of collaboration than conflict.'[8] He drew attention to the links between Welsh Nonconformists and Jews, both being 'people of the Book', whereas Ursula Henriques properly insisted that the examples of religious conflict presented in *The Jews of South Wales* related to Baptists only and were not intended to be a portrayal of attitudes among all Nonconformist denominations. More research was needed in this area before generalizations could be made, she insisted. That research remains to be carried out. Furthermore, Abse's insistence on collaboration as the dominant relationship between Jews and the Welsh led him to dismiss the Tredegar riots of 1911 as an unimportant skirmish. In so doing, his comments prefigured a bitter academic debate that would begin later in the 1990s.

A revisionist view of the Tredegar riots of 1911 was launched by the historian William D. Rubinstein in 1997.[9] Rubinstein argued that the violent events of that year were not anti-Semitic at all but were simply the consequence of acute social and economic conditions. The anti-Jewish element of these riots, he maintained, was exaggerated at the time to create a press sensation, and contemporary terms such as 'pogrom' or 'near-pogrom' were very wide of the mark. In contrast to the received view of the disturbances as being fundamentally anti-Semitic in nature, he argued the precise opposite, claiming that *philo*semitism (respect or admiration for the Jews) was largely ubiquitous in south Wales at that time. This fitted in with a broader argument he constructed about the English-speaking world being characterized by philosemitism.[10]

This revisionist view was startling because the riots at Tredgar and elsewhere in south Wales in 1911 had been the subject of intensive research that came to very different conclusions to those of Rubinstein. The evidence for the riots has been worked over systematically by a number of historians, all of whom have been convinced by the evidence that the disturbances were anti-Semitic in character (although Anthony Glaser in this volume concluded that they were an enigma).[11] Geoffrey Alderman's response to the revisionist approach accused Rubinstein of ignoring evidence that did not conform to his preconceptions about the prevalence of philosemitism in British and Welsh society: where Rubinstein had encountered evidence that contradicted his views he had either failed to discuss it or questioned its veracity or significance without good reason.[12] In the sense of historians assessing the evidence for certain truth claims about the past, the revisionist approach to the riots was scrutinized and was found wanting.

Whether knowingly or otherwise, the revisionist argument recycled ideas of Wales as a tolerant society (under the guise of philosemitism) that had been questioned and largely discredited by scholars over the previous decades.[13] Toleration presupposes a defined power relationship, specifying the place of minorities as subordinate to an assumed national consensus; in a 'tolerant society' the majority endure, not embrace, minority cultures, extending to them the space to nurture their beliefs and customs rather than endowing them with the rights to do so. In such circumstances toleration is not unconditional. Implicit in such a relationship is the proviso that toleration can be revoked should the majority feel that their identity is under threat. Thus, in an important and paradoxical sense, the way in which the conception of a tolerant society has been articulated holds within it the possibility of a negative response to minorities as well as a hospitable one, on the grounds that a minority culture will not be endured where it is perceived to threaten the values of the host society. Such a threat can be perceived to have emerged without changes occurring in the culture or behaviour of the minority; a change in external circumstances (as in economic depression or war) can be sufficient to precipitate a hostile reaction. It can be argued that this is precisely what happened in the western valleys of Monmouthshire in 1911. The idea of philosemitism is too imprecise and all-encompassing to capture this kind of circumstance adequately. Furthermore, it assumes that opposition in some quarters to violence against Jews is equivalent to a positive attitude to Jewish people, a claim that is very difficult to substantiate.

If it is desirable to adopt a more nuanced approach to what has been characterized as philosemitism, it is also necessary to distinguish between different types of hostility. The Tredegar riots have been scrutinized so assiduously precisely because they were not a common occurrence. In an attempt to clarify the terminology used to describe the various complex expressions of hostility, Colin Holmes discerns a qualitative difference between 'prejudice' and 'antipathy'. The former is seen as the intense pathological hostility of some individuals arising from a personality disturbance and remains a constant feature of their psychological make-up, while the latter is generated by social and cultural factors and varies in intensity according to conditions external to the individual's psyche. This distinction at the analytic level is particularly useful. When applied to ethnic conflict in Welsh society in the nineteenth- and early-twentieth centuries, it allows us to identify antipathy (as defined above) not prejudice as the dominant expression of enmity.[14]

While debates about anti-Semitism and philosemitism have taken centre stage in publications about Jewish communities in recent decades, our understanding of the growth and decline of Welsh Jewish communities has developed in other ways, too. The 1990s was a seminal decade for research about Welsh Jews. The unpublished thesis by David Morris has answered many of the criticisms of Tony Kushner by locating the study of these communities in a new academic context.[15] Among the important features of his important study is a discussion of the professionalization of Welsh Jews after 1945, an analysis of the process of secularization, and a consideration of the problematic nature of assimilation. In addition to Morris's work, cultural historians have placed broader Jewish–Welsh interactions under the microscope, including literary and political interactions, as well as the distinctive cinematic depiction of Jewish–Welsh relations in the Oscar-nominated film *Solomon & Gaenor*.[16]

The context for the study of the Welsh Jewry has changed in important ways since *The Jews of South Wales* was first published. This can be demonstrated most clearly by examining how current debates about Jewish history and culture compare with those relating to other minority ethnic groups. A recent study of the Italians in modern Wales, for example, has shown how devolution and the creation of the National Assembly for Wales in 1999 has been accompanied by a new ideology of inclusivity that the Italians and their cafés appear to epitomize.[17] While the Italians are presented as a 'model' minority in this culture of inclusivity, it has been difficult to portray Welsh Jews in those terms because of the continuing debate about the Tredegar riots of 1911 and because the most important examples of awareness of Jewish heritage in popular culture also relate to that incident.

The extent to which the history of the Jews in Wales can be considered one predominantly characterized by conflict or co-operation remains a live issue. In 1993 Leo Abse made the pessimistic assertion that 'the full story of the South Wales Jews is, I fear, never to be told'.[18] If by 'the full story' Abse meant an acknowledgement of the diversity of Welsh Jewry, his fears were misplaced. The study of the history of Jews in Wales was not closed down by *The Jews of South Wales*, as Abse implied it would be. Instead, it sparked an unprecedented period of historical and cultural enquiry that continues unabated.

Notes to the Foreword to the New Edition

1. Colin Hughes, *Lime, Lemon and Sarsaparilla: The Italian Community in South Wales, 1881–1945* (Bridgend, Seren Books, 1992); Paul O'Leary, *Immigration and Integration: The Irish in Wales, 1798–1922* (Cardiff, University of Wales Press, 2000); Charlotte Williams, Neil Evans and Paul O'Leary (eds), *A Tolerant Nation? Exploring Ethnic Diversity in Modern Wales* (Cardiff, University of Wales Press, 2003); Paul O'Leary (ed.), *Irish Migrants in Modern Wales* (Liverpool, Liverpool University Press, 2004); Alan Llwyd, *Black Wales: A History of Black Welsh People* (Cardiff, Hughes and Sons, 2005).
2. Review in *English Historical Review*, 111/440 (1996), 239–40.
3. Review in *Albion*, 25/4 (1993), 746–8.
4. Leo Abse, 'A tale of collaboration not conflict with the "People of the Book"', *New Welsh Review*, 22 (Autumn 1993), 16–22.

5. Ibid., 17.
6. Frank Greenaway, 'Mond family (per. 1867–1973)', *Oxford Dictionary of National Biography* (Oxford, Oxford University Press, 2004); online edn, January 2011 (*http://www.oxforddnb.com/view/article/51124*, accessed 5 December 2012); Jasmine Donahaye, 'Introduction' to *Eunice Fleet* by Lily Tobias (Dinas Powys, Honno Press, 2004), pp. ix–xxii; eadem, ' "The link of common aspirations": Wales in the work of Lily Tobias', in Claire Tylee (ed.), *In the Open: Jewish Women Writers and British Culture* (Newark, Delaware, University of Delaware Press, 2006), pp. 147–63.
7. Ursula Henriques, 'The Jews of south Wales', *New Welsh Review*, 23 (Winter 1993/4), 85. See also Robin Reeves, 'Multiculturality in Wales', in Eberhardt Bort and Neil Evans (eds), *Networking Europe: Essays on Regionalism and Social Democracy* (Liverpool, Liverpool University Press, 2000), pp. 297–310.
8. Abse, 'A tale of collaboration not conflict', 19.
9. W.D. Rubinstein, 'The anti-Jewish riots of 1911 in south Wales', *Welsh History Review*, 18 (1997), 667–99.
10. W.D. Rubinstein and Hilary L. Rubinstein, *Philosemitism: Admiration and Support in the English-Speaking World for Jews, 1840–1939* (New York, St Martin's Press, 1999); see also Tony Kushner and Nadia Valman (eds), *Philosemitism, Antisemitism and 'the Jews': Perspectives from the Middle Ages to the Twentieth Century* (Aldershot, Ashgate, 2004).
11. Geoffrey Alderman, 'The anti-Jewish riots of August 1911 in South Wales', *Welsh History Review*, 6 (1972/73), 190–200; eadem, 'The Jew as scapegoat? The settlement and reception of Jews in south Wales before 1914', *Transactions of the Jewish Historical Society of England*, 26 (1974–8), 62–70; Colin Holmes, 'The Tredegar riots of 1911: anti-Jewish disturbances in south Wales', *Welsh History Review*, 11/2 (1982), 214–25; Anthony Glaser, 'The Tredegar riots of 1911', below, pp. 151–76.
12. Geoffrey Alderman, 'The anti-Jewish riots of August 1911 in south Wales: a response', *Welsh History Review*, 20 (2001), 564–71. Some of Alderman's work on south Wales is reprinted in Herbert A. Strauss (ed.), *Hostages of Modernization: Studies on Modern Antisemitism, 1870–1938/9* (Berlin, Walter de Gruyter and Co., 1992), pp. 365–75; Geoffrey Alderman, *Controversy and Crisis: Studies in the History of Jews in Modern Britain* (Brighton, MA., Academic Studies Press, 2008), pp. 53–82.
13. See, for example, Williams, Evans and O'Leary (eds), *A Tolerant Nation?*; Louise Miskell, 'Reassessing the anti-Irish riot: popular protest and the Irish in south Wales, c.1826–1882', in O'Leary (ed.), *Irish Migrants in Modern Wales*, pp. 101–18; O'Leary, *Immigration and Integration*; Paul O'Leary, 'When was anti-Catholicism? The case of nineteenth- and twentieth-century Wales', *Journal of Ecclesiastical History*, 56/2 (April 2005), 307–25.

14. Colin Holmes, *A Tolerant Country? Immigrants, Refugees and Minorities in Britain* (London, Faber, 1991).
15. David Morris, 'The history of the Welsh Jewish communities, 1750 to the present', unpublished PhD thesis, University of Wales, 1999.
16. Grahame Davies (ed.), *The Chosen People: Wales and the Jews* (Bridgend, Seren Books, 2002); Jasmine Donahaye, ' "A dislocation called a blessing": three Welsh Jewish perspectives', *Welsh Writing in English: A Yearbook of Critical Essays*, 7 (2002), 154–73; eadem, ' "By whom shall she arise? For she is small": the Wales–Israel tradition in the Edwardian period', in Nadia Valman and Eitan Bar Yosef (eds), *The Jew in Late-Victorian and Edwardian Culture: Between the East End and East Africa* (Basingstoke, Palgrave, 2009); eadem, *Whose People? Wales, Israel, Palestine* (Cardiff, University of Wales Press, 2012), 161–82; Steve Blandford, *Film, Drama and the Break-Up of Britain* (Bristol, Intellect Books, 2007), pp. 89–91; Paul O'Leary, 'Film, history and anti-Semitism: *Solomon & Gaenor* (1999) and representations of the past', *North American Journal of Welsh Studies*, 7 (2012), 38–52 (http://welshstudiesjournal.org/article/view/25).
17. Marco Giudici, 'Migration, memory and identity: Italians and nation-building in Wales, 1940–2010', unpublished PhD thesis, Bangor University, 2012.
18. Abse, 'A tale of collaboration not conflict', 21.

Introduction

URSULA R. Q. HENRIQUES

I

The Jews were expelled from England in 1290. They did not return openly until they were invited unofficially (since no parliament could be relied on to legitimate them), by Oliver Cromwell.[1] In the second half of the seventeenth century a small group of Jewish merchants of Sephardi origin (that is from the Latin countries, Portugal, Spain and later Italy), were living in London where in 1701, moving from a room in Creechurch Lane, they founded their own synagogue, Bevis Marks. Their numbers were soon augmented by a growing body of Ashkenazi Jews from central Europe. Throughout the eighteenth century the population slowly increased until by the end of the century there were some eighteen to twenty thousand Jews living in London, with small colonies in some of the provincial towns and the large ports. An unknown number of Jewish pedlars wandered about the country selling trinkets, needles, scissors and other articles of use to the housewife who had no access to shops, often returning to base in one of the towns on Friday evenings for the Sabbath. A despised minority, they were rejected by the churches and subject to vicious stereotyping in the broadsheets.[2] However, they were, on the whole, tolerated by a British society already, perforce, getting used to a variety of sects, and generally more moderate and tolerant than its Roman Catholic continental neighbours.[3] Although there was harassment there were no serious anti-Jewish outbreaks in the eighteenth century, apart from the London riots of 1753 in response to a bill to enable long-resident Jews to become naturalized, precipitated by the jealousy of London merchants for the richer elements in the London Jewish colony.

During the nineteenth century, Jewish immigration into Britain speeded up. It came from Russia, which included a large part of Poland, and central Europe where nationalist movements, under a liberal flag, were accompanied by anti-Semitism. In Russia the Jews were mostly compelled to live in the 'Pale of Settlement', extending along the Russian-Polish border from the Baltic to the Black Sea. They were restricted in education and occupation, and conscripted into the Russian army where they were automatically excluded from promotion to officer. Sir Moses Montefiore, the Anglo-Jewish philanthropist, returning from a journey to Russian Poland, reported to the Russian minister Count Kisseleff that the Jews in that part of the Russian empire were subject to gross discrimination. They could not work for nor employ a Christian, they paid extra taxes, could not live near towns nor on the frontier, could own no land and were recruited by force into the army.[4] With the accession of the Czar Alexander II some of the anti-Jewish restrictions were relaxed. But the assassination of Alexander in 1881 was followed by a wave of anti-Jewish pogroms. Starting in Elizavetgrad in April of that year they spread through the neighbouring districts until by December some two hundred villages had been attacked and looted. For the next three decades these sporadic populist attacks continued. In 1882 there were pogroms in the Ukraine and on the considerable Jewish population of Odessa on the Black Sea. In 1903 a mob at Kishinev killed forty-nine Jews and injured some five hundred more.[5] The Russian government encouraged the violence and the looting and responded to it by further repressive edicts. Such an outlet for popular discontent was useful in distracting attention from the shortcomings of the regime.

From 1881 onwards Jewish emigration from Russia, Poland and Romania (which was equally violent in its anti-Semitism) became a tidal wave. The main destination was America, and most of the immigrants landing in London or the north-east ports headed for Liverpool and Glasgow, hopefully on their way to the New World. Some remained, and the East End of London, the industrial towns of Leeds, Bradford, Liverpool and Manchester all acquired Russo-Jewish colonies.

South Wales was not on the main emigrant route, and Jewish settlement there came comparatively late and in relatively small numbers. The first known settled community (as opposed to visiting pedlars and a few individual residents) was in the third quarter of the eighteenth century in Swansea, then a flourishing sea port.[6] The Cardiff community was founded in 1813, and there were already Jews living in Merthyr Tydfil in 1848. During the nineteenth century numbers in south Wales increased fairly rapidly, attracted by the opportunity to make a living in the rapidly industrializing ports and valley settlements of the area. Exactly how they came is not at present clear, although it may have been under the heading of 'chain immigration', i.e. newcomers joining or bringing in their families. Their journeys were facilitated by the new railways. A striking number of British-born Jewish families in the mid-century census returns included an elderly relative born in Poland. Although some of the Jewish families in England had a long ancestry there, most of the Welsh Jews were comparatively recent arrivals, and the Jewish settlements were built up by successive waves of immigrants.

II

The Jews are apt to regard themselves, and to be regarded by others, as a unique phenomenon in history. They did exhibit certain special features. There was a diaspora in every country of a people without a country, professing a religion repudiated by and repudiating the majority religions of their hosts, distinguished by its own languages — Hebrew and Yiddish or Ladino — bound by a detailed code of dietary laws and religious customs and sometimes dress, all calculated to prevent it dissolving into the societies in which it lived. The Jews were thus particularly vulnerable. Much of the poverty of those in eastern Europe, which would have classed them today as 'economic migrants', was artificially induced by persecution or discrimination. However, recently historians have begun to see the Jews in the context of other immigrant communities in nineteenth- and twentieth-century Britain.[7] Comparisons are made with the Italians, the Germans, the Chinese, and above all, the Irish, not to mention the more recent immigrants from the West Indies, Africa, India and Pakistan.[8] The comparison is not unreasonable, seeing that many of these immigrant groups encountered similar experiences. In this context it is illuminating to consider what disadvantages were most likely to arouse the hostility of the receiving populations against them, and endanger peaceful settlement in their new land.

Whatever the well-meaning may say there is always danger to immigrants when they arrive in such large numbers that they appear to swamp the long-settled natives. Fortunately this danger was not overwhelming in south Wales where all the coastal towns and industrial valleys were in fact immigrant colonies, successively filled with incomers from rural Wales and the neighbouring English counties, and where there was a very small long-resident population.[9] None the less, the Irish, already present in south Wales as diggers of canals and builders of railways, were not popular when they flooded in during the Irish famine years of 1846–9. Thereafter, impelled by starvation, evictions and an oppressive colonial-type regime, they kept coming until the flow slackened in the 1880s.[10] The full force of the flood was caught by Liverpool and Glasgow, but many came to Cardiff where their congregation in the dock area made them conspicuous. They were not legally foreigners since they were British subjects until 1922, but with their peasant background, poverty, and attachment to the Roman Catholic Church, they seem to have been regarded as people from another and inferior country. But for their British nationality it is not unlikely that they would have preceded the Jews as subjects of an Aliens Immigration Act such as that passed in 1905. Where there are destitute immigrants compassion is soon exhausted, and the main enemies of the very poor are often the classes just above them. Because of their numbers and destitution the Irish were felt to endanger employment by undercutting wages and forcing the local people out of jobs, and this fear turned to fury when Irish labourers were occasionally imported as strike-breakers. Irish masons, carpenters and smiths were kept out of skilled jobs by jealousy and fear of competition and forced down into the mass of unskilled heavy labourers.[11] Later, in the Rhondda, they were effectively excluded from the more highly paid underground jobs in the coalmines.

It was said of the Irish in London that they could undersell even the Jewish orange-sellers, since the Jews went home at night to a warm room while the Irish lay down in the gutter. With the fear for employment goes the fear for housing and the competition for shelter. In Cardiff high rents led to multi-occupation, and the festering slums of mid-nineteenth-century Cardiff housed many more Irish than Jews. One small house in the Irish quarter was said to house thirty-six tenants by day and more at night. However, once fully established in their own quarter north of the docks, they in turn violently repelled coloured and Asian seamen trying to spread northwards from Tiger Bay.[12]

Comparable with the Irish, although much fewer in number, were the Chinese immigrants whom the vagaries of the East India trade dumped in the south Welsh ports in the later nineteenth century. Hired as crew on the tramp steamers which carried coals from Cardiff and Barry around the world, they also were felt to undercut the wages of British seamen and, being docile, they also acted as strike-breakers. Curiously the Chinese fell foul of another cause of hostility to immigrants — sexual jealousy. This is usually associated with rich rather than poor newcomers, for example the popular saying about the gallant American soldiers in Second World War: 'They're over-sexed, over-paid and over here'. The Chinese were not rich, but in addition to smoking opium they were perceived to be too successful in attracting English and Welsh women, whether as mistresses or as wives, and in this case the jealousy was obviously associated with colour prejudice. In the first decade of the twentieth century the Chinese suddenly appeared in the trade directories as owners of most of the smaller laundries in Cardiff. They were the targets of a furious riot in 1911 which, first directed against Chinese sailors, ended in the destruction of the laundries.[13] Later, when they turned to the restaurant business, the hostility died away.

Rather than arousing sexual jealousy the Irish were associated with drunkenness, prostitution and petty crime. But they also fell foul of two other general causes of immigrant unpopularity, religion and politics. Violent Irish nationalism, and especially the Fenians and the Phoenix Park murders, engendered a media attack and a hatred which spread into a prejudice against even the most innocent of Irish residents. This was slightly mitigated in Welsh circles by sympathy with Irish aspirations to Home Rule. But the Irish were Roman Catholics, and not infrequently wore their religion as a sign of their nationalism. In Nonconformist Wales the Catholic Church was probably more unpopular than the synagogue.

Perhaps the least unpopular of the immigrant groups, and those who in some respects most closely resembled the Jews in Wales, were the Italians. Theirs was a small migration, rising from only 243 in the census of 1871 to 1,531 in that of 1921. Most of the Italians who settled in the valleys had been sharecropping peasants in the valley of the Ceno in northern Italy. They were fleeing not from persecution but from desperate poverty. Their forerunners in Wales had been street musicians and organ grinders, but the immigrants from Ceno took up ice-cream selling and the running of cafés and fish and chip shops. Their numbers were not menacing, they were well spread out, they did not compete for the main industrial jobs, and they performed a useful service in the towns and villages where they lived. Their Roman Catholicism does not seem to have aroused religious hostility as it did against the Irish. They remained in touch with their roots in Italy, but those who had not been naturalized shared with the Jewish refugees from Germany in the Second World War the traumatic experience of being arrested as enemy aliens, thrown into concentration camps, and shipped abroad in unprotected ships, at least one of which was torpedoed with many casualties.[14]

The Jewish immigrants in Wales, more by luck than wit, steered clear of most of the obvious dangers to new settlers. Even after 1882 their numbers did not compare with those of the Irish. The trades they brought with them or adopted on arrival did not compete with the main kinds of industrial employment. There were few Jewish seamen or dockers. A small group of steel workers in Dowlais soon left for Canada. The few who went down the pits were for the most part only temporary miners, and those who stayed in the industry joined the Union, which was seen as a guarantee against undercutting wages. In Cardiff, after an initial tendency to cluster in Bute Street, they soon spread out through the developing town, while in the valleys their occupations as shopkeepers and pawnbrokers encouraged dispersal. There were never the large Jewish areas of bad housing and sweat shops which invited accusation that they were a danger to public health as in east London or Leeds. They did not compete on a large scale for housing, although a minority tended to be unpopular landlords. Their trade as pawnbrokers could not have endeared them to their local communities, as did the ice-cream carts and cosy cafés of the Italians, and probably served to reinforce the 'money bags' image. Yet it provided a vital service in working-class areas. Their village shops could be an alternative to company stores. They did not, as a rule, add to the burden of the poor rate since they took care to relieve their own poor, although this has sometimes been exaggerated by their defenders — there were a few Jews in the workhouses. They did not compete for the favours of young women since marrying out of the Jewish faith was taboo. They were not associated with unpopular political causes. Even Zionism, which began to gather some political reality at the end of the nineteenth century, was little recognized by the general public. It is a curious phenomenon that Jews, the only immigrants without emotional ties to a foreign state or nation, many of them passionately attached to Britain, were frequently accused by anti-Semites of divided loyalties. Since the establishment of the state of Israel the old accusation has rarely been heard; but there is usually an element of irrationality in anti-Semitism. One prejudice the Jews could not avoid was racism. This by-product of slavery and of colonial rule over peoples perceived as less civilized than the white races of Europe did little damage to Jews throughout most of the nineteenth century. Disraeli in his romantic novels praised the Jews as a superior race. Only when the French philosopher and diplomat Gobineau exalted racism into a pseudo science, which was adopted by German nationalists towards the end of the century, did it begin to form a substantial basis for anti-Semitism. In Britain, while the physical results of poverty and ghetto-dwelling were sometimes mistaken for racial characteristics, racism after the Second World War was to menace coloured and Asian migrants more than the Jews. If the Jews of south Wales formed one minority among several, their position in the local society was not less favourable than most, and more favourable than that of the Irish. There were anti-Irish riots and attacks on Irish houses in 1848, 1882 and indeed all through the nineteenth century. In 1911 there were riots against the Chinese, and in 1919 serious riots against coloured seamen in Cardiff. There was only one serious attack on the Jews, in 1911 at Tredegar. There was an undercurrent of popular semi-automatic anti-Semitism, usually not very dangerous. Mrs Bernstein, retired owner of a small drapery store in Abertillery, remembering her childhood before the First World War, said she was called 'B— Jew' in school. Yet she still retained friends from her schooldays. The neighbours were respectful. They would talk about 'B— Jews; we don't mean you'.[15] At Brynmawr, the *cheder* (religion school) had a fighting team led by a stout lad called Lennie Myers which used to fight with a well-known Christian gang called the J.C.Gs.[16] As we shall see in Chapter 3 a more serious form of anti-Semitic prejudice tended to surface in the local courts, and there was a nasty incident at Pontypridd in September 1903 when a girl was supposed to have been abducted for ritual purposes, wrapped in a sheet and pricked with needles. But when questioned she said she had 'been doing it for a lark'.[17] Despite this, the Jews made economic and social progress and although they had arrived as impoverished immigrants, it would be fair to say that they became, generally speaking, reasonably well accepted in south Wales.

Notes to Introduction

1. H.S.Q. Henriques, *The Return of the Jews to England* (London, Macmillan, 1905); Cecil Roth, *History of the Jews in England* (Oxford, Clarendon Press, 1941), *passim*.
2. See a board game kept in the Mocatta Library (now Jewish Studies Library), University College, London. The aim of the players was to get their dice onto the Jew's money bag.
3. U.R.Q. Henriques, *Religious Toleration in England 1787–1833* (London, Routledge and Kegan Paul, 1961), *passim*.
4. L. Loewe (ed.), *The Diaries of Sir Moses and Lady Montefiore* (London, Griffith Forman & Co., 1890), 381–2.
5. Martin Gilbert, *Exile and Return* (London, Weidenfeld and Nicholson, 1978), 38, 58.
6. Neville Saunders, *The Swansea Hebrew Congregation 1730–1980* (1980), 29.
7. Colin Holmes, *John Bull's Island: Immigration and British Society, 1871–1971*, (London, Macmillan Education, 1988). Colin Holmes (ed.), *Immigrants and Minorities in British Society* (London, George Allen and Unwin, 1978). Neil Evans, 'Immigrants and Minorities in Wales, 1840–1940: A Comparative Perspective', *Llafur*, 5 No.4 (1991), 5–26.
8. Paul O'Leary, 'Anti-Irish Riots in Wales, 1826–1882', *Llafur*, 5 No.4 (1991), 27–36.
9. Philip N. Jones, 'Population Immigration into Glamorgan, 1861–1911: A Reassessment', *Glamorgan County History VI* (1988), 122.
10. O'Leary, op.cit., *Llafur*, 5 No.4 (1991), 27–36.
11. Ibid. See also Paul Brendan O'Leary, 'Immigration and Integration: A Study of the Irish in Wales 1798–1922', (unpublished University of Wales Ph.D. thesis, 1989). John Hickey, *Urban Catholics* (Catholic Book Club, 1967), 78.
12. Neil Evans, 'The South Wales Race Riots of 1919', *Llafur*, 3 No.1 (1980), 5–18.
13. Colin Holmes, *John Bull's Island*, 30. Joanne M. Cayford, 'In Search of John Chinaman: Press Representations of the Chinese in Cardiff 1908–1911', *Llafur*, 5 No.4 (1991), 45–6.
14. The *Arandora Star* was lost with 486 Italians and 175 Germans. Albert Colin Hughes, 'The Italian Community in South Wales, 1870–1943' (unpublished University of Wales MA thesis, 1988), 110 and *passim*.
15. Mrs Bernstein, widow, lately of 1 Dorchester Court, Brandreth Road, Cardiff; now deceased.
16. David Morris reminiscing in a seminar on the 'Valley Communities' held in Cardiff, reported in CAJEX, 26 No.4 (1976), 42. Fred Hopkins tells us that when the son of an Italian immigrant made the local anti-Semitic sign, crossing his index fingers and spitting over them, Lennie promptly knocked him down.
17. *Jewish Chronicle*, 25 September 1903. Evidently she didn't know much about ritual practice!

1

The Jewish Community of Cardiff, 1813–1914

URSULA R. Q. HENRIQUES

I

The first Jewish settlers arrived in Cardiff in 1813. In the course of the eighteenth century, pedlars and traders had visited the town but none had stayed. Indeed, there was little to keep them. In 1800 Cardiff was a small town situated at the mouth of the River Taff. It was surrounded by hills on the north, and marshes and tidal mudflats on the west, south and east. It probably owed what importance it had to its position on the highway (now the A48) from England into south and west Wales. It was the third guardian of that route, west of Chepstow and Newport, and possessed a ruined Norman castle, a fine late-medieval church and a cluster of small streets. These stretched southward from the castle to Bridge Street, where the newly opened Glamorganshire Canal Basin allowed boats and barges up to 200 tons, in addition to those which used the Taff quays abutting on the west side of St Mary Street, to come close to the town centre. Its two main streets, St Mary Street and Crockherbtown (now Queen Street), met at right angles in front of the castle, and already housed its main shops and businesses. An ancient borough, with its administrative wards based on the two parishes of St John and St Mary (extended to four wards in the late eighteenth century), it had changed comparatively little since the seventeenth century. Although the new canal linking Cardiff and Merthyr Tydfil foreshadowed more expansive days ahead, such a small community had little to offer the immigrants of whom provincial Jewry was largely composed. The primary need was to make a living, and small British market or fishing towns before the Industrial Revolution had few unfilled niches which could afford opportunities for this.

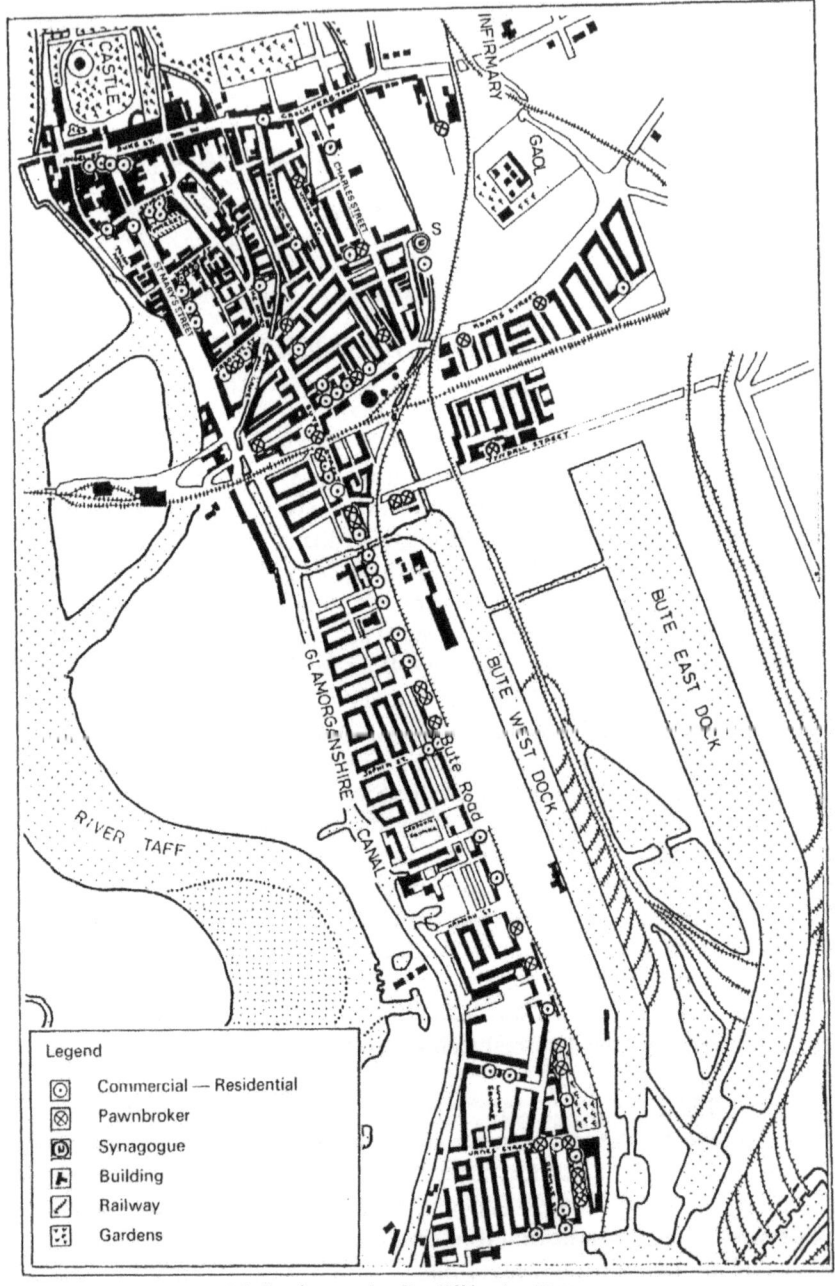

Jewish Settlement in Cardiff in the 1850s

In 1801 the total population of Cardiff was still under 2,000, but it was beginning to grow. In 1811 it was given as 2,457. By mid-century it had reached 18,351, or 20,258 if the growing suburbs are included. Moreover, following the 1835 Municipal Corporations Act, it had changed its administration from that of an archaic closed borough to something approximating a modern municipality based on a £10 rent-payers' franchise.[1] Equally important, the growth of Welsh Nonconformity had broken the monopoly of the Church of England, and while some of the chapel sects were by no means friendly to Jews, it was easier for a Hebrew congregation to maintain a toehold in a religiously pluralistic society.

The first arrivals in Cardiff were Michael and Levi Marks. They had been born in Neath where, it seems, a few Jewish families had settled as an offshoot of Swansea, the oldest Jewish community in south Wales. Why they decided to come is unknown, but Levi set up as a slop-seller (or vendor of cheap ready-made working clothes) and Michael as a watchmaker, both typical immigrant trades. In 1829 Mark and Solomon Marks, sons of Michael, were recorded as watchmakers and jewellers in Angel Street (now Westgate Street), while Mark also remained a slop-seller in St Mary Street. This successful establishment in Cardiff may have attracted other members of the family. The census enumerator's report of 1841 reveals a Samuel Marks, dyer, at No.3 Arcade, Church Street, off St Mary Street. He and his father came from Middlesex, but his wife, Anne, was from Neath.

The Marks were no starving pedlars but at least second-generation in Britain, and well assimilated. In 1858 Mark wrote proudly to the *Jewish Chronicle* that his father had been a volunteer in Neath during the French invasion of Fishguard in 1796, that he and his brother had served in the East Glamorganshire Militia, and that he personally had been on duty in the Merthyr Riots of 1831.[2]

The brothers were ambitious, and Mark set up as an auctioneer and valuer. But he evidently overreached himself, for in 1835 he went bankrupt and had to be released on petition from the debtors' wing of Cardiff gaol.[3] Thereafter, the family prospered. By 1858 Mark was established as a house and estate agent, appraiser and auctioneer at 9 St Mary Street.[4] Solomon was registered as Marks & Co., Watch and Nautical Instrument Maker, 101 Bute Road.[5] Later he became well known in the life of the docks, and was one of those who signed a petition to Parliament in the Bute interest against the scheme for building a rival dock at Barry. He was awarded a testimonial in 1877.[6] He died at the age of 83, and a memorial was erected to him in Highfield cemetery in gratitude for his many services to the Hebrew Congregation — although he had married his wife, Mary Ann, in St Mary Redcliffe, Bristol. Mark's eldest son Barnett, as well as being a well-known portrait painter, became, like his father, a pillar of the Hebrew Congregation, while the next two sons, Levi and Nelson, were baptized in 1853.[7] In 1841 it was to Mark, Solomon and Samuel Marks that the second Marquis of Bute donated the land at Highfield for a Jewish cemetery which marked the formal start of an independent Jewish community in Cardiff (before that the dead had to be shipped to Bristol for burial).[8] It is no exaggeration to attribute to this somewhat wayward clan the foundation of the Cardiff Jewish community, which they continued to dominate until well into the second half of the nineteenth century.[9]

Cardiff, as its historians have pointed out, took its rise as a great coal-exporting port from the opening of the Bute West Dock in 1839. Before that, most of the coal from the south Wales valleys had been exported via Newport and Swansea. The opening of the Taff Vale railway in 1841 gave fast access from the mines to the docks. Between 1843 and 1863 the coal and coke carried by rail increased from 152,000 to over 2,772,000 tons per year.[10] The 1841 population of over 11,000 included many Irish immigrants imported to construct the dock and railway. The Irish famine of 1846–8 unleashed a further flood; and by 1851 the population had almost doubled. By 1871 it was 57,363, by 1881, 82,761, the port attracting foreign settlers from all over the world.[11] Thereafter (allowing for a change of statistics to include the widening of the old town's boundaries), the population continued to rise following the successive openings of East Bute Dock in 1858, Roath Dock in 1887, and Alexandra Dock in 1907. Cardiff's greatest expansion began in the 1880s when the valuable high grade steam coal seams in her hinterland were fully exploited. The development of Barry in the 1890s by rivals of the Bute interest did not prevent Cardiff from becoming, by 1913, its peak year, the greatest coal-exporting port in Britain, if not the world, although Barry edged ahead the following year. The census report of 1911 recorded greater Cardiff's population as 182,259.

The Cardiff dock developments not only created a situation in which there would be opportunities for immigrants to make a living; they also altered the topography of the town. The army of dock and railway construction workers had to be housed. The pleasant suburban gardens were filled and filled again until they became a small but potent area of the worst slums in Britain. The streets between St Mary Street and Charles Street, Crockherbtown and Bridge Street became something like an Irish ghetto which spread eastward into Newtown.[12] There was little attempt at clearance before the 1880s. Cardiff also extended north to south. Butetown was built in the 1840s and 1850s. The retail markets and commercial centres of St Mary Street, the Hayes and Queen Street flourished, but a large industrial and commercial district associated with the docks emerged to the south. The connecting link, constricted by the configuration of the River Taff and West Bute Dock, was Bute Road (later Bute Street). This road became the hub, or rather the ribbon, of Jewish settlement.

As early as 1855 it is possible, from contemporary street maps and trade directories, to plot on a contemporary map of Cardiff some twenty-seven shops or businesses in Bute Road registered in what appear to be Jewish names. We are, of course, faced with the familiar difficulty that many apparently Jewish names were Welsh, and vice versa. None the less, there was undoubtedly a concentration of Jewish businesses in that street, the owners mostly living above them. There were other businesses elsewhere. St Mary Street had some half-dozen, while, avoiding its high rents and rates, more gathered in the small streets linking St Mary Street with Charles Street or the canal, which formed the eastern boundary of built-up Cardiff north of Bute Road. In the 1850s Bute Terrace, Bridge Street and Caroline Street, abutting on the Irish-occupied slum area, were already well stocked with Jewish shops, especially pawnbrokers. Later, many sprang up in Wood Street, round the corner near the railway station and clear of St Mary Street rents which reached £300 or even £500 a year. By 1884 Caroline Street had some nine Jewish-occupied houses and shops out of a total of forty-five, Bute Terrace at least five out of thirty-five. Bute Street had some thirty Jewish premises out of 300, and at least five more rented by non-Jewish occupiers from Jewish landlords. There was never anything approaching a Jewish ghetto in Cardiff, but there were certain streets in which Jewish businesses congregated. Yet as early as the 1850s, Jewish shops and houses could be found spread out through the old part of Cardiff as well as in newly-built Butetown. As the great landowners, the Marquis of Bute, Lord Tredegar and the Homfrays, leased out their lands for building estates, Jewish shops and houses appeared even before the estates were completed. They were thickest in main shopping streets such as Castle Road (now City Road), Clifton Street, Roath, and the long Cowbridge Road. But the rather drab streets south of Newport Road and in Riverside, Grangetown and Cathays contained a proportion of Jewish tobacconists and corner shops among those which punctuated the long rows of small terraced houses. By the 1880s a few had prospered to the stage at which one shopkeeper owned several shops, or could even afford to keep a carriage and live in a villa in Roath or Canton, away from his work place.

There were also a number of Jewish landlords. The rate book for 1884 covering Bute Street gives the names of Jacob, Weichert, Bernstein, Solomon and Anna Friedman, Louis Barnett, Ephraim Harris and Solomon Blaiberg, each letting one or two houses. Only Solomon Blaiberg leased and sublet property on a really large scale, becoming the third largest houseowner in Cardiff.[13] He died in 1907 leaving £95,120, an enormous sum for those days.

The trade directories and the census surveys up to 1881 suggest a fairly steady growth in the Jewish population from the 1860s, rising more rapidly in the 1870s and swelling to spate after the Russian pogroms of the 1880s and 1890s induced a mass flight from central Europe. Jewish population figures are much more difficult to estimate than those of the total population, which have been intensively analysed by Professor Brinley Thomas and others. The figures for Jews rest on the Jewish Year Books — that is, largely on guesswork. Even in the early twentieth century, when numbers were reaching their peak, the Year Books estimate the Jewish population of Cardiff at 1,250, a round number which they repeat for several years running when we know there was intensive immigration. Compilers seem to have depended on irregular reports from the provinces; and if, as seems likely, the reporters counted only synagogue subscribers, they omitted many families without synagogue affiliation, producing a serious underestimate.[14] There are many examples of this difficulty. For instance, the Blaibergs were prominent in synagogue activities. The Brukewiches, one successively recorded as Maravski, Morris and Maurice, hairdresser, hosier and draper, the other Selig, sailmaker, ship's chandler, warehouseman and coal exporter (one of the immigrant success stories), never appear in accounts of synagogue activities. Such a wealthy and prominent citizen as Selig could hardly have failed to occupy a prominent position in any congregation he joined. Were they Jewish? Among the working-class estates it is even more difficult to tell. Whatever the number, Cardiff Jewry was never large compared with that of London, Manchester or Leeds. Since Cardiff was not on the route from Hamburg — via Hull, Newcastle or Edinburgh to Liverpool — for those escaping from the continent, it did not catch the drop-outs from the great migration to America. Also, the increase in the number of Jews in Cardiff and south Wales was small compared with that of the population as a whole. Nor is it easy to generalize about how the Jews reached Cardiff. Some early families can be identified from the census reports as coming from Neath (Marks), Bristol and Plymouth (Cohens). Others, such as Barnett Lyons, are simply reported as born in Poland. Some, notably watchmakers, were certainly refugees from the continental revolutions of 1848–51, including a German contingent. Some came via intermediate stopping places — the south coast ports or Merthyr Tydfil. Some joined relatives already settled. Others presumably came on reports of livings to be made; apparently employers wanting skilled workmen sent messengers to engage them directly off the immigrant ships. Quite a lot came, and went, through marriage (the marriage registers indicate that families in the same trade but in different towns often intermarried, presumably through business association). The Cardiff community was the largest centre in an immigrant Jewish population scattered among the industrial ports, towns and villages of south Wales, between which there was frequent communication. This population brought with it a desperate need to earn a living.

II

Maurice Dennis, historian of Cardiff Jewry, observed that from 1858 the Jews carried on an astonishing variety of occupations.[15] While in a sense true, this deserves further investigation. The Cardiff trade directories, published throughout the nineteenth century, enable us to identify not only the number of Jews in various trades but their proportion to the total numbers engaged in them. There are difficulties. One is the usual trouble with names which, to be sure of their identity, should be confirmed from synagogue lists (now mostly vanished) or tombstones, burial and marriage registers. Another is that only professionals or successful businessmen would get their names into the directories. Pedlars, glaziers, servants, factory workers, jobbing tailors and other working-class employees never appear. We know of their existence from marriage certificates and burial registers, but little about their numbers. Worrall's *Cardiff Directory* for 1875 lists two auctioneers and valuers with Jewish names, two or three restaurant keepers, all in Bute Street; seven innkeepers out of 155, a hardware dealer, an iron merchant and two ironmongers, a photographic artist, three private schoolteachers, a hatter, two tailors, four milliners and dressmakers (largely female occupations) out of sixty-three, six drapers out of thirty-two, fifteen clothiers out of forty (the distinctions are unclear, but surprisingly the section on travelling tailors contains few Jewish names and many Scottish ones), nine jewellers out of twenty-seven, some managers of loan societies (a euphemism for money-lenders) and twenty-one pawnbrokers out of twenty-three. Other directories, census reports and marriage registers provide further information. Newport directories show several farmers, and at least two more appear in Cardiff marriage registers. Samuel Marks, the Church Street dyer, had no successors in the trade, and the numbers of Jewish café proprietors tended to decline, perhaps because their places were taken by other immigrants. Many Butetown cafés were run by Italians, boarding houses by Greeks, and laundries by Chinese. Among a few Jewish brewers and publicans, another Samuel Marks ran the Canton Hotel, Llandaff Road, and William Jacobs the Albion Hotel, Cowbridge Road. The marriage registers show a large class of persons calling themselves General Traders, and another, rather mysteriously, called Commission Agents. As the numbers of immigrants increased, the occupations multiplied, and there appeared more grocers, butchers, bakers and confectioners, tobacconists, stationers, chemists, painters and decorators (heirs, perhaps of the glaziers). But the fact that no trade was closed to Jews does not affect the preponderance of the traditional immigrant occupations.

Throughout the period, there is a heavy emphasis on the clothing and allied trades—clothiers, drapers, milliners, dressmakers, hatters, boot and shoe makers, and tailors. By the turn of the century, some tailors achieved entry in the trade directories. No doubt, many more worked for the clothiers or for private customers in the bespoke trade. Then came the furniture trades and watchmaker-jewellers. Furniture dealers, including wardrobe dealers, cabinet makers, picture-frame makers and upholsterers tended to increase; and some clothiers turned to furniture, for example, Isaac Samuel of Samuel & Co., clothiers, who founded the Atlas Furnishing Co. The watchmakers and jewellers included a few highly-skilled chronometer and nautical instrument makers such as Solomon Marks, and William Weichert whose name adorns the clock face on the tower of the Coal Exchange. Clothing and jewellery had the advantage that they were easily combined with pawnbroking.

Clothing, furniture and jewellery were traditional trades, often drawing on skills imported from eastern Europe by urban Jews. In the East End of London as in Leeds, sweat shops employing immigrant labour for long hours in unhealthy, crowded conditions, through subcontractors to the big clothiers, became an incubus on the penniless 'greener' for several generations.[16] There is no evidence that the system ever developed far in Cardiff. There was a Tailors' Association founded in 1889 which protested against the evils of sweating in May 1890,[17] but it was not specifically Jewish. There was a Pawnbrokers' Association, and when the Chief Rabbi visited Cardiff in May 1899 he addressed a meeting of Jewish pawnbrokers and also a meeting of Jewish tobacconists in the Angel Hotel.[18] Little is known of these associations, and there are no reports of Jewish trade unions in Cardiff such as appear in the appendices (H of C, Parl. Papers, 1894, Vol. XXXV) to the Royal Commission on Labour of 1892 for Leeds and Manchester.

Were there Jewish workmen in the docks and railways such as we know existed for a time in the Dowlais steelworks and Merthyr coalmines? They are difficult to identify and probably few in number. Even the poorest observant Jews preferred self-employment in which they could stop work on sabbaths and holy days. Hence the prevalence of small traders, who sometimes appeared briefly in the newspapers when they fell to the temptation of opening on a Sunday and were caught under the Sunday Trading Acts.

It was also long before Cardiff Jews entered the middle-class professions in any numbers. The marriage registers described several bridegrooms as 'clerks'. There were a few private schoolteachers, notably Julian Marks, a son of Mark Marks, and his sisters Julia and Louise who kept a school for young ladies in Dumfries Place. A group of Board School teachers appear in the marriage registers, probably drifting into the profession (but it was hardly recognized as such) via the pupil-teacher system. This was, perhaps, surprising since teaching was no career for an ambitious Jew, who could not expect to become a headmaster or headmistress unless willing to take Christian prayers, even up to the Second World War. There were many Jewish moneylenders, but few bankers or insurance agents. In the 1870s a Samuel Solomons, solicitor, of 70 Bute Street, often defended pawnbrokers in the courts. In Owen's *Cardiff Directory*, 1889-90, Braham Barnett and William Gottwaltz, as well as a doubtful Hier Jacob, appear in the list of solicitors, but in the *Directory* of 1894-5 only Jacob is left. Jewish doctors were equally scarce. In 1894-5, A.H. Joseph MB, MRCS, Oakfield Street, and H.L. Goodman, dentist, are included in very long lists of medical practitioners. Even as late as 1924 only one or two solicitors, four physicians, five dentists and one dental surgeon appear. By 1937 the numbers were rising sharply, reflecting the advent of women doctors and the ascent of the sons of well-established trading families, Cohen, Rapport and Shibko, into the trained professions. The surge of Jews into these skilled middle-class occupations reflects a change of emphasis from the need to make money to a desire for status which occurred mainly after the Second World War.

How far did Jews participate in the mainstream of Cardiff's commercial life: coal, shipping and railways? Apart from Marks, Weichert and Brukewich, already mentioned, the names of Menasseh Angel, 17 Mount Stuart Square, and J.F. Cohen & Co., Pierhead Chambers, are entered as coal exporters and shipowners in the 1880s. M. Angel, Shipowners, were still going strong in 1914, and C. Angel & Co., coal exporters and merchants, 36 Mount Stuart Square, were listed in 1924. The Bielski family were also in shipping as were G. Berg & Co. The Jewish identity of Thomas Diamond & Co., Engineering Works, Bute East Dock, was more doubtful. At the turn of the century, a small group of Jewish families seems to have been contending for a solid foothold in the shipowning and coal-exporting world, although none appears among the mineowners whose offices were in Mount Stuart Square, nor in the railway company offices. At the start of the twentieth century, the young and brilliant brothers, Samuel, Theodore and Alfred Einstein, were climbing into the shipping world. Samuel, manager of the Compagnie Maritime Boulonnaise, was in 1903 appointed to supervise Cory & Co.'s new line of steamers plying between Boulogne, Southampton and Cardiff. By 1906 he was a partner of Messrs Einstein Holmes & Co., running a regular line between Cardiff and Boulogne. By 1908 he was senior partner of S. Einstein & Co., and an elected member of the Cardiff

Chamber of Commerce.[19] His brother Alfred, who married a daughter of the wealthy Swansea pawnbroker and synagogue president, Hyam Goldberg, was prominent in synagogue affairs. But in 1914 the family changed its name to Instone, and thereafter moved by stages to London.

The other notable family was the five sons of Moses Samuel, originally from Poland. In the 1880s they were clothiers, pawnbrokers, and not inconsiderable landlords. By the 1890s, two sons, Louis and Isaac, had founded the Atlas Furnishing Co. and were rich enough to give £500 for a medical scholarship to the new University College, with other donations for its building fund and for the National Museum of Wales. In 1896 Louis became Cardiff's first Jewish JP, an honour of which the Jewish community was immensely proud. When he died in 1906, Isaac was made JP in his place. Isaac also sat on the Council of University College, on the Committee of the Royal Infirmary, was vice-president of the Lifeboat Fund and treasurer of the local Freemasons. In 1907 he was partner in W.T. Symonds, I. Samuel & Co. Ltd., owning the S.S. *Kathleen* registered at Penarth, and the S.S. *Nora* on the Tyne.[20] The contribution of Cardiff Jews to shipping, considering the small size of the community, was not inconsiderable. Of course, they were massively outnumbered by other shipowners and exporters of all nations, and they were never in the league of the Butes, the Corys or the Daviesses. But they did throw up a business élite which had succeeded by grasping the opportunities which the expansion of Cardiff presented, by diversifying interests, widening goals, by energy and persistence in many fields. The Samuel family, especially Isaac, had these qualities in abundance, and as well as making their fortunes and emerging into public life, they dominated the Cardiff Jewish community in the early twentieth century as the Marks family had dominated it in the early and mid nineteenth century. Of Louis Samuel's four sons, Henry and Albert became medical doctors, Herbert became a solicitor and Wilfred a London theatre manager — illustrating once more the progression from business and money-making into the middle-class professions.

This account of the Cardiff businessmen neglects the principal means by which immigrants climbed from poverty and insecurity to comfort and affluence — pawnbroking. This profession was a way of life for at least two generations of Jewish immigrants. Every trade directory between 1850 and 1914 included a growing list of names which were at least 80 per cent Jewish. Some pawnbrokers employed non-Jewish assistants and some of these tried to set up in the trade but very few succeeded. Only Jan Dirk Zussen (a Dutch name, and apparently without synagogue connections) reappeared annually from 1871 for some twenty-six years. According to oral information, not all the Jewish pawnbrokers succeeded; some almost starved.[21] But a survey of well-established Jewish families reveals that most had some connection with the trade. A few avoided it, including, possibly, most of the Marks at the beginning of the century, and the Einsteins at the end. The majority of synagogue wardens and communal leaders owed the foundation of their family fortunes to it, not only in Cardiff but throughout south Wales.

Pawnbroking has not enjoyed a good press, either in the Jewish or in the wider community. The children of those enriched by it have tended to want to forget it. So records and account books have been destroyed, and it has proved almost impossible to obtain detailed information as to how the business was managed. Moreover, for some unknown reason, the parliamentary select committees of 1870, 1871 and 1881 which examined pawnbroking in London and other cities where Jewish pawnbrokers were a proportion, but probably not a majority of the trade, neglected south Wales where they had almost a monopoly.

Pawnbroking filled a social need.[22] The poorest of the working class, the unemployed, part-time and casual labourers, the insecure and those entangled in debt, who used it and sometimes survived through it had no access to banks. Few Jews were bankers.[23] Not surprisingly, the two groups came together. The result was unfortunate, since it placed Jewish traders in daily dependent relationship with the most despised, poorest and, in some cases, the most feckless sections of the population. The criminal and legal aspects of this situation have been examined elsewhere.[24] The relationship gave rise to at least two sets of conflicting legends. One saw the pawnbroker either as the receiver of stolen goods and organizer of criminal gangs, or as the thief-catcher and ally of the police. The other saw him as either the heartless, grasping exploiter of the defenceless poor, or as the golden-hearted befriender of the sick and defenceless, always ready to extend credit to those in desperate need. Probably it varied with the individual. Great insecurities bred high interest rates, inadequately controlled by the law, and necessitated both caution and toughness if the pawnbroker were to stay solvent.

Pawnbrokers were roughly divided into a higher class which lent money on the security of watches or jewellery, business often being transacted on a counter at the back of the jewellery shop; and a lower class which accepted pledges of clothing, bedding and household articles, in conjunction with a slop-selling or credit drapery business which might, when prosperous, be done in a different shop. Periodically, both types held sales of unredeemed pledges. In Cardiff the distinction was blurred, many pawnshops accepting both kinds of pledges; even more so in the valleys towns. But both kinds had undesirable features. The jewellery shops attracted counterfeiters, thieves and burglars. The clothing shops attracted petty thieves and also received bundles of contaminated or infested garments which had to be handled by the assistants. There were fraud risks and fire risks and severe risks of infringing laws or police regulations and being hauled before unfriendly magistrates. In the circumstances, the surprising element is the extraordinary success of many. A small business in Bute Street or Bridge Street might expand with the expansion of Cardiff, and the owner endow his sons with new premises as they grew up and married, while he, possibly by then a landlord or the owner of a loan office, possessed shops in several Welsh towns.

Charles Abrahamson, who had migrated from Poland via Liverpool, Plymouth and Newport, was in 1881 living in Lower Grangetown. By 1885 he owned two pawnshops; his son, Joshua, had another; his daughter, Rebecca, married Abraham Freedman of a well-established pawnbroking and brewing family. His relative (probably brother), Louis Abrahamson, clothier, jeweller and pawnbroker in Newport, helped to found Newport Royal Infirmary and became a town councillor. Solomon Blaiberg from Poland, beginning in 1865 with a small pawnshop in Bute Terrace, had by 1871 offices in Charles Street and in Merthyr and Newport. He also became a big landlord. Louis Barnett, born in Cardiff in 1835, the son of an immigrant draper, by 1884 was in partnership with his son Solomon as clothier, pawnbroker and money-lender at 19 and 49 Bute Street, 6 and 9 Caroline Street and had shops in Swansea and Newport. Several of his sons became pawnbrokers. He died in 1901, perhaps the patriarch of them all. The list could be extended indefinitely. There was a veritable web of interrelated pawnbrokers, many of whom became leaders of their Jewish communities. Probably their fortunes did not compare with those of the coal exporters and shipowners, but they laid the foundation from which their grandsons could migrate to the more prestigious professions, distancing themselves from the most profitable of all the immigrant trades. By the 1920s the pawnbrokers were beginning to decline in numbers, and now they have vanished, leaving behind a few money-lenders, drapers and jewellers.

III

Judaism is as much a community as a religion. Orthodox Jews repudiate Reform and Liberal Jews, but co-operate with them in Zionist and charitable affairs. Observant Jews repudiate secular Jews and, still more, converts to Christianity, but claim them when their actions reflect credit or renown on the Jewish community. Was Disraeli a Jew?

Yet the centre of most community life in the diaspora was, and still is, the synagogue. As soon as enough Jews settled within walking distance to supply a *minyan* (ten adult males), they would hire a room for prayer and, if possible, procure a plot to bury their dead. Then they would buy, borrow or beg *sepharim* (scrolls of the law), elect wardens, seek a *shochet* (or ritual slaughterer) so that the members could eat meat, a *mohel* so that their sons could be named, and a *chazan* (also often the *shochet* and *mohel*) to lead the prayers. Finally, they would hope to rent or build a real synagogue and appoint a trained rabbi or an English minister. Judaism being a non-sacramental religion, the rabbi's function was to act as authority on ritual matters, as teacher, preacher and pastoral visitor. He was the senior religious official of the synagogue and moral mentor of the community, which could manage without him but suffered spiritually and socially when the rabbi was unsatisfactory or missing. Unfortunately, this happened all too often. Provincial synagogues were strongly oligarchical and hierarchical. The president, treasurer, secretary and auditors were elected annually at general meetings of paid-up members, but they might be re-elected and hold office for several years. To be treasurer or president (usually in succession) entailed work and responsibility as well as prestige. Inevitably, the offices fell into the hands of those with wealth and leisure to devote much time to synagogue management. We do not know for certain, although we suspect, that subscriptions in the Cardiff Hebrew Congregation were devised to underpin the hierarchical system, as they were in Swansea. As in Swansea, the Cardiff officers were mostly substantial businessmen, the majority being pawnbrokers. The ministers, generally appointed on three-year contracts, were, like Nonconformist ministers, chosen from those invited to take a service and perhaps preach a sermon to the congregation. They were men of vocation (the insecurity and pitiful salaries were not calculated to attract the financially ambitious), trained on the continent, or in Jews' College, London, in Biblical and Talmudic scholarship; and their education and interests were often very different from those of the businessmen who hired and sometimes controlled them. Inevitably, there were misunderstandings, quarrels, odium and departures. So the history of the Cardiff synagogue shows a succession of 'low' periods and poor morale alternating with periods of vigour and prosperity.

According to Maurice Dennis, the earliest synagogue in Cardiff was a rented room in Trinity Street near the market.[25] As Bute Street became the focus of settlement, the congregation moved to larger premises near the railway bridge there. The census survey for 1851 mentions Lazarus and Menasseh Cohen, aged 60 and 23 respectively, born in Poland, lodgers at William Griffiths, Wharton Street. Lazarus is described as leader of the Jews' congregation. The meaning is unclear; perhaps he was a *chazan*, but in any case, living where he did he was obviously desperately poor. A local pawnbroker, Mr Jehiel Phillips, seems to have acted as reader and celebrant of marriages, while in October 1856, a meeting of the congregation elected Mark Marks as president, Louis Barnett as secretary and treasurer, and Solomon Marks and Ephraim Harris as wardens of the burial ground. Money was already being collected for a proper synagogue; and in May 1858 East Terrace Synagogue, at the end of a row of terraced houses overlooking the canal, was consecrated with due ceremony. Indeed, the celebrations set a precedent for larger occasions in the future. The new minister delivered 'a short impressive sermon on the importance of peace and concord', the Chief Rabbi sent a specially composed prayer which was read in Hebrew and English. Many Jews from neighbouring towns attended, and after the service they all adjourned for a 'sumptious dinner' (*sic*) at the house of Mr Freedman, at which toasts were drunk 'to the army and navy', to 'prosperity' and to 'Christian contributors to the synagogue'. The occasion ended with a quadrille party for the younger members which broke up very late. The *Jewish Chronicle* commented that 'the Jews of this town will for many years remember the event of the opening of this synagogue'.[26]

With the opening of East Terrace, the Hebrew congregation appointed its first minister, the Revd Nathan Jacobs, and this seems to have ushered in a period of consolidation and progress, in which the Holy Days of autumn 1859 saw the synagogue well attended, 'numerous and respectable'. However, in 1865 a row broke out between the synagogue elders and Gerson Gryham of 243 Bute Road, apparently over ritual. Gryham accused the Cardiff Jews of countenancing disgraceful scenes after the sabbath service, taking their quarrels before the local, non-Jewish magistrates, and totally neglecting the religious education of their children.[27] The accusations were vigorously rebutted by Nathan Jacobs, but the shake-up may have been partly responsible for the institution by Jacobs of regular sermons in English as well as a move to turn weekly Hebrew classes into a proper Jewish school.[28] The school was later boosted by the Lyons case or 'Jewess Abduction Case' of 1867 in which a Jewish girl was enticed away from her family and converted by the wife of a Cardiff Baptist minister and her friends, which showed how vulnerable young, disaffected and uninstructed Jews were to the wiles of conversionists. In May 1867 the children from Jacobs' classes were examined before a large audience not only in Hebrew and Scripture history but in English history, grammar, geography and spelling. This reveals that no mere classes in religion were intended, but rather the full curriculum of a superior public elementary school of the period. In August 1870, the school obtained a professional headmaster, the Revd J.H. Cohen, who had taught at the famous Jews' Free School in London. In July 1871 the delegate Chief Rabbi, Hermann Adler, came to examine the children and reported most favourably on the work of Revd Cohen and his wife, especially praising the prowess of the girls in mental arithmetic.[29] Then the whole project collapsed. Apparently, many synagogue members were uninterested in the school and resented its cost. Cohen's request for a reasonable salary was refused and he resigned, taking with him the minister, Nathan Jacobs. The inevitable recriminations followed. The president, Solomon Marks, wrote to the *Jewish Chronicle* deploring the faction-fighting, and the lack of interest both in education and the general weal. Only a few 'English residents' had supported the school, and in view of the reduced salary offered and the conditions attached to it, he would 'caution anyone against coming to Cardiff in hope of a permanent appointment'.[30]

For over a year there was no minister in Cardiff. The next two appointees, M. Lewis and Revd Samuel Fillo, made little mark. The school remained closed, but the gap in religious teaching was filled by classes taken by Revds J.C. Myers and Louis Minski. The congregation's attention was focused on a new synagogue as East Terrace was becoming too small for the rapidly growing Jewish population of Cardiff. The cost of the new building was estimated at £800, and efforts were made to raise the money; but the upshot was only a fairly radical renovation of East Terrace.

The early 1880s were not a particularly prosperous time for the Cardiff congregation. Frequent elections and changes among the officers suggest faction-fights and lack of leadership. The nadir was reached with a bitter schism in which a section of the congregation broke away to form a new synagogue. Better times were foreshadowed with the election in February 1887 of Revd J.H. Landau, a scholar of the Jews' Free School and a graduate of London University. He inaugurated a succession of young, able and well-educated ministers who, although none remained for more than three or four years, revived the sermons, introduced, cautiously, some improvements in the services, and restored the efficiency of Hebrew teaching for the rapidly growing numbers of children. Landau revived the religion classes (there was no further attempt to institute a full Jewish school) and, inspired no doubt by neighbouring Sunday schools, began the custom of summer picnics and winter Chanucah parties for the pupils. He also organized a choir of children trained by the *chazan*, Revd L. Rubenstein. He preached, by invitation, in Unitarian chapels and kept on good terms with the local Christian clergy. When he resigned in August 1890 to go to a congregation in Sydney, Australia, it was reported that 'he had caused the name of the Jewish Minister to be respected and esteemed, which was a new departure for Cardiff'.[31] He was succeeded by Revd D. Wasserzug, a solicitous preacher assisted by an able *chazan*, H. Caminetsky, and *shochet*, J. Hamburg. He was followed in 1895 by Revd J. Abelson, who had graduated from Jews' College the year before. Supported by the president, Isaac Samuel, he introduced Bible readings on alternate sabbaths, preceded by the Ten Commandments in English. Such small developments modernized the services without ever acknowledging the influence of Reform. (It could be said that Reform made a virtue of change and adaptation while the Orthodox changed in fits of absence of mind.)

In April 1888, East Terrace was formally reopened after extensive renovation. That this sufficed for the time being was possibly due to the opening of new synagogues in the valleys which took some pressure off Cardiff, but even more to the foundation of a new synagogue in Edwards Place. The immediate occasion of the secession was a dispute over a member's request that his young son should be circumcised in the synagogue on Yom Kippur, an action disapproved of by the Chief Rabbi. According to the wardens, Louis Barnett and Isaac Samuel, differences of opinion on the management of communal affairs had arisen in the spring of 1887. Despite Hermann Adler's attempts to reconcile the differences, a group withdrew, established themselves in a rented room and began to collect funds to buy a house for conversion into a synagogue. It was quite unnecessary, wrote the wardens; there was 'sufficient accommodation in the present building for the whole Jewish community'. Their refusal to abide by the delegate Chief Rabbi's decision was proof of the weakness and worthlessness of their grievance. No doubt their opposition would crumble and disappear, but publicity was necessary so that co-religionists would not, under misapprehension, support a movement 'which does not deserve, and we feel sure, will not receive assistance'.[32] But the group's opposition did not crumble, while the delegate Chief Rabbi's did (he was periodically faced with the alternative of countenancing schism or losing the allegiance of new congregations). In March 1889, Adler withdrew his ban on the new congregation engaging its own *shochet*, Edwards Place was established as Cardiff's New Synagogue, and it acquired its own marriage secretary in 1897.[33]

The underlying causes of this secession are not difficult to guess, despite lack of hard evidence. They probably included personal and family jealousies between the older established families, possibly reinforced by resentment at the growing influence of the Samuel brothers. Other causes were obscured because, as with similar fissures in Swansea, there was no clear division between the established and the incoming immigrants. The New Synagogue's first *chazan* and *shochet* was Revd B.J. Rittenberg, of a family of furniture dealers, who had performed the same service at East Terrace. The founders included J.W. Joseph, a pawnbroker originally from Pontypool, and his son Leopold, a pharmacist, later to be chairman of Cardiff's

Pharmaceutical Society. Less familiar names include J.S. and L. Bomash, one a jeweller and pawnbroker with shops in Queen Street and Penarth, the other a money-lender; both possibly descended from a Polish glazier called Beaumarsh. There was Abraham Melcher, who started a hire-purchase furniture business in Clifton Street, Roath, in 1884 and went temporarily bankrupt in 1888 through difficulties in collecting the payments; and I. Tumpowsky, of whom little has been ascertained except that he married into the rich Abrahamson family.

By 1890 the new congregation in Edwards Place had acquired its own burial ground and an elected minister, Revd Elias Plaskowsky. Despite its relatively well-established leaders, it was a minority and comparatively poor congregation. For some time it had no religion school and its children learned Hebrew privately with Revd Louis Minski. There were some differences in custom. Circumcisions could be celebrated in the synagogue on Yom Kippur.[34] Barmitzvah celebrants were required to recite most of the service and a special prayer as well as their portion of the Law — an innovation, not unknown in Reform synagogues but soon copied by the Old Congregation.[35] More significantly, the New Synagogue was soon known as the 'Furriners' Shul' while Cathedral Road, the successor to East Terrace, was called the 'Englishe Shul'.[36] Edwards Place, with a strong Lithuanian element in contrast to the Polish majority in East Terrace, was evidently the focus of the newer, poorer, less assimilated immigrants of the 1880s and 1890s, while the Old Congregation retained the support of the Anglo- or Welsh-Jewish establishment. Bad feeling between them continued, although their members learned to co-operate in charitable and secular activities.

Despite the temporary relief, by the 1890s East Terrace was again unable to accommodate the rising numbers of Jews in Cardiff. It was becoming impossible to cram the would-be attenders on High Holy Days into the building, and overflow services conducted by second ministers, *chazanim* and visiting readers had to be held in hired halls. Moreover, with the movement of the Jewish population into the new developments of Grangetown, Riverside and Canton, East Terrace was becoming less convenient for sabbath walkers to synagogue. The Chief Rabbi, on a pastoral visit to Cardiff in 1894, more or less demanded the building of a new synagogue. But the real inspiration for action seems to have come from a newcomer to Cardiff, Colonel Albert Edward Williamson Goldsmid.[37]

A descendant of the famous eighteenth-century banking brothers Goldsmid, Albert had been born in 1846 into a branch of the family converted to Christianity. Educated at Sandhurst, as a young man he had rediscovered his Jewish roots and was now managing to combine a career in the army, including service in India, with a great enthusiasm for Judaism and Jewish causes. Before being appointed to Cardiff, he had taken two years' leave (which may have affected his prospects of really high promotion) to administer the Jewish colonies of Baron de Hirsch in the Argentine. Although mainly an administrator on the General Staff, he was to see fighting in the South African War. He was a founder of Chovevei Zion, the predecessor of Herzl's political Zionism which, after Herzl had visited him for a famous interview in Cardiff, he later espoused. He proclaimed that there was no conflict between Jewish nationalism and English patriotism — he was devoted to both. He helped to found both the Maccabees and the Jewish Lads' Brigade, a somewhat militaristic counterpart to the Church Lads' Brigade, which recruited British army NCOs to drill its members. On appointment as colonel in command of the 41st 'Welch' regimental district in Cardiff in 1894, he sent the regiment with bands playing and flags flying on its first recruiting march through south Wales. Then he turned his attention to the Jewish community. As the *Jewish Chronicle* later remarked, he came to Cardiff with misgivings at a time when it had not the sweetest of reputations. 'Young aspirants for a ministerial career were not enamoured at the prospect of gaining their first experience among the Jews of Cardiff, and businessmen had as much reason to scrutinize closely the credits given to them.' The *Chronicle*, however, kindly allowed that things had vastly changed in recent years, and Goldsmid soon discovered his misgivings to be unjustified.[38]

In fact, Goldsmid seems to have taken the Old Hebrew Congregation by storm. Having organized a local 'tent' of Chovevei Zion with a lively programme of lectures and meetings, he tackled the problem of a new synagogue. Probably his high military rank, his aristocratic connections, his vigorous interest in the affairs of this somewhat neglected provincial community dazzled the synagogue members and disarmed opposition. Evidently he had no difficulty in getting on with the governing élite. In July 1894 a new Synagogue Sites and Collecting Committee was set up with Isaac Samuel, then president of the congregation, as its chairman but with Goldsmid as its president. In December the plans were laid before a general meeting of the congregation which decided, without a dissentient voice, to move the synagogue, as the Chief Rabbi had urged. After some search, a site had been secured from the Marquis of Bute at a nominal rent in Cathedral Road, 'a handsome thoroughfare containing some of the best houses in Cardiff' to which, it was suggested, the synagogue would be an ornament.[39]

The planning may not have proceeded quite as smoothly as the reports in the *Jewish Chronicle* suggested. Revd Wasserzug, who resigned in June 1895, foresaw in his farewell sermon a good future for the Cardiff congregation, 'if only the members laboured for the common weal, and did not fritter away their energies and their ability by pulling in different directions'.[40] Six months later his successor, Revd J. Abelson, was preaching the need to give sympathy and whole-hearted co-operation to the Building Committee.

The hesitations were understandable since the Old Congregation had saddled itself with a very expensive undertaking. Mr Delissa Joseph, one of the group of architects who designed synagogues for the London United Synagogue, was commissioned, and a contract made with Cardiff builders, J. Lissarman, for £5,164. The full cost was estimated at £6,000 and eventually turned out to be nearer £7,000. Over £1,000 had already been promised in donations and East Terrace could be sold for about £700. The rest could be raised by a mortgage of £3,000 and the balance by appeals.[41]

The construction of the new synagogue necessitated two separate ceremonies. On 29 April 1896, the foundation stone was laid by Goldsmid, while the corner stones were placed by the Chief Rabbi, the mayor of Cardiff, Lord Windsor, Lord Tredegar and the local Conservative MP, J.M. Maclean. This underlined the importance attached to the approval of civic representatives of the Christian community. After the ceremony, the stonelayers were presented with silver trowels by the wives of the congregation leaders, and they made speeches. Lord Tredegar (the largest landowner after the Butes) said he would have given land for the site if he had had any suitable. Maclean, the MP, admitted that he had had 'some diffidence in accepting the invitation . . . but when he found the Mayor and Lord Tredegar willing he had followed them'; and he descanted on the decay of religious persecution and animosity. The Chief Rabbi compared Wales with the Holy Land and called for further donations, for 'living is giving'. Goldsmid exhorted British Jews to show a spotless record of good behaviour and welcomed the

Christian guests. He praised Christianity which, he declared, was spreading the knowledge of religion and morality, and thus performing the Jews' mission for them. In the evening a banquet was held in the rooms of the Jewish Institute, followed by a reception hosted by the Chief Rabbi and attended by members of all the congregations in south Wales.[42]

Such a grand occasion would only be exceeded by the consecration ceremony a year later. Its euphoria was only slightly marred by an angry report in the *Church Times* berating the Church dignitaries, especially the vicar of St Stephen's, Revd A.G. Russell, for attending the foundation of a synagogue. In a curiously contorted argument, it asked what conscientious Jews must have thought of the principles of those professing Christians, especially when they heard Maclean declare that the Gospel could be preached in the synagogue, when finished, as truly as in any Christian church? This was immediately answered by Goldsmid in a strong letter in the *Western Mail*. Goldsmid saw nothing incongruous in Christians assisting at the foundation of a synagogue, in which their Master had been wont to worship and preach. He himself had lent a hand for Christian denominational purposes without being the less staunch to his race and faith.[43] The incident was something of a damper on rejoicing — a reminder that anti-Semitism still lurked beneath the surface of British society.

Cathedral Road Synagogue was officially opened on 12 May 1897 — none too soon for Goldsmid, who had been appointed assistant adjutant-general and would soon leave Cardiff. On the ceremonial morning, a closing service was held at East Terrace. In the afternoon, the new building was filled with a crowd of 'prominent persons' including leaders of the congregation such as Louis and Isaac Samuel, Barnett Jacobs and Solomon Blaiberg. Among the distinguished visitors was the fashionable London portrait painter, B.S. Marks, long ago president of the Cardiff Hebrew Congregation. The Chief Rabbi attended, along with the ministers and presidents of the Swansea, Newport, Merthyr and Bristol congregations. Non-Jewish representatives included the deputy mayor (the mayor was away) and the new commanding officer of the Welch Regiment.

The official opening was performed by F.D. Mocatta, President of Berkeley Street, the leading Reform synagogue in London, and an advocate of harmonious relations between the various sections of Judaism; he was invited no doubt by Goldsmid, to whom he was related by marriage. First, Goldsmid offered the carved and gilded key of the synagogue to Mocatta, who opened the door. Then, the Chief Rabbi entered at the head of a procession bearing *sepharim*. They made seven circuits of the synagogue and placed the scrolls in the Ark. Then, the Chief Rabbi preached a long and somewhat florid sermon, alluding to the growing prosperity of Cardiff and of the Hebrew Congregation, exhorting his hearers to pay off the building debt, and impressing on them the importance of Jewish education. A list of subscribers to the synagogue and of donations of furniture, *sepharim* and ritual objects was read out. The prayers were accompanied by a choir specially trained by the *chazan*, Caminetsky. In the evening a banquet was presided over by Goldsmid with his wife and two daughters, and attended by 'several leading Christians'.

Many Jewish residents of Cardiff, present and past, hastened to endow the new synagogue. Recorded subscriptions ranged from £250 from the Samuel brothers down to £25. Goldsmid donated a stained-glass window in memory of his cousin, Sir Julian Goldsmid, and B.S. Marks presented a life-size bust portrait of Albert Goldsmid painted by himself. There were scrolls of the law, mantles and silver bells, curtains for the Ark and a pair of oak doors contributed by M.L. Fligelstone in thanksgiving for his recovery from an illness. But most striking were the many stained-glass windows, mostly in memory of relatives of the donors, which today form an unusual and decorative collection of late-nineteenth-century glass in the *art nouveau* style.[44]

While the new building celebrated a prosperous community in a prosperous city, it left a continuing burden of mortgage debt. By February 1899 the congregation was in financial trouble. A long mining strike was depressing trade, several wealthy supporters had left Cardiff and the wardens were looking round for a means of economizing. Abelson's three-year contract had ended and it was decided to replace him with a *chazan* who could act as teacher and whose salary would be £100 a year instead of £150. The scheme was leaked to the *Jewish Chronicle* by an angry correspondent signing himself 'Provincial', who accused the congregation of victimizing Abelson in order to save £20 on his salary (since £30 out of the £150 was paid by the Provincial Ministers' Fund in London).[45] Fortunately, he was snapped up by Bristol which, also economizing, had been for some time without a minister and was now glad to engage him. Isaac Samuel wrote to the *Chronicle* explaining that the need to dispense with a fully qualified English minister had been forced on the congregation by straitened circumstances and suggesting that ministers should be salaried from a general fund, so that rich London communities could help the outlying ones. As usual the correspondence ended in accusations of callous neglect of the provinces by the wealthy London Jews. However, on closer examination, it appears that economy was not the only motive. Abelson, in his final sermon on 21 April 1899, hoped that the relations between the wardens and their future ministers would henceforth be of a mutually amicable and respectful nature, and that no spot or stain would ever again attach to them either in deed or in the written word.[46] Evidently, he and the wardens had, for some reason, fallen out. He was given an enthusiastic send-off with an illuminated address, but the wardens were not present.[47] Abelson behaved with dignity and magnanimity, and was soon back in Cardiff lecturing to the Dorshei Zion Society. His place was taken by the Revd Philip Wolfers of Swansea. But it was obvious that the unifying and harmonizing effect of Goldsmid's leadership had faded away.

By June 1899 Isaac Samuel and his colleagues on the Building Committee were being presented with illuminated addresses, and the crisis was over. The congregation were settled in the new and palatial synagogue, which soon proved to exercise some uniting power of its own. In 1896 the New Synagogue in Edwards Place founded a Talmud Torah School which then established itself, quite amicably it would seem, as the Talmud Torah and Holy Law Congregation, served by Revd H. Caminetsky (the *chazanim* apparently moved freely between congregations in Cardiff, though the ministers did not). It elected a rabbi, Revd S. Katz, and by 1899 had secured a site from the Marquis of Bute, on which to build a new school and synagogue in Clare Road, Grangetown. This *Beit Hamedrash* or *Beth Hamedrash* — alternative spelling — (House of Study) pursued an independent career for six years, attracting to itself a number of bright young newcomers, including Joseph Bogod, an engineer, and Alfred Einstein, youngest of the shipowning brothers. In 1900 the synagogue in Clare Road was formally opened with a silver key amid appropriate rejoicings,[48] but only four years later it amalgamated with Cathedral Road Synagogue, and its leading members soon appeared on the Cathedral Road council.

Years later, the New Synagogue in Edwards Place (which in 1918 had moved to Windsor Place), after much disputation, was persuaded by the Chief Rabbi to join with Cathedral Road in forming Cardiff

United Synagogue. The differences between Furriners and English had gradually dwindled, and it took a new wave of immigrants from Hitler's Germany to re-create the profound divisions which turned petty quarrels into a schism — and led to the foundation of a Reform synagogue in 1947.

For some fifty years the observant life of Cardiff Jews centred on its great synagogue, its wealthy élite living in Cathedral Road while its rabbis and poorer congregants lived round the corner in Canton and Riverside. Not until the building of the middle-class suburbs of Cyncoed and Pen-y-lan after the Second World War did the need arise for another synagogue building nearer the new residential districts. Then Cathedral Road began a long, sad decline into dereliction. Meantime, the difficulty of obtaining and keeping a suitable minister continued until 1908 when a young Russian immigrant educated at the Jews' Free School was appointed. Revd Harris Jerevitch proved to be a renowned preacher and a doughty defender of the Jewish community against the tide of Fascist anti-Semitism of the 1930s. He stayed with the congregation for forty years.

IV

No Jewish community can be understood merely as a group of immigrants worshipping in a synagogue. Religion is only one aspect of community activities, which touch many sides of life. Jews were noted for taking care of their own poor; it was a virtue often praised by British Judaeophiles. Occasionally, there were exceptions. The brothers Morris and Solomon Joseph were summoned in 1878 for allowing their father, David Joseph, to become chargeable to the Cardiff Union, and they were ordered to pay 3s. a week each. There was also a scandal about Jewish (probably illegitimate) children in Swansea's workhouse.[49] But these cases seem to have been the fruit of family quarrels. As a rule, local communities supported destitute Jews, even if only as a means of warding off an anti-immigrant backlash. Unfortunately, relief records in Cardiff have vanished along with the synagogue books. We know only that there was, as elsewhere, a long-standing custom of distributing *matzos* and other relief to indigent Jews at Passover, and that there existed a succession of charitable committees under various names.

In 1883 the Hand in Hand Benevolent Society elected J. Fligelstone as its president. It was probably an offshoot of the synagogue administration. Its annual report gave 'a favourable résumé of the Society's usefulness in assisting the casual Jewish poor'. But by 1885, in the face of increasing immigration, its effectiveness was being questioned, and its founder Louis Fligelstone, with Charles and Samuel Abrahams, encouraged the establishment of a local Jewish Board of Guardians. This Board, conceived in the image of a Victorian Poor Law Union, relieved in 1900 approximately 230 cases, in 1901 some 240 cases, in 1902 200 cases, in 1903 250 cases. According to the *South Wales Jewish Review* edited by Alfred Einstein, which gave the figures, approximately one-third of these were 'professional beggars' and not in any sense new immigrants. The honorary officers exercised 'a wise and careful discretion' and would help only bona fide cases of destitution.[50] The contemporary distinction between 'deserving' and 'undeserving' poor was reflected in Jewish circles in the distinction between resident and itinerant poor, the latter being objects of suspicion, often denounced as 'schnorrers'. This is hardly surprising: starving wanderers, unattached to any synagogue, were apt to fall into criminal habits, or to live on their wits, indulging in sharp practices, bringing respectable Jewish communities into disrepute, and fostering anti-Semitism.[51]

There were also less deterrent charities. The Benevolent Society, probably founded in the wake of fund-raising efforts for the victims of the 1892 Russian pogroms, was soon taken over by the women of the Old and New Congregations and became the Jewish Ladies' Benevolent Society. It specialized in fund-raising through soirées and concerts, and its annual dinner in the Town Hall Assembly Rooms became famous, as did the benefit performances at the New Theatre, lent annually by the proprietor, Mr Redford. There were other, more specialized charities: individual endowments for poor families, a Workmen's Benefit Society which ran evening classes to teach immigrant workmen English, a Naturalization Society which nominated members for naturalization certificates under the 1905 Immigration Act, a number of societies for young people, including Goldsmid's Jewish Lads' Brigade and a branch of the Young Men's Jewish Association. In 1886 the YMJA, under its chairman Louis Samuel, ran a successful fancy dress ball in the town hall, devoting the proceeds as follows: £3 to the Mayor's Distress Fund, £3 to the Rifleman Explosion Fund (a colliery disaster), £2.2s. to the Cardiff

Infirmary, £1.1s. to the Deaf and Dumb Association and £3.3s. to the local Jewish poor.[52] The Jewish community never confined its charitable donations to Jewish causes alone. There were numerous contributions to mayors' relief funds and to the victims of the colliery disasters of the 1890s. These charitable endeavours were generous and were also, perhaps, encouraged by a desire to conciliate Christian neighbours, emulating the admired philanthropist, Sir Moses Montefiore, and combating the anti-Semitic stereotype of Jewish meanness.

The beneficial results were not confined to the recipients. Collecting for charity promoted a varied and cheerful social life, including dances, concerts and outings. It also helped to paper over the religious squabbles and fissures. It provided a role on committees and an opportunity for administration to the wives of the synagogue grandees, and an important if domesticated function to all the women of the congregations, who were rigidly excluded from the ceremonial and administrative activities of the synagogues. The same could be said of many communal activities not religious or strictly charitable in purpose.

On 27 January 1888, the *Jewish Chronicle* announced that Cardiff Jewish Literary and Musical Institute had given its first soirée in Roath Hall. The Revd J.H. Landau, its founder, had performed the inaugural address, pointing out the Institute's many social advantages. This was followed by songs and recitations contributed by members of the Old Congregation.[53] The soirée was a kind of extension of the Victorian family evening round the piano, to encourage local talent. The Jewish Literary and Musical Institute was probably not the first, and certainly not the last, association of its kind. It continued until 1890. In 1892 we hear of a Hebrew Social Club with lectures, and in December of that year a Jewish social club (possibly the same) recently founded to provide recreation and social enjoyments for the younger members of the community; it opened with an inaugural dance. In January 1893 it held a debate on the question, 'Should Jews in English courts of law swear with their heads uncovered?' Although Isaac Samuel defended the proposition, it was lost by a large majority.[54]

In 1894 a new Institute — for the benefit of the entire Jewish population of Cardiff — was inaugurated with a smoking concert and a dance. St John's Hall was hired with the intention of opening it every evening for concerts, dances, chess, draughts and dominoes, and every Saturday for English classes for foreigners (it is not clear if this was instead of, or as well as, those run by the Workmen's Benefit Society).[55] Isaac Samuel was elected president and the initiative seems to have come from the Old Congregation, although members of the other synagogues participated. By October 1895 it had obtained newly decorated premises in the Old Masonic Hall in Working Street.[56] In December 1895 a variety performance and a farce were performed by members of the community, followed by a dance.[57] In March 1896, the children of the Old Congregation's Hebrew School were examined at the Institute, Mrs Isaac Samuel giving away the prizes; after that, the examinees sat down to a 'sumptuous tea', followed by various entertainments given by the children themselves.[58] In April there was a Sunday evening debate on 'Whether civilisation or savagery conduces more to the happiness of the state?'[59] Debating themes in whatever society or venue seem to have ranged from the religious to the moral and secular.

After January 1897, there was a long silence from the Institute. Then, in March 1903, we read of a meeting in the new rooms of the Jewish Literary and Social Society for a debate, 'Does the Jewish Ritual need Reform?' — which was carried (of course) in the negative.[60] In April there was another debate, with Samuel Einstein in the chair. The Society continued its monthly Sunday evenings until November 1904, when it amalgamated for a time with the Dorshei Zion Society. Then it broke down under protests from the Zionists, but was revived separately in 1907 as the Jewish Literary and Debating Society with (in 1909) a club and free library.[61] Despite these alternations of activity and apathy, the needs of the community for society, entertainment and some intellectual pabulum were generally met, the women doing most of the theatricals and the men most of the debating. Sometimes speakers were invited from similar societies in the valleys towns, or from London or Manchester. Sometimes friendly Christian speakers were engaged.

In 1891 Zionism came to Cardiff with a meeting to establish a 'tent' of Chovevei Zion. Charles Abrahamson took the chair and was elected treasurer, Isaac Tumpowsky was voted hon. secretary and Revd E. Plaskowsky auditor.[62] Clearly this was an initiative of the New Congregation or Foreigners' Shul. Cardiff already possessed a branch of the much older Anglo-Jewish Association, founded in the 1870s as a rival to the French Alliance Universelle (an international charitable movement to found Jewish schools and assist oppressed

Jewish communities abroad). This was generally associated with the elders of established congregations in Cardiff, Swansea, Newport and Merthyr. That the Zionist movement did not split Cardiff according to the Old and New Congregations was partly due to Goldsmid, who from Chovevei Zion turned to political Zionism. In 1900 a meeting 300-strong was addressed by M. Halpern, a Zionist lecturer from Manchester, and a resolution to support the Basle Programme was carried by acclamation. At the next meeting Barnett Jacobs, then president of Cathedral Road Synagogue, was elected president, the Revds Wolfers and Katz, ministers of the Old and Beit Hamedrash Congregations, became vice-presidents, with B. Shatz of the Beit Hamedrash, treasurer.[63] Thus, there was Zionist support across synagogue lines. Nevertheless, when the Jewish Territorial Organization (or ITO) was founded in London in 1906 by the well-known Jewish writers, Israel Zangwill and Lucien Wolf, looking for a place of refuge other than Palestine, there was support for that too, also across synagogue lines, Isaac Samuel becoming president of the Cardiff branch and Leo Joseph of Edwards Place its hon. secretary.[64] Most long-established Anglo-Jewish families feared and opposed Zionism as a threat to their credentials as patriotic Britons, but in Cardiff there were complicated cross-currents. Inevitably, the nationwide controversies, loud with accusations of disloyalty to the mother-country and counter-accusations of faint hearts and cowardice, were echoed in south Wales. But the ministers of all the synagogues were active in the Dorshei Zion (Universal Zionist) societies, and there is little doubt that the prevailing feeling in Cardiff and south Wales was strongly Zionist.

Predictably, the initial enthusiasm waned, and the Cardiff Dorshei Zion Association tended to turn into yet another lecture and debating society. But it was prevented from losing its identity by the periodic elections of delegates to the regional and national conferences as well as by the strong network of Zionist societies which was built up all over south Wales. In April 1903 a South Wales Zionist District Committee was set up with its headquarters in Cardiff, with Councillor Louis Abrahamson of Newport in the chair and with representatives from Brynmawr, Newport, Abertillery, Pontypridd, Merthyr, Aberdare and Swansea.[65] However remote a pipe-dream Zionism must have appeared to many in the early 1900s, it was, perhaps, the most powerful institutional link between Cardiff and the other communities of south Wales. By 1910 the Dorshei Zion societies had recovered from their doldrums and were strong again, listening to addresses from leading London Zionists and collecting for the Jewish National Fund.

V

The interest of Cardiff Jewry as a community lies less in its uniqueness than in its typicality. Although its economic life never developed the full industrial structures and class antagonisms of London's East End or of Leeds, its only truly peculiar feature was the remarkable preponderance of the pawnbrokers. The religious and administrative divisions of its synagogues were repeated in many other communities. At least until 1947 Cardiff (indeed, south Wales) was noted for its orthodoxy. If it had a name for quarrels and disputes, so do many other small inward-looking communities. Its social and cultural activities were also typical of provincial Jewries all over Great Britain. Its literary and social societies had counterparts in many towns and were mostly connected with nationwide movements with their headquarters in London, as were its Anglo-Jewish, Zionist and ITO associations. Its charitable activities were also common to many towns. Its preoccupation — not always successful — with the religious education of its children only differed from that of Swansea and other smaller and poorer communities in that the Old Congregation never hesitated to include in its classes the children of parents who were not members.

As far as we know, relations between Jews and their non-Jewish neighbours were also not untypical. We have little information about the degree and success of individual contacts. Jewish children were educated in the local schools and, as the *Jewish Chronicle* recorded, won many prizes and scholarships. Several became students at the new University College in Cardiff. Members of several leading Jewish families sat on the College Council, served on the committee of the Royal Infirmary and on various relief committees. The *Jewish Chronicle* published an enthusiastic letter of thanks to Joe Abrahamson for his work as treasurer of the relief committee occasioned by the coal strike of 1898. 'We desire it to be known among the Hebrew race how highly we value the work done by one of your brethren in time of need.'[66] After the Russian massacres of 1881, the public protest meeting in the town hall featured Christian clergy and ministers on the platform, although it appears that this was carefully organized behind the scenes by the London secretary of the Anglo-Jewish Association.[67] As we have seen, local clergy and political figureheads were always invited to special occasions like the opening of new synagogues. In turn, presidents of the Hebrew Congregation, especially the Samuels, rabbis and other notables such as Goldsmid were regularly invited to the mayor's banquet and civic receptions. Relations with the local dignitaries were always correct. The marquises of Bute, or their estate managers, donated plots of ground at nominal rents for burial grounds and synagogues. The third marquis joined the Cardiff branch of the Anglo-Jewish Association and sent a subscription of ten guineas to Isaac Samuel.[68] Jews were not excluded from political life. In 1890 the South Ward Liberal Association elected one of the Samuel brothers chairman for the year, while another, Isaac, was chairman of the South Ward Conservative Association. Most of the grandees who were active in politics favoured the Bute connection and the Conservative cause. But the name of the vice-president of the Shop Assistants' Union, formed in 1890 to fight for shorter hours, was Thomas Levy.[69]

In their social organization the Jews assimilated so far with their Christian neighbours as to imitate them without joining them. There were the Jewish Lads' Brigade, the Young Men's Jewish Association, the Jewish Workmen's Benefit Society. A branch of the Maccabees for sport was started in 1907. There was even a Cardiff Jewish Cycling Club. Participation in the widespread Friendly Societies movement was managed by the *Achei Brit*, of which a detailed description appeared in the *South Wales Jewish Review*.[70] There were various explanations of this separateness. Sometimes the national movement was rendered unacceptable by religious connotations, sometimes by holding meetings on Saturdays or by offering trefa food. Even the festivities at the coronation of Edward VII necessitated a separate Jewish committee. But also, especially where the young were involved, there was the pervasive fear of close social contacts leading to intermarriage. So participation remained through imitation not intermingling. Only in Freemasonry was there complete and equal mixing. The movement's religious practice was entirely nonsectarian. Jews were welcomed, joined with alacrity and rose to senior positions.

Inevitably, the undercurrent of anti-Semitism which existed everywhere surfaced occasionally in Cardiff. There were incidents. In

1864 Rabbi Abraham Spiro was assaulted outside East Terrace Synagogue by an Irish labourer who said; 'You are a b—old Jew, you killed Christ', and tried to kill him with the handle of a knife.[71] A current of hostile conversionism which started with the Lyons Case of 1867 fostered a lasting hostility between the Jewish community and the Welsh Baptists.[72] In 1888 a leader in the *Western Mail* alleged that Jews had joined with the Irish in defeating a candidate 'in revenge for the publication of some report affecting one of the community'. This was vigorously denied, as was the idea of a Jewish vote.[73] In 1892 a magistrate rebuked the headmaster of a local school for trying to tamper with a witness against one of his staff accused of assaulting a Jewish boy in class.[74] In 1907 Isaac Samuel protested about a Welsh counsel's untrue and offensive remarks in court about his alien origins, but Mr Harold Lloyd refused to withdraw them.[75] In the 1930s there emerged the inevitable admirers of Hitler, including Fosdike, a former mayor of Cardiff, with whom Revd Jerevitch engaged in furious controversy.[76] No doubt instances could be multiplied, as they could elsewhere. On the other hand, when the Science and Art Department in London insisted on setting its public examinations on a Saturday, thereby debarring two Jewish boys in the higher grade of Cardiff Board School from competing for scholarships (it would kindly allow them to sit the papers on another day on payment of £10, but not enter them for a scholarship), the School Board Committee vigorously supported the Jewish protests.[77] Other favourable instances could be adduced.[78] Even allowing for the trauma of the unexpected, unique and disastrous near-pogrom which broke out in 1911 in Tredegar and the Upper Rhymney Valley, there is no suggestion that the Jews of Cardiff were ever made a scapegoat. The serious riots of 1919 were directed against black and Arab seamen in Cardiff Docks, not against the Jews. Nor is there any indication that the Jews of Cardiff lived in fear of their neighbours, nor that they felt repressed. And they certainly knew how to enjoy themselves. With respect at least to this city the picture painted by Dr Alderman in 'Into the Vortex' seems too sombre.

Rather than persecution, Cardiff Jews feared assimilation, intermarriage and conversion. There were conversions; the famous Marks family seem to have provided one or two in each generation. There were intermarriages, though in what number is unknown. Who, for instance, was Rees Gershon Levy, headmaster of Cardiff Grammar School in 1875? Yet despite the warnings and croakings of well-wishers, the community as a whole remained remarkably solid. Difficult, quarrelsome, apathetic, enthusiastic, mean, generous, orthodox and persistent, Cardiff was probably typical of its kind. The waves of immigrants who, each in turn, went through the trauma of arrival, often in desperate poverty and insecurity; the gradual settling into comparative stability, comfort and anglicization, and then the experience of assimilating the next wave of immigrants, torn between sympathy and anxiety as to the effect this influx might produce upon their own hard-won security and status — such experiences were the common lot of British Jews.

Notes to Chapter 1

1. William Rees, *Cardiff: A History of the City* (City of Cardiff 2nd edn, 1969), 229–32, 235–44, 297; A.M. Williams, 'Social Change and Residential Differentiation: A Case Study of Nineteenth Century Cardiff' (unpublished University of London Ph.D. thesis [LSE], 1976), 165.
2. *Jewish Chronicle* (hereafter *JC*), 25 June 1858, 22.
3. Glamorgan Quarter Sessions Order Book 18, p.317, in South Glamorgan County Archive.
4. See advertisement in the *Cardiff Directory and Handbook* for 1858, 100.
5. *Worrall's Directory of South Wales and Newport, Mon.*, 1875. The full entry is 'Marks, Solomon and Son, Chronometer, Watch and Nautical Instrument Maker, Jewellers and Opticians, Bute Dock Observatory, 101 Rothesay Terrace, Bute Docks'.
6. *Western Mail*, 14 December 1877. He died in 1883; Mark died in 1871.
7. The baptisms are entered in Cardiff Parish Register, St Mary the Virgin, on 9 December 1853. Levi was 25 and Nelson 23. The information about Solomon's marriage comes from a notice in the *Western Mail*, 15 May 1877, on the celebration of his golden wedding. But the statement that he was married at St Mary Redcliffe could refer to the parish rather than the famous church.
8. See the plaque on the cemetery wall at Highfield.
9. The name of Solomon's wife on the tomb at Highfield is Rebecca. Was she converted or is this another person? There were several Marks families in nineteenth-century Cardiff, and it is almost impossible to disentangle them.
10. E.L. Chappell, *History of the Port of Cardiff* (Cardiff, Priory Press, 1939), 85.
11. M.J. Daunton, *Coal Metropolis: Cardiff, 1870–1914* (Leicester University Press, 1977), 10; Brinley Thomas, 'The Growth of Population' in J.F. Rees (ed.), *The Cardiff Region* (Cardiff, University of

Wales Press, 1960), 111-17. The figures vary somewhat, depending on the author.
12. John Hickey, *Urban Catholics* (London, Chapman, 1967), Chap.5, gives an excellent account of the Catholics in Cardiff, especially the Irish.
13. Daunton, op.cit., 118, 120.
14. Cf. Preface iii.
15. Maurice Dennis, 'The Cardiff Jewish Community. Part II: Consolidation, 1858-1897', CAJEX, 1 No.4 (July 1951), 27.
16. Cf. Joseph Buckman, *Immigrants and the Class Struggle: The Jewish Immigration in Leeds, 1880-1914* (Manchester University Press, 1983), *passim.* See also Harold Pollins, *Economic History of the Jews in England* (Littman Lib. Associated Press, 1982), 42-51.
17. *Western Mail*, 14 December 1889, 9 January 1890, 1 May 1890.
18. *JC*, 5 May 1899, 27.
19. *JC*, 30 October 1903, 30; 12 October 1906, 26; 24 January 1908, 31. Theodore's daughter edited 'Music Magazine', a well-known radio feature, Alfred's daughter became a doctor and his eldest son a successful commercial barrister. I knew the family well, in London. After the war Samuel became a pioneer in air transport.
20. *JC*, 12 June 1896, 21; 19 March 1897, 35; 3 March 1899, 29, etc.
21. I owe this information to the late Mr Louis Hamburg, who told me many interesting things about the Cardiff community.
22. Cf. Melanie Tebbutt, *Making Ends Meet: Pawnbroking and Working Class Credit* (London, Methuen, 1983), *passim*; Kenneth Hudson, *Pawnbroking: An Aspect of British Social History* (London, Bodley Head, 1982), *passim.*
23. Maurice Dennis records Samuel P. Kernick, Pharmaceutical Chemist, as an agent of three insurance companies. But it seems the Kernicks were not Jewish.
24. Cf. 181.
25. Maurice Dennis, 'The Cardiff Jewish community, Part I: The Earliest Days', CAJEX, 1 No.3 (April 1951), 30.
26. *JC*, 14 May 1858, 173.
27. *JC*, 1 September 1865, 5.
28. *JC*, 2 November 1866, 8. The school, which obviously owed some inspiration to the Reform movement, was also partly a reaction against it. The reporter hoped other congregations would adopt the same course so that 'the community at large would be enabled to resist those "wolves in sheep's clothing" who would endeavour by the abolition of our sublime liturgy in our vernacular, to undermine the whole foundation of our sacred and ancient faith'. Interestingly the writer uses the medieval ecclesiastical catchphrase for heretics.
29. *JC*, 14 July 1871, 9. A public elementary school was a school grant-aided by the Committee of the Privy Council for Education.
30. Ibid., 11 August 1871, 3.
31. Ibid., 29 August 1890, 16.
32. Ibid., 30 November 1888, 12.

33. G. Alderman, op.cit., 4, from M. Dennis, 'The History of the Cardiff Jewish Community, Parts XIII and XIX', CAJEX, 19 No.3 (September 1969), 14–19; 20 No.1 (March 1970), 26–7.
34. JC, 17 October 1890, 15.
35. JC, 9 January 1891, 15; 28 August 1891, 13.
36. Maurice Dennis, 'The Cardiff Jewish Community, Part II: Consolidation 1858–1897', CAJEX, 1 No.4 (July 1951), 29.
37. Goldsmid died in 1904. For his obituary, see JC, 1 April 1904, 9, with details of his life.
38. Ibid., 7 May 1897, 16.
39. Ibid., 2 October 1896, 11; 14 May 1897, 24.
40. Ibid., 28 June 1895, 22.
41. Ibid., 28 February 1896, 17. For present-day equivalents, multiply by at least twenty.
42. Ibid., 1 May 1896, 18. That Goldsmid's remarks were not considered patronizing is an interesting reflection on contemporary attitudes.
43. Ibid., 5 June 1896, 10.
44. Ibid., 14 May 1897, 24.
44. The best of them are now in the care of the National Museum of Wales at St Fagans.
45. Ibid., 17 February 1899, 9; 21 February 1899, 8 (Abelson); 3 March 1899, 9; 10 March 1899, 10; 17 March 1899, 12, 13; 24 March 1899, 8 (A. Green); 31 March 1899, 9 (I. Samuel).
46. Ibid., 21 April 1899, 25.
47. Ibid., 14 April 1899, 27.
48. Ibid., 26 June 1896, 21; 4 August 1899, 24; 28 September 1900, 29.
49. Western Mail, 10 October 1878.
50. The South Wales Jewish Review, No.3 (4 March 1904), 33.
51. For example the starving pedlar in the valleys who, it is said, ate the crust of his lunch-time slice of bread, rolled the crumb into pills which he sold in the local market as a cure for all diseases — and netted a fortune.
52. JC, 9 April 1886, 7.
53. Ibid., 27 January 1888, 13.
54. Ibid., 27 January 1893, 16.
55. Ibid., 23 November 1894, 19.
56. Ibid., 25 October 1895, 22.
57. Ibid., 3 January 1896, 20.
58. Ibid., 13 March 1896, 22.
59. Ibid., 10 April 1896, 20.
60. Ibid., 20 March 1903, 30.
61. Ibid., 19 April 1907, 26; 26 April 1907, 28; 5 February 1909, 32.
62. Ibid., 26 June 1891, 16.
63. Ibid., 9 February 1900, 23.
64. Ibid., 5 January 1906, 33.
65. Ibid., 10 April 1903, 31.
66. Ibid., 4 November 1898, 26.

67. Records of this meeting are stored in the basement of Cardiff City Hall: Box 304.
68. The A.J.A. canvassed leading Christians for subscriptions.
69. *Western Mail*, 1 March 1890.
70. An account of this Jewish Insurance Society appeared in the *South Wales Jewish Review*, December 1904, 187.
71. *JC*, 22 January 1864, 2.
72. See Chap.6.
73. *Western Mail*, 21 January 1888.
74. *JC*, 9 December 1892, 19. An assistant master was summoned in the Police Court for assaulting Lazarus Marks, pupil. Magistrates elicited that the headmaster had tried to make it appear that the witness, a servant in the parent's house, had been compelled by her mistress to give false evidence. Magistrates severely censured the headmaster and fined the assistant master 10*s.* and costs, or fourteen days.
75. *JC*, 17 May 1907, 33.
76. 'Extraordinary Men are Ordinary to G-D', CAJEX, 29 No.3 (1979), 19–29.
77. *Western Mail*, 17 May 1887; *JC*, 27 May 1887, 12. The chairman of the Cardiff School Board wrote expressing the willingness of members of the Board to give up their own time to invigilate the boys on a different day.
78. For example, the Revd C.J. Thomson took a leading part in protest meetings against the Russian pogroms in 1882.

2

The Valleys Communities

ANTHONY GLASER and URSULA R. Q. HENRIQUES

I

Jews began settling in the valleys of south Wales from about the middle of the nineteenth century.[1] The small mercantile communities which they formed in the valley towns reached their high point in the decade before the First World War. By the end of the 1930s they were in decline and some had all but disappeared. The young people, the lifeblood of the communities, were leaving or had left for larger Jewish centres, sometimes for Cardiff, often for Manchester or London. Many of the parents, when they could, had sold up their homes and followed the children.

There was a temporary slowdown in the population decline just before 1939 when the valley settlements were augmented by a small number of central European refugees, but many of these latecomers had also left by the time the war ended. The contribution they made to the establishment and growth of the trading estate at Treforest is examined in Chapter 8. In the valleys at present only a few isolated couples and individuals remain. Most are in their seventies or eighties.

The Jewish presence in the valley towns, then, lasted about 100 years. It was closely associated with the rapid expansion of the iron and steel industry around the Merthyr–Dowlais region in the middle decades of the nineteenth century and with the explosive growth of the coal industry in the Rhondda and Cynon Valleys from the mid 1870s to the end of the century. When these industries declined, so eventually did the Jewish communities.[2]

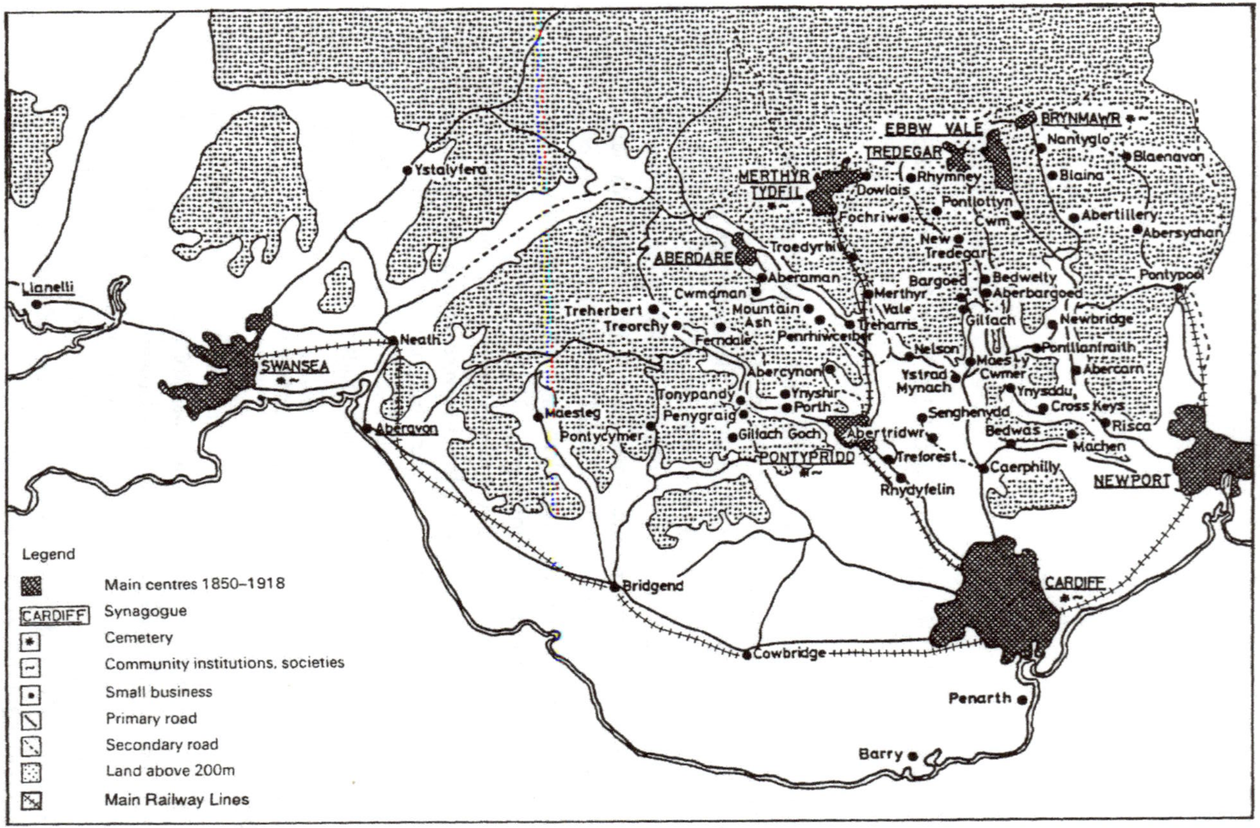

Jewish Communities in Industrial South Wales

II

The first of the valley Jewish communities to be established (though predated by Swansea and Cardiff) was at Merthyr Tydfil. Its foundation was officially recognized in 1848 with the erection of a small synagogue in Victoria Street, but there is evidence of Jews living and working there well before that date. As early as 1830, when the total population of the town was approximately 24,000, six out of the seven dealers in old clothes listed in the trade directory bore Jewish names. On 23 February 1833 the *Merthyr Guardian* reported a court case in which a witness, Solomon Harris, was sworn on the Pentateuch. Harris claimed that two men had obtained from him a gold chain for which they had promised to pay by a certain date, but failed to do so. He accused them of theft and they called him a 'Jew', obviously as a term of opprobrium. In the following year the same newspaper reported the committal for trial of Jane Truman who was accused of stealing from Henry Lyons, a Jewish slop-seller.[3]

In Pontypool, *Pigot's Trade Directory* for 1830 lists four out of five furniture brokers with Jewish names. Even before these two very early settlements pedlars and travelling salesmen had wandered into the valleys from the ports and border towns. By the 1850s there were Jewish shopkeepers resident in Aberdare, Tredegar and Pontypridd. Pontypridd opened its synagogue in 1867 and Tredegar tried to do so in 1875 but failed, amidst a scandal, for lack of money. The local synagogue, crown of permanence and prosperity, was only possible in the larger valleys communities. But by 1895 small Jewish businesses were to be found in almost all the industrial towns of south Wales. The moment when each of these small groups could be considered a community is difficult to establish, the reasons for their being there less so. Essentially the valleys Jewish communities resulted from the coincidence of two unrelated historical events. One was the opening up of the iron, steel, copper and tinplate industries in the middle of the nineteenth century followed by the rapid expansion of coalmining from about 1870 onwards. These developments sucked in a flood of workmen and their families from rural Welsh counties such as Carmarthenshire, Radnor, Pembrokeshire and Montgomery and from neighbouring English shires, Somerset, Gloucestershire, Wiltshire, Devon, and Cornwall.[4] To these were added immigrant inflows from Ireland, Spain and Italy. In the developing pithead and heavy industry towns there were openings for various commercial services to supply the new population. The other event was the increase in Jewish immigration from Russia, bolstered and intensified by the persecutions which followed the assassination of the Czar Alexander II in 1881. While south Wales was not on the main emigration route from northern Europe to America, which crossed the north of England, the opportunities for making a living in the fastest growing industrial area in Britain were too good to miss. As the mines were sunk in the later part of the century so Jewish names appeared among the commercial lists, not only in Merthyr, Aberdare and Pontypridd, but in subsidiary villages such as Hirwaun and Troed-y-rhiw. In 1895 there were few Jewish names in the Rhondda and Rhymney Valleys where the exploitation and opening up of coal seams was just beginning. When the mines and their attendant towns were established Jewish settlement appeared.[5]

Exactly how the process of colonization proceeded is far from clear. But it is certain that, once firmly settled, the newcomers sent for their families in Poland and Russia and later from the Baltic states. Businesses, once established, could not cluster in competition with each other and tended to spread out in a network. Flourishing pawnbrokers in Cardiff or Swansea endowed their sons and relatives with subsidiary shops in Neath or Newport. The marriage registers show that there were business contacts between men in the same trade, such as furniture dealers, all over the United Kingdom. Jews isolated in a not very friendly world desire to meet, and it is probable that news of new mining communities and new opportunities were passed on from one to the other. Much of this is speculation, but these mining towns were almost all linked up by branch railways, and what is certain is that the communities spread.

In each valley town the actual numbers of Jews as well as their proportion to the total population was always very small. Dr Alderman in his article 'The Anti-Jewish Riots of August 1911 in South Wales' suggests that, at that date, the 135 Jews of Brynmawr represented just over 2 per cent of the town's population.[6] Surprisingly, Brynmawr had the third largest percentage of Jews of any town in Great Britain, coming third after Leeds (5.8 per cent) and Manchester (5.5 per cent). In London, Jews accounted for 2 per cent of the total population.[7] Tredegar Jewry amounted to 0.75 per cent of the town's inhabitants, while the Jews of Aberdare constituted 0.5 per cent. Even Cardiff, with the largest Jewish population in south Wales estimated (very roughly) at 1,800, comprised only just over 1 per cent of the town's total population.[8] But the Jews, mostly first-generation immigrants, speaking English (or Welsh) with a foreign accent, and usually clustered in a limited number of businesses and occupations, appeared conspicuous in their new surroundings.

How many of the Jews who settled in south Wales valleys were British born and how many arrived direct from eastern Europe is difficult to ascertain, though a random selection of seven Jewish households listed in the 1851 Merthyr population census provides some useful information about the occupants' country of origin. The seven households were all located in High Street, in the Pontmorlais district of Merthyr. Six heads of the households were born abroad; three in Poland and one each in Russia, Germany and Austria. Only one was British born, actually in Merthyr. In five of the homes the wife was in residence on the census day. Two of these were born in Poland, one in Germany, one in Merthyr and one in Bristol. Of the six relatives, visitors or lodgers present, five came from Poland. Although no firm conclusions can be drawn from such a small sample, it does suggest that most at least of the early valley settlers were first-generation foreign immigrants.

III

Kelly's Directory for the year 1895 gives, along with much other information, a list of commercial addresses in the market and mining town of Aberdare. Among these are some twenty-five premises under Jewish or probably Jewish names. They include five pawnbrokers (one in the outlying village of Aberaman, one listed as pawnbroker, outfitter and furniture dealer), three jewellers (of whom one is listed as watchmaker and jeweller), one watchmaker (but it may be assumed that watchmaker meant watch-repairer, and that such repairs were usually carried on in a small jewellery shop), three tailors, or tailors and drapers, a milliner, an outfitter (who presumably sold second-hand clothes), two bootmakers, two furniture dealers (one of the pawnbrokers was also an outfitter and furniture dealer), a hairdresser, two 'shopkeepers', one provision merchant and confectioner (his name was John Isaac and he may have been a Welshman with an Old Testament name), and the owner of the Central Hotel, Josiah Emanuel, who likewise may or may not have been Jewish.

The remarkable feature of this list is that it was unremarkable. If we turn to Tredegar and New Tredegar at the same date we find five pawnbrokers (one with two shops), four clothiers (presumably second-hand) and an outfitter, two furniture dealers, a bootmaker, a butcher, a tobacconist. The smaller mining and iron town of Ebbw Vale had two pawnbrokers, an outfitter, a furniture dealer and a shopkeeper. Aberavon's commercial enterprises under Jewish names included a pawnbroker, two furniture dealers and two picture-frame makers (the surprising number of picture-frame makers in these lists seems to require some explanation beyond the popularity of heavy carved gilt picture-frames in Victorian times — did they also make small items of furniture?), two drapers, a painter, a tailor and a grocer. The grocer was Levi Harris junior, presumably son of Levi Harris the tailor, which may suggest that the son had taken a step up in the world. Many other commercial lists include much the same range of occupations. The only unexpected feature is the comparatively small number of tailors and glaziers, both traditional Jewish occupations. But a look at the Merthyr Jewish marriage register reveals that they were there.[9] Presumably only a well established business with a certain amount of fixed capital merited inclusion in the directories.

A fairly central date in the era of mass Jewish immigration into Britain (and the Welsh valleys) is 1895. As time went on the range of occupations widened. There had been a distiller in 1888, a corn dealer in 1892, a baker was recorded in 1902, and also an auctioneer (not the first). An engine fitter and a chemist were both married in 1908.[10] These were, generally speaking, exceptional. In the advancement of even the occasional Jew to the learned professions such as law and medicine the valleys were a long way behind the big coastal towns such as Cardiff and Swansea. Even in these there was little advancement towards the professions requiring long education and training until the 1920s and 1930s. However, in the first decade of the twentieth century there were Jewish labourers in the Dowlais steel works and Jewish miners underground. An editorial in the *South Wales Jewish Review* of 1904 refers to an alleged attack upon Jewish workmen at the Dowlais Iron Works.[11] The Chief Rabbi Dr Hermann Adler sent a special mission to them, and Revd Fyne was permitted by the Swansea community to provide occasional ministration to the Jewish colliers and their children at Merthyr in 1902.[12] That there were Jewish miners is also attested by Mr Joseph of Cardiff who recalls that his grandfather, Benjamin Joseph, was employed as a miner at the Old Pit colliery, Abertyswg, near Bargoed. Born in Jerusalem but a refugee from Turkish conscription, he worked underground and later on the surface, but died aged sixty-seven of pitch cancer, a disease believed to have been contracted by long association with the by-products of coke.

These examples show a gradual tendency of the valleys Jews, once settled, to gravitate in small numbers, usually temporarily or for one generation, towards the occupations of the host communities. On the other hand, it was important to many of them to stay in employment in which they could observe the sabbath, leaving work on Friday evenings and not working on Saturdays, or the High Holy days. In London, this promoted the employment of 'greeners', or new immigrants, by Jewish employers in established tailoring concerns, very often in sweat shops. In Leeds it induced two generations of immigrant Jews to work for other Jews subcontracted to large clothing firms or in slipper-making or cap-making workshops.[13] In south Wales, where employment was mainly in heavy industry owned by large capitalists, Jews tended, on the whole, to remain outside the main industrial complex, and find their niche in commercial services to the working inhabitants of the industrial towns.

It has been observed that the nature of such services was in part guided by the skills which the immigrants brought with them from central Europe. There had been Jewish innkeepers in Russia, sometimes established by the local nobles to sell the products of their vineyards. The occasional Jewish innkeeper appears in the valleys, although there were more of them in Cardiff. The general question has been addressed by Harold Pollins in his *Economic History of the Jews in England* who shows that according to the population census recording immigrants born in Russia, Poland and Romania (the vast majority of whom would have been Jews) most worked in the clothing and footwear industries.[14] The Poor Jews' Temporary Shelter, located near the London docks, kept records of the occupations of newly arrived immigrants who turned to it for help. Of the 9,047 such immigrants between 1895 and 1908, 29 per cent were garment makers, 23 per cent were in trade or commerce, 9 per cent were boot or shoe makers, 7 per cent carpenters and 2 per cent agricultural workers of some description.[15] There was a rough correlation between these occupations and the majority trades of the valley dwellers — the clothiers, glaziers, furniture dealers, picture-frame makers, jewellery sellers and watch-repairers and boot makers (or repairers) — often an adaptation of the original skills or trades. Even the small multi-occupational business was a pattern not infrequently found in the east European *stetl* or small Jewish township. On the whole the Jews engaged in a very limited range of occupations. But of these the dominant and by far the most important trade was that of pawnbroker.

IV

The pawnbroking trade in south Wales during the latter half of the nineteenth and well into the twentieth century was a Jewish domain. It was another traditional Jewish occupation, for pawnbroking and money-lending had been connected with Jews since the Middle Ages. While the Catholic Church passed laws against 'usury' they were evaded by the sophisticated bankers of Lombardy and ignored by the Jews who, not being Christians, were not only not subject to them, but were also forced to rely on money-lending by being excluded from the ownership of land and the membership of craft guilds. A law regulating Jewish pawnbrokers was passed in Augsburg as early as 1276 recognizing the pledge as legal evidence of debt. They were never popular. Charges of excessive interest were often an excuse for anti-Jewish riots.

The creation of an industrial working class in England and Wales during the nineteenth century ushered in the great era of pawnbroking. Faced with the hardships of unemployment, sickness, or sometimes fecklessness, they turned to pledging what small pieces of property were available. A study in Birmingham suggests that the average loan advanced was often very small, between ten and fifteen shillings (50–75p) while in the poorer parts of the town five shillings (25p) was considered quite a large amount.[16] On the other hand, apart from the Sun Alliance founded by Moses Montefiore there were no Jewish insurance companies or high-street lending banks, and few Jewish bank employees, since banks remained open on Saturday mornings. Pawnbroking therefore provided finance for the poor and employment for Jewish traders. It was not, however, in Jewish hands throughout the United Kingdom. In London the trade seems to have been shared between Jews and non-Jews. *Kelly's Birmingham Directory* for 1852 lists 96 Birmingham pawnbrokers of whom only

16 were known to be Jewish. In 1871 there were 210 in the trade, of whom 22 were Jews. Similarly in Bristol the business was largely in Gentile hands.

The reasons for the near monopoly of pawnbroking in south Wales by Jews are not clear, though the fact can be seen in all the trade directories. (It is possible that the slight 'apartness' of the Jews and their tendency to remoteness from village gossip may have assisted this confidential trade). In the valley towns, figures taken at intervals from local trade directories emphasize the point. In 1871 56 out of 61 pawnbrokers were Jews. In 1894 84 out of 91 were Jews. In 1901 the figures were 81 out of 95, in 1910 66 out of 85 and in 1920 72 out of 88. When new mining towns were established almost the first Jewish shop to open seems to have been the pawnbroker. The larger towns had several of them; we have seen that in 1895 Aberdare with Aberaman had five. Pawnbrokers had pledges to sell, and the trade was frequently combined with jewellery and watchmaking or (the lower class) with drapery and second-hand clothing, or in the valleys where such class distinctions did not apply, with both. In mining villages the pawnbroker's was often a counter in the back premises of a general store.

Pawnbroking was in many ways an unpopular and disagreeable trade. Subject to strict licensing laws intended to protect the poor from exploitation, the insecurity of the loans still made for high interest rates. There was a long-standing association of pawnbroking with the receiving of stolen goods, although the Pawnbrokers' Act of 1872, initiated largely by the pawnbrokers themselves, which laid harsh penalties for receiving, did something to remove the 'Fagin' image.[17] Pawnbrokers were a magnet both for fraud and for burglary. But pawnbrokers could expect little sympathy from the courts. On 24 December 1884 the *Western Mail* reported that Julian Gittelsohn of Brecon Street, Dowlais, had been summoned for overcharging by $3\frac{1}{2}d$. The magistrate pointed out that the Pawnbrokers' Act had been passed to protect poor people, and he imposed a fine of £5. There were numerous adverse references in the press to Jewish pawnbrokers; they seem to have invited anti-Semitism. Possibly this was partly due to envy, since pawnbrokers could flourish when times were bad.

Not all pawnbrokers were successful. As in Cardiff there are verbal reports of traders in a condition of failure and near starvation. Yet the advantages of the trade were enormous. It required little initial capital, provided self-employment, and could be pursued in combination with other traditional occupations. It offered the freedom to close on Saturdays and festival days (although not to open on Sundays). To the successful there were great rewards. We have seen that in Cardiff and the coast towns the majority of sizeable fortunes were based on pawnbroking. It is unlikely that it was as profitable in the mining towns, but the fact of its multiplication and persistence suggests that it formed the basis of modest Jewish prosperity in the valleys. At the same time numerous working-class families could not have survived without the services of the pawnbroker. The trade was as important to the mining and heavy industry labourers and their families as it was to the Jews.

Some of the pawnbrokers figure in the Merthyr marriage register. In the twenty-eight years between 1886 and 1914 thirty-four bridegrooms claimed to be pawnbrokers. In the twenty-five years between 1915 and 1940 there were only three. The last year recording such an entry was 1925. Pawnbroking was dying out, although probably more slowly than the marriage register suggests. The last pawnbroking counter in a Cardiff jeweller's was abandoned about 1986. Meantime, the range of Jewish occupations was gradually expanding, slowly in the 1920s, more rapidly after 1930. In the 1930s the Merthyr marriage register contains entries such as museum clerk, tool-setter, textile mechanic and precision-grinder, all non-traditional skilled occupations. From 1938 there is evidence of women being employed outside the home, an indication of the important social changes beginning to happen in the Jewish community. (Women had been employed in munitions factories during the First World War, but there is no indication whether there were Jewish women among them.)

Representatives of the professions began to appear among the Jewish communities in the 1920s. Their numbers were small. Only six were found in the register during thirty-five years from 1915 to 1950; a doctor, an accountant, a solicitor, a chemist and two schoolmasters: sixty-eight engaged in non-professional occupations were mentioned in the same period. Of course this is not a complete tally of the Jewish residents, and more could probably be found in the increasingly voluminous directories. Nor is there any way of knowing how many young Jews moved away from the valley towns to take up professions elsewhere. We only know of those who remained, and they were heavily outnumbered by those who clung to the traditional Jewish occupations. Such occupations continued to be the bedrock of the

Jewish economy in the valleys — even when the Jewish communities, the industrial towns, and the industries which supported them declined. Participation in trades and professions always lagged behind that in the large coastal towns. Some means of subsistence remain to be explored. We do not know how many Jews acquired property and became landlords in the valleys — the one who came to notice in Tredegar acquired an unsavoury reputation and was accused of being a contributory cause of the Tredegar Riots of 1911.[18] The economic limitations on the Jews in the valleys reflected the economic and social limitations on their host communities. The pedlars who had started it all died out, but they left their heirs in the market stall holders and travelling salesmen and commercial travellers. The pawnbrokers provided finance, the clothiers sold working clothes to the miners and metal workers, the furniture dealers helped to furnish the miners' cottages. Historians of these communities may well enquire not only how the Jewish immigrants made their livelihoods, but also how much they contributed to the life of the places in which they lived.

V

The crowning event of a valleys Jewish community was the acquisition of a purpose-built or converted synagogue. Most of the early settlers, as soon as a *minyan* could be found, borrowed or rented a room in which prayers could be said. The congregations preceded the synagogues. On the High Holy Days as many as could get there flocked to Cardiff or Swansea where the sudden multitudes necessitated overflow services in those towns. The building of synagogues (as well as the payment — or under-payment — of rabbis) was always difficult, and the smaller the community the greater the burden. Several attempts collapsed; yet by the first decade of the twentieth century there were synagogues at Merthyr, Tredegar, Pontypridd, Brynmawr, Aberdare, Ebbw Vale, Aberavon, Ystalyfera and Llanelli. There were also Jewish cemeteries at Merthyr, Pontypridd and Brynmawr.

The first purpose-built synagogue in Merthyr Tydfil took only a year to build. A plea for financial help for the project appeared in the *Jewish Chronicle* in February 1852. Eighteen Merthyr Jewish residents had already contributed, and their efforts were supplemented by donations from Jews in Pontypridd, Tredegar and Carmarthen and by the princely sum of ten shillings from the Chief Rabbi, Dr Nathan Marcus Adler.[19] A site near the railway station was purchased, the foundation stone was laid on 29 May by Joseph Barnett, a leading member of the congregation who had donated ten guineas to the building fund, and the synagogue was ready for its ceremonial opening eight months later.[20]

Perhaps the most noteworthy feature of the building of the Merthyr synagogue (and no doubt of the other valleys synagogues) was its close resemblance to similar enterprises in the larger towns of Cardiff and Swansea. As in Cardiff there were two ceremonies; at the laying of the foundation stone and at the consecration of the building. As in Cardiff leading Christians in the town were invited to take part in each ceremony, and made suitable speeches in the course of which they remarked that they 'were glad to observe that the prejudices which had formerly existed were dying away'.[21] These were days of rejoicing for the congregation. All Jewish shops were closed; the stone-laying was followed by a dinner with speeches, and the opening ceremony by festivities provided by Joseph Barnett and attended by the Christian guests.

Unfortunately, as in Cardiff, this acquisition of a focus for Jewish religious and social life for the Jewish residents of Merthyr and the neighbouring villages involved the congregation in a considerable burden of debt. This is more apparent in the history of the second synagogue, necessitated by the increasing numbers of Jewish residents, built on a hillside commanding a view of the town and inaugurated in March 1876, with a service followed by a grand banquet and ball.[22] The cost of the site and the building was given as £1,800. Of this the congregation managed to raise some £400 including a gift of £200 from the Rothschild family, and took out a mortgage of £1,000 for the rest. There were additional expenses of £850.[23] Years later the mortgage was still being repaid, and the difficulties were intensified by the economic recession of the late 1870s which put miners out of work and reduced the takings of many of the Jewish shops. Repayments were continuing even as late as 1918.

Two other communities which attempted to build synagogues in the 1870s were Tredegar and Pontypridd. Tredegar, having been offered a site free by a generous, Christian gentleman, entered into a contract with a local builder and proceeded to lay the foundation stone. Despite donations, which included £50 from Baron Lionel de

Rothschild, the project soon ran into difficulties. The shopkeepers who should have contributed were affected by poor trade due to a lockout of workmen in the town; there was interference by a mysterious 'eminent party residing in London', and the committee in charge was rent by dissensions.[24] Eventually the partly completed building was sold by auction.

At Pontypridd the issue of a synagogue was raised as early as 1867.[25] An appeal for funds to convert the building into a synagogue brought donations from places as far afield as London, Bristol, Birmingham and Penzance, as well as from Merthyr and Cardiff.[26] But nothing happened, and although the issue was raised again in 1873 and had the active backing of the Goodman brothers, well-to-do pawnbrokers, it seems that even in 1879 there were barely enough Jews in the town to form a *minyan*. It was impossible to build with such small numbers of Jewish residents; the development had to await the great influx of immigrants which began in the 1880s. Eventually both Tredegar in 1883 and Pontypridd in 1895 obtained their synagogues.

VI

One of the Minute Books of Merthyr's synagogue has been preserved. Unfortunately it does not begin until 1918, and covers only the period 1918–34. Yet it reveals a form of synagogue administration closely resembling those of Swansea (and probably Cardiff) at a much earlier date. Like the congregations of the greater towns, Merthyr's was governed by a small oligarchy of comparatively wealthy men with the leisure and enthusiasm to devote themselves to synagogue affairs and to monopolize power. As in Swansea the best seats near the *bima* were reserved for those who paid the highest subscriptions, while between 1918 and 1934 the offices of secretary, treasurer and president were held by just eight men, the honorary secretary and treasurer moving up towards the presidency roughly every three years.[26] Once only, in 1921, a ballot was held for the presidency of the congregation, and in 1923 for secretary. After that the administration relapsed into its former state of conservatism and oligarchy.

As in other towns the problems which preoccupied the Merthyr leadership were the appointment and control of the salaried synagogue officials, the ceaseless struggle to make ends meet, the upkeep of the communal buildings, the distribution of relief to destitute congregants, the provision of religious education, the conduct of relations with neighbouring communities, and the seemingly endless skirmishing with the congregation's kosher butcher.

Ideally the staff of a synagogue included a rabbi or minister, a *chazan* or reader, a *mohel* or qualified circumciser, a *shochet* or ritual butcher (usually working in an independent butcher's shop), a Hebrew and religion teacher and a *shammas* or beadle. Usually, in fact, most of these offices were combined. The rabbi was expected to organize the religion school and to teach in it. He and the *chazan* often acted as *mohel*, supplementing their meagre salaries with fees for the circumcision of babies in other towns. The *chazan*, as well as the rabbi, might kill chickens as well as teach in the school.

In south Wales attracting and keeping a minister was always a problem. The smaller valleys congregations could not generate enough income to support an independent minister, even with the aid of the Provincial Ministers' Fund in London (which they complained was never enough). They frequently borrowed or hired the services of ministers from the larger towns. Rabbis or ministers were sometimes obtained direct from congregations abroad or were graduates of Jews' College in London.[27] They were on short-term contracts which made for insecurity, and their salaries were miserable. In 1919 Revd Eli Bloom was being paid £100.10s. a year, and Revd Israelstam, *chazan* and teacher in the Merthyr religion school, £33. These were unskilled workmen's wages, although probably supplemented by free accommodation, by an occasional grant towards the expenses of a holiday (which had to be asked for) and by some earnings for services to other congregations and to private clients. Between November 1918 and April 1920 there were six requests for salary increases from the two ministers, none of which produced more than vague promises for some future date. Revd Israelstam encountered opposition from some members of the synagogue committee who were dissatisfied with his standard of teaching, and in March 1920 he was sacked with four months of his three-year contract to run. Later a Mr Freedman came from London on a six months' trial contract, to combine the offices of teacher and beadle or caretaker. When he left Revd Eli Bloom agreed to take on the task of *chazan*, and actually got an extra £1 a week. Within a month the committee was receiving complaints from the congregation that he was giving private Hebrew lessons. It seems that most of the rabbis did this, and the objection was not to their obtaining a little badly needed money, but that the parents who took private lessons for their children avoided contributing to the congregation's school fund. An entry in the Minute Book for 9 May 1920 records an instruction to Revd Bloom to stop teaching the children of the Bargoed congregation until the terms of payment to the congregation for these services had been agreed. There were also complaints that he was killing chickens for the Bargoed and Aberdare communities.[28]

Complaints of the poor standard of teaching in synagogue schools were common in the larger as well as the smaller congregations of south Wales, and probably elsewhere. Synagogue administrators never seemed to learn that low pay and the combination of teaching with menial offices ensured that standards would not rise. Contempt for teachers on the part of the comparatively rich was, in fact, a specifically English disease, while a tendency to bully the ministers has already been detected in Swansea and Cardiff. All things considered, Merthyr was singularly fortunate to keep its minister, Revd Eli Bloom, for thirty-eight years, from 1901 to 1939.

The south Wales Jewish congregations had some excuse for their tendency to treat their ministers shabbily and to drive hard bargains with their smaller neighbours, because they were always hard up and usually in debt. There were various ways of raising cash, most of them unsatisfactory. In April 1920 the Merthyr congregation had overspent by £150. A subcommittee proposed raising the rental of all the synagogue seats, of which there were four grades ranging from 3s. (15p) a week down to 6d. (2$\frac{1}{2}$p), by 3d., apart from the lowest grade which would be doubled. They also raised the licence fee of the two kosher butchers from 5s. (25p) to 15s. (75p).[29] These measures produced immediate complaints. Several of the seatholders refused to pay, as did one of the butchers, who was promptly told to pay up or lose his licence. Nevertheless, seat subscriptions rose annually. Even Revd Bloom's regular annual passover grant had to be withdrawn.[30] South Wales had now run into a period of industrial decline and the population of the Jewish communities was dwindling. A few of the more agreeable events survived, such as an annual children's outing to Barry Island (which took up so much of the time of the synagogue council and space in its minutes). But discussion of financial matters continued to be interminable and financial problems increasingly insoluble. Such perpetual and increasing financial strictures help to account for the synagogues' habit of driving hard bargains for the services of rabbis to other congregations, for the lending of Scrolls of the Law, for burial plots in their cemeteries, and for religious teaching (although this was often balanced by fear of denying poor children a Jewish education and possibly losing them to Judaism). In the history of these communities there is a curious contrast between communal meanness and not infrequent acts of outstanding generosity by individuals.

VII

There is an obligation on every Jew to give charity (literally, *tsedaka* or justice) to the less fortunate. One of the highest forms of giving is helping another to help himself, often adapted to modern circumstances as an interest-free loan to enable someone to start a business. No Jewish community, however small or insolvent, could avoid its obligation towards its own poor. This responsibility to indigent Jews also had the advantage of keeping them off the local poor rate and thereby, to some extent, disarming anti-Semitism. As early as 1864 the *Jewish Chronicle* published a report of the plight of Youtaff Levy, who a few years before had been a subscriber to the synagogue fund, but was now appealing for assistance to the Merthyr community.

> Having four small children ill with fever for some time, and one buried only a few days since ... he has been reduced to the greatest distress, his wife expecting to be confined daily. He has been well-known as a respectable tradesman for the last sixteen years. The undersigned believe that if sufficient funds could be raised to enable them to place him in a little way of business so as to enable him to obtain a living for himself and family ... [sic].[31]

The Merthyr and Cardiff congregations gave £5 each and Swansea £8.15s.

By 1900 Merthyr, in common with many other Jewish communities, had a Board of Guardians. In 1904, at the invitation of a minister, the Revd I. Raffalovich, the ladies met and set up a Benevolent Society to help refugees from Russia. On its committee sat the wives of the congregation elders. Doubtless this replaced earlier and less formal societies which looked after local long-term poor and, as was the custom of Jewish communities, distributed unleavened bread, wine and *matzo* meal to the poor at Passover. But the Board of Guardians also took responsibility for the casuals who passed through the town. Being off the main migrant routes the south Wales valleys were not overwhelmed by floods of these, but there were enough to be a problem. As the *South Wales Jewish Review* put it:

> No doubt . . . a great number of the 284 casuals that passed through Merthyr have also been relieved in other towns and so the monies — by no means plentiful — of the different Boards (i.e. Boards of Guardians) are spent mostly and in some cases solely, in paying the railway fares of a wandering tribe, who in time, may develop into a class such as are to be met with in Poland. Surely it is time that some scheme should be worked out by which means the poor shall be relieved in a more effective manner, without sending them from place to place benefiting nobody and frittering away the hard collected subscriptions.[32]

The casuals were generally regarded in settled communities as 'undeserving poor' and a nuisance. It is curious that, while responsibility for them was not repudiated, their presence had produced a reversion to older English 'remedies' under which 'sturdy beggars' were removed to their place of settlement. But the wandering immigrants had no place of settlement. Instead such agencies as the Jewish Colonization Association might step in to help dispose of the newcomers. In 1903 a party of refugees from Russia took temporary jobs in the Dowlais steel works, hoping to finance their onward journey to North America.[33] They attracted hostile attention from the Irish steel workers (whose families constituted a large part of the town's population) and the Association and the Merthyr community together contributed to their fares, doubtless glad to see them go. Unfortunately they failed to find employment in Canada, and it seems that some of them came back. Wisely the *South Wales Jewish Review* had already pointed out that trouble from the immigrants could be easily overcome 'by a constant mixing with them, and by an endeavour to raise them from their abject condition, to which centuries of long persecution has plunged them'.[34] After all, many of the members of the Board of Guardians had themselves (or their parents) been homeless wanderers not many years ago. They had, more or less, assimilated themselves to their present English or Welsh background, and they saw safety and stability in persuading the newcomers to do likewise as quickly as possible.

Judging from the entries in the Merthyr Congregation Minute Book little attempt was made to pay regular pensions to the indigent. Admittedly the Board of Guardians had lapsed during the war years, but the congregation continued to pay out sums to applicants on an *ad hoc* basis for special needs or special purposes. A Mr S. Hyman of Dowlais obtained a grant of 30*s*. (£1.50p) for two or three weeks 'to enable him to rest' — probably convalescent money.[35] Mrs Solomon received the considerable sum of £15 to enable her family to visit London.[36] Unfortunately no estimate can be made as to the consistency or effectiveness of these charitable grants without more information about the cases. Large sums could be raised for emergencies. At a meeting of the congregation on 8 June 1919 to protest against the atrocities perpetrated on the Jews in Poland — a copy of the resolution was to be sent to the Prime Minister — ten guineas were voted for the Polish Jews' relief, and the nineteen committee members present pledged a further sixty-two guineas.[37] As the years passed and the Merthyr community dwindled in size and the average age of its members increased, charitable giving became more of a strain. But the communities helped each other in relieving individual emergencies, and there is no sign that *tsedaka* ever died out, as long as Jews remained in the valleys.

VIII

The small Jewish communities, isolated from each other in the Welsh working-class towns of the valleys, established and maintained contact with other Jews. In the early years of the twentieth century these contacts burgeoned into a movement for literary societies. Mr Louis Harris of Tredegar, in an address to the Merthyr District Jewish Literary and Social Society on 3 December 1903, defined their aims:

> It is hardly necessary to observe that under the term Literary Society are embraced and included all such branches as Debate, Discussion, Reading Courses, in short, anything which bears a connection with or relation to Literature . . . It is from an occasional gathering of earnest-minded young men and women for the purpose of interchanging ideas, the discussion of topics, and the debating of subjects that their minds develop, expand and gain in intellectual growth . . . It is at such societies that they learn the discipline of order and method . . . the

training of their mental and the strengthening of their intellectual faculties . . . In conclusion, I claim for the utility of the Literary Societies namely that the young men and women of today are the responsible men and women of tomorrow . . .[38]

Literary, musical and theatrical societies already existed in Cardiff and the larger towns. There was a Union of Jewish Literary Societies which met in London, and was a target of such complaints of inactivity as are usual in these movements. However, Merthyr's Literary Society does not seem to have been formally inaugurated until May 1903, while Tredegar's society started about the same time. A wave of enthusiasm swept the valleys. Tredegar offered five lectures or discussions within three weeks: 'The Jewish Capacity for Self Government' (20 February), 'An Evening with Dickens' (21 February), 'The Jew and the Stage' (28 February), 'Humorous Readings' (6 March) and 'The Universal Influence of the Psalms' (13 March). The Merthyr Society offered a lecture by Julius Prag on 'Alien Immigration into Britain', a topic of red-hot political interest to the community since a Royal Commission was currently gathering evidence designed to lead to the Aliens Immigration Act of 1905.[39]

These societies had some remarkable features. Their programmes included secular as well as religious, political as well as literary topics. They were independent of the synagogues; their membership included men and women, apparently on terms of equality, and they seemed to have been angled largely at the young. They displayed a moral earnestness typical of Edwardian Britain. They started on a wave of enthusiasm which, again typically, did not last. Although a large delegation from south Wales attended the third conference of the Union in London in June 1903, by the following year the *South Wales Jewish Review*, which had enthusiastically reported these activities, was complaining of waning interest. It seems that the literary societies were reverting to the social clubs of former days, or being taken over by new Zionist societies.[40]

Paradoxically, some of the valley literary societies may have been saved from collapse by the Zionist movement. A 'tent' of Chovevei Zion (Lovers of Zion), forerunner of the Zionist movement in Britain had been established in south Wales by Col. A.E.W. Goldsmid along with a detachment of the Jewish Lads' Brigade.[41] Following his celebrated meeting with Theodore Herzl in 1903 Goldsmid had become sympathetic to political Zionism. The English Zionist Federation was founded in London in January 1899, and this form of

Jewish nationalism quickly penetrated the valleys. In Cardiff as in London, where there was already a wealthy and well-established élite, Zionism provoked serious conflict in the Jewish community. The élite feared that Zionism with its goal of a Jewish state would undermine the position that successful and loyal Jews had won for themselves in Britain. But in the valleys, where the majority of Jews were newer immigrants, where life was still precarious and a professional class had barely formed, such a division was hardly visible. On 21 October 1900 a Zionist conference was held in the Central Hotel, Cardiff, followed by a public meeting in the new and prestigious synagogue in Cathedral Road.[42] A South Wales Zionist Federation had already been established. In December 1903 the Federation met in conference in Newport. It was unfortunate that the movement was now split by the controversy surrounding Herzl's proposal for temporary Jewish emigration from Russia to Uganda. But neither this nor Herzl's death in 1904 destroyed the Zionist movement in south Wales. While in various places the literary societies melted into the Zionist societies, these social and literary groups now had a strong cause to hold them together. Despite some complaints of apathy and poor attendance at the Merthyr meetings membership of the local Zionist societies remained remarkably high. In May 1904 the combined Tredegar and New Tredegar Zionist Society had a membership of 55 out of a total Jewish population of 90, Newport 30 out of 120, Merthyr 40 out of 300, Aberdare 30 out of 90, Brynmawr and Abertillery 70 out of 200, and Pontypridd, astonishingly, 57 out of 100.[43] The accuracy of these figures, which the *South Wales Jewish Review* took from the Jewish Year Book, cannot be trusted, yet they do suggest a well-supported movement. The *Review* made an interesting comparison between the Zionist fervour and the Nonconformist religious revival currently sweeping the valleys:

> At the present time Wales is attracting world wide notice by reason of an exceptional development of religious fervour. Whether it is a question of environment or not, we cannot say, but it is undeniable that some of the recent Zionist meetings in the district have been unique in their enthusiasm.[44]

IX

The south Wales valleys communities were unique. The only settlements which could be in any way compared with them were those of the Durham coalfields, also situated in scattered mining villages. Life was the reverse of that in a continental ghetto; spaced instead of cramped, isolated instead of crowded. It was not even comparable with the villages and towns of the Russian-Polish border, where the proportion of Jews was so much higher. The Jews in Wales were very dependent on their Christian neighbours, who were their classmates in school (there were no Jewish secular schools) and the customers in their shops. That their acceptance was sometimes hazarded by the role of so many as pawnbrokers, and that there was anti-Semitism in the valleys is proved by the Tredegar Riots of 1911, if by nothing else. That the Jewish families had friends who would shelter them in times of danger is also shown in the events of those riots. But all in all the Jews held together, maintaining their religious and social lives and their Jewish identity despite the difficulties of communication and the hazards of bad times. Perhaps this was partly because the period of the Jewish settlements in the valleys was comparatively short. Also the scattered nature and small size of the communities seems to have produced in them a clinging to traditional forms of Judaism. South Wales Jews were, on the whole, noted for their orthodoxy. There was no sign of a Reform or a Liberal Jewish movement, even in Cardiff, until after the Second World War.

In the nineteenth century Jewish names were conspicuously absent from the lists of town councillors and permanent officials in the directories. Even after the First World War there were only two solicitors of note, Benjamin Hamilton (the name was changed from the German-sounding Himmelstein during the war) and Leo Roskin. Exceptionally, the very first Jewish JP in south Wales was Israel Fine of Rhymney. The absence of a middle-class élite was not due to absence of talent but to the very restricted opportunities afforded by the valley societies. They produced several noteworthy and talented people,[45] but they had to go elsewhere to fulfil their promise. None the less the communities of the Welsh mining valleys offer an interesting chapter in Jewish history. There is room for further research upon them.

Notes to Chapter 2

1. Jews were certainly present in the south Wales area in medieval times as reported by Gerald of Wales in *Speculum Ecclesiae* written in 1218. He reports that a monk from Margam Abbey 'became a convert to Judaism and even allowed himself to be circumcised according to the Jewish rite'.
2. See Epilogue pp. 215f.
3. *Merthyr Guardian*, 26 April 1834. Brinley Thomas, 'The Migration of Labour into the Glamorganshire Coalfield (1861–1911)'.
4. W.E. Minchinton (ed.), *Industrial South Wales 1750–1914*, (London, Cass, 1969), 37–56.
5. *Kelly's Directory*, 1895 et seq.
6. *Welsh History Review*, 6 December 1972, 191.
7. Ibid.
8. Ibid. The figures were taken from the Jewish Year Books, which are often suspect.
9. The Merthyr Jewish marriage register from 1886 to 1914 has been preserved. It brings to notice Jews in the humbler occupations who would not appear in the directories.
10. Merthyr Jewish marriage register.
11. *South Wales Jewish Review*, no.1 (January 1904), 16. Cf. note 33.
12. Special Committee Meeting. Minutes of the Swansea Hebrew Congregation, 13 July 1902.
13. Joseph Buckman, *Immigrants and the Class Struggle: The Jewish Immigrant in Leeds 1880–1914* (Manchester University Press, 1983), *passim*.
14. Harold Pollins, *An Economic History of the Jews in England* (Littman Library, Associated Presses, 1982), 142.
15. L.P. Gartner, *The Jewish Immigrant in England 1810–1914* (London, George Allen and Unwin, 1960), 57–8. The figures were taken from the annual reports of The Poor Jews' Temporary Shelter for the years 1895–6, 1899–1900, 1901–2, 1903–4, 1907–8.
16. Birmingham Jewish Research Group, 'Birmingham Jewry 1759–1914' (1980), 44.
17. A. Hardaker, *A Brief History of Pawnbroking* (London, Jackson Ruston and Keeson, 1892), 276–86, 358–64.
18. See Chap.1. Any estimate of the numbers and property of Jewish landlords in the valleys would require an extensive investigation of surviving rate books from the valley towns.
19. *Jewish Chronicle*, 27 February 1852, 168.
20. It is now a roofless ruin. CAJEX 19 No.4 (December 1969), 70.
21. *JC*, 28 May 1852, 267.
22. Ibid., 22 June 1877, 12.
23. Ibid., 23 October 1874, 482, 30 October 1874, 491, 1 March 1878, 5. It has been pointed out that Nonconformist congregations sometimes incurred similar burdens of debt in building their chapels.

24. Ibid., 27 August 1875, 351. Could the mysterious 'eminent party residing in London' have been the Chief Rabbi?
25. Ibid., 24 May 1867, 8.
26. Merthyr Congregation Minute Book 1918-34.
27. Not all ministers were officially 'rabbis', i.e. had graduated or received 'semicha' from a training seminary.
28. Merthyr Congregation Minute Book, 9 May 1920.
29. Ibid., 25 April 1920.
30. Ibid., 7 February 1932.
31. *JC*, 8 April 1864. Merthyr Tydfil was notorious for its lack of sanitation and periodical epidemics.
32. *South Wales Jewish Review*, No.11 (November 1904), 171.
33. Cf. note 11. It appears that the refugees had been invited to Merthyr by the parents of Benjamin Himmelstein (later Hamilton), who had immigrated from Lithuania. Some of them settled in the New World, and returned to visit Hamilton in Dowlais as American soldiers in the First World War. Benjamin Hamilton, 'Recollections', p.24 *et seq.*
34. *South Wales Jewish Review*, No.2 (February 1904), 30.
35. Merthyr Congregation Minute Book, 2 November 1919.
36. Ibid., 27 April 1927.
37. Ibid., 8 June 1919.
38. *South Wales Jewish Review*, No.1 (January 1904), 6–7.
39. Ibid., No.3 (March 1903), 44.
40. Ibid., No.11 (November 1904), 168, 176, 180. Einstein feared that the new Zionist societies were weakening the literary societies with which they amalgamated.
41. Cf. p. iv.
42. *JC*, 26 October 1900, 25–6,. Cf. pp.29f.
43. *South Wales Jewish Review*, No.5 (May 1904), 68.
44. *South Wales Jewish Review*, No.12 (December 1904), 192.
45. Cf. Epilogue, p.216.

3

The Jews and Crime in South Wales before the First World War

URSULA R. Q. HENRIQUES

How many Jews were criminals? What sort of crimes did they commit? Were Jewish immigrants a menace to the society in which they lived? On the whole nineteenth-century anti-Semitic stereotypes did not follow this line. Jews had more of a reputation for getting round the law than for breaking it. But this was not universal. For instance Dickens, who was apt to get his plots from Government Blue Books, depicted Fagin in *Oliver Twist* as the archetypal receiver of stolen goods, organizing gangs of young thieves. And it was generally believed that this role was played by Jews in mid-nineteenth-century London. Wales was not London, but this reputation could have followed the provincial community as it developed there.

Many Jewish immigrants were newly arrived, speaking a foreign tongue, penniless, rootless and forced to scratch a living by peddling, hawking or, if settled in one place, working as under-paid tailors, seamstresses, cap-makers or coal-miners. They were caught in sweated occupations which must have made crime seem an easy option. But the same was true of the populations of miners, port-workers or sailors among whom they lived. So how did the records compare?

The opportunity to examine this question was afforded by the existence of the very full materials retained in the Glamorgan Archive in Cathays Park, Cardiff, together with a helpful staff of archivists ready to show them to the enquirer. They include a long run of printed calendars of the prisoners held in Cardiff and Swansea gaols (including those bailed) who were tried at the Glamorgan Assizes and Quarter Sessions. The Assizes were usually (although not invariably) held quarterly, in spring, summer, autumn and winter. Well-known

High Court judges came down from London to preside. The Quarter Sessions Courts were also held quarterly, usually before a bench of three Justices of the Peace. Both courts were located, more or less alternately, in Swansea and Cardiff Town Halls, although after 1907 those at Cardiff were generally held in the newly-built Cardiff Law Courts. The Cardiff Quarter Sessions cases, once started in 1890, were heard before the Recorder of Cardiff, Benjamin Williams Esq., QC. Until that date the Assizes and Quarter Sessions Courts covered the trials of those charged with offences committed in the whole of Glamorgan, from Swansea in the west to Cardiff in the east, and Merthyr Tydfil in the north. For a time the Assizes also dealt with cases from Brecon, Carmarthen and Hereford, although these rural areas produced very few crimes of note. After 1890 crimes committed in Cardiff were heard in the separate Cardiff Quarter Sessions, although the most serious ones still went to the Assizes. The latter dealt with the most important cases of murder, rape, robbery, fraud, forgery, etc; Quarter Sessions dealt with the other cases considered serious enough to require a jury. Below these two tiers the Petty Sessions, courts of summary jurisdiction presided over by JPs or a stipendiary magistrate, sat in subdivisions of the county and heard the minor offences. The records of these, including the well-known Cardiff Police Court, are in the Glamorgan Archive. They are mostly hand-written notes taken during the trials, and are sketchy, illegible and far too voluminous for systematic coverage by a single researcher.

On the other hand, the prison calendars of cases before the Assizes and Quarter Sessions are printed. By 1860 they had settled into a uniform format giving the name of each prisoner, the place and nature of the crime with which he was charged, the authority or person bringing the charge, the verdict of the court, the sentence (if any), and a list of his previous convictions. An index in the front of each calendar gives the names, in alphabetical order, of the prisoners in each of the two prisons, and on bail from them. In the later years each prisoner's degree of education was assessed on a scale, and an analysis of the different types of charge was given, along with the numbers charged. Thus the printed calendars enable a reasonably systematic study to be made of the more serious criminal cases heard in Glamorgan throughout the period. This can be supplemented by some consideration of the endless lists of drunks, disorderlies, prostitutes, beggars, minor assaults and petty thieves who came

Table 1: The Growth of Crime in Glamorgan from 1861 to 1908

	VALLEYS			CARDIFF			GLAMORGAN		
	No. tried	Probable Jews	%	No. tried	Probable Jews	%	No. tried	Probable Jews	%
1861–66							1849	11	0.59
1873–78							1748	12	0.68
1879–84							1534	17	1.11
1885–90	1813	10	0.55	50*	1	2.00	1863	11	0.59
1891–96	1832	20	1.09	671	8	1.19	2503	28	1.11
1897–1902	1658	23	1.38	448	14	3.12	2106	37	1.75
1903–08	2056	20	0.97	738	9	1.22	2794	29	1.04

* 1890 only

before the Petty Sessions. Finally, a great many of these cases were reported in more detail in the *Western Mail* and other local papers, where further information can be found.

The numbers of those charged with crimes at the Quarter Sessions and Assize Courts for Glamorgan in any one year fluctuate so much that they mean very little. To help in identifying trends I have grouped them into totals for six years at a time which fits in with the list of calendars preserved (there is a gap between 1866 and 1873). The results can be seen in Table 1 (above).

It appears that the total number of criminal charges for the whole of Glamorgan remained more or less constant between 1860 and 1890. When Cardiff became a County Borough in 1890 the establishment of the separate Cardiff Quarter Sessions to try crimes committed in the borough increased the total by about 600 (why is not clear), and thereafter it continued to rise, unevenly but surely. After 1908 the numbers rose more rapidly, including those tried at Cardiff Quarter Sessions. In 1891 the Cardiff Court had dealt with ninety-eight criminal charges. These, of course, included a fair proportion ending in a verdict of No True Bill, or Not Guilty (which, judging by the speed with which the 'innocent' person was often again before the court, could merely mean exonerated for lack of evidence). Nor did the calendars differentiate between the cases of new offenders and those of many habitual criminals who appeared before the judges time after time, thus inflating the statistics.

Glamorgan is not the whole of industrial south Wales. The eastern industrial valleys, which also contained Jewish communities such as those of Newport and Tredegar as well as groups of families in the smaller mining villages, lay in the county of Monmouthshire. The Monmouth Quarter Sessions were held at Usk, and their calendars are now kept in the Gwent County Hall archive at Cwmbran. Unfortunately many of the earlier records have been lost, and there are many gaps. Even in 1903 only two out of the four Quarter Sessions calendars remain, although from 1904 onward the records are complete. Gwent also has some Petty Sessions books from the various Monmouthshire divisions, although with much less detail than those for Glamorgan. The Monmouth Assizes were part of the Oxford Assize Circuit. Their calendars form part of the Oxford Assize Circuit minute books held at the Public Record Office in Chancery Lane, London. Putting together the Glamorgan Assize and Quarter Sessions calendars, the Monmouth Quarter Sessions records, and the Oxford Assize records for Monmouth we have a reasonably comprehensive record (so far as it has survived) of the more serious criminal proceedings in south Wales, at least during the period 1903-8. Only the westernmost industrial towns and villages such as Llanelli, which contained a Jewish community of about seventy, remain outside. The population numbers were small, and it can be presumed that the proportions and nature of the criminal elements were much the same as in the rest of the south Wales industrial area.

To this, however, a caution must be added. Although the cases on record increased rapidly towards the end of the nineteenth century and became very numerous after the turn of the century, they were still numbered by hundreds. In fact the numbers were paltry in proportion to those of the exploding population. They cannot represent more than the tip of the iceberg, that is the criminals caught and brought to justice (including those found not guilty)—by no means all the crimes committed. They must reflect the degree of efficiency of the police as much as the extent of crime.

But what of the Jews? Here again it is necessary to start with a caution. The Jews accused of crime present the usual problems of identification. Only a few can be found among the known, locally settled families whose names appear on synagogue subscription lists, marriage registers or the burial books of Jewish cemeteries. Among the Welsh offenders we encounter many members of those working-class families who, in the early nineteenth century, took biblical names. Statistically it is even possible that Welsh criminals wrongly identified as Jewish by Old Testament names are partly cancelled out

Table 2: Proportion of Jews Tried to Total Numbers Tried on Criminal Charges in South Wales, 1903–1908

	VALLEYS			CARDIFF			GLAMORGAN	
No. tried	Probable Jews	%	No. tried	Probable Jews	%	No. tried	Probable Jews	%
2056	20	0.97	738	9	1.22	2794	29	1.04

		MONMOUTHSHIRE			S. WALES		
		No. tried	Probable Jews	%	No. tried	Probable Jews	%
Q.S.*		138	3				
Ass.		108	4				
		246	7	2.84	3040	36	1.18

* Two out of four in 1903

Table 3: Proportion of Persons Tried on Criminal Charges to Total Population of South Wales, 1903–1908

	POPULATION (1901)	NUMBERS TRIED	%
Glamorgan	860,000	2794	0.32
Monmouthshire	298,000	246	0.08
South Wales	1,158,000	3040	0.26

Table 4: Proportion of Jews Tried on Criminal Charges to Estimated Jewish Population of South Wales, 1903–1908

	JEWISH POPULATION		PROBABLE JEWS TRIED	%
Cardiff	either	1500	9	0.6
	or	1250	9	0.72
South Wales	either	5000	36	0.72
	or	6000	36	0.6

by Jewish criminals overlooked under English or Welsh names. Despite the formulation of statistical tables, the results of a study of this kind can never produce more than approximations or even guestimates of the actual situation. All the same, such a study is not without interest.

In Table 1 an attempt has been made to trace the statistical growth of criminal cases in Glamorgan and to work out the number and proportion of Jewish cases among them. Tables 2, 3 and 4 (see above) cover the shorter, if peak period of 1903–8, adding Monmouth (always recollecting that only two out of four of the Monmouth

Quarter Sessions calendars for the year 1903 remain). Table 2 shows the percentage of Jews tried to the total tried; Table 3 gives the total tried to the total population, and Table 4 gives an estimate of the percentage of Jews tried to the Jewish population. Another disadvantage on the Jewish side is that the numbers were so small that a variant of even one or two in the figures produces a large variation in the percentages. Allowing for this the results are palpable if not dramatic. We find a very slightly higher proportion of Jews tried on criminal charges to the Jewish population of south Wales than of total numbers tried to the total population: 0.6 per cent to 0.26 per cent. The proportion of Jews tried for crimes to the total tried for crimes is 1.18 per cent to 0.26 per cent. However, these numbers and proportions are so low that by no stretch of the imagination could the Jewish immigration be seen to produce a large increase in the crime rate or a crime wave in south Wales. Indeed, if the numbers of Jewish names in the calendars are compared with the numbers of Irish names (which as late as the Glamorgan Autumn Assizes for 1908 constituted over 14 per cent of those on the lists) it will be apparent which of these influxes of penniless refugees provided the larger share of criminals. And this impression is reinforced by the long lists of drunk and disorderly Irishmen and women who appeared before the Cardiff Police Court.

What sort of crimes did Jewish criminals commit? Were there any specifically 'Jewish' crimes which marked their perpetrators out from the rest of the criminal fraternity? Before considering this question it would be useful to look at the nature of crime in south Wales.

The calendars suggest that the majority of the more serious crimes committed were crimes against property. In every list of cases both at Glamorgan Assizes and Quarter Sessions the greatest number of charges were for larceny (theft). These were often divided into simple larceny, larceny from the person (i.e. picking pockets), bailee larceny (i.e. the theft or conversion of property being held in trust, usually in a case of bankruptcy, and sometimes larceny by a servant or a post office worker). To these were added housebreaking, shopbreaking, warehouse and counting house breaking, all of which became burglary if done at night. Secondary to these was the receiving of stolen goods. Then there were various kinds of frauds and the obtaining of money or goods by false pretences. The most serious — forgery and counterfeit coining — generally went to Assizes. A combination of offences against property and against the person was the frequent crime of robbery with violence. The serious cases usually went to Assizes, along with murder, manslaughter, rape, malicious wounding, and the infliction of grievous bodily harm. Monmouth Assizes in particular had numerous cases of rape and carnal knowledge of children under the age of sixteen. The less serious cases of wounding, attempted rape or indecent assault, and malicious damage to property valued at more than £5 went to Quarter Sessions. There was an overlap between the cases heard in the two courts, and the principles of division are not altogether clear. Bigamy, a surprisingly common offence, and probably often an attempt to acquire property, was usually heard at Assizes. So was homosexuality, usually described as 'gross indecency' and severely punished with imprisonment. Pimps, along with persistent beggars as 'incorrigible rogues', were sent to prison for several months at Quarter Sessions, while their flocks of prostitutes were sentenced to shorter periods at Petty Sessions.

The separation of Cardiff Quarter Sessions from Glamorgan Sessions from 1890 (recollecting that the graver cases still went to Glamorgan Assizes) highlights some differences between the crimes typical of Cardiff and the ports and those typical of the valleys. Each had special circumstances likely to augment its crime figures. Cardiff, a big docks and shopping centre, was haunted by prostitutes, and the arrival of merchant ships was reflected in the calendar by foreign names, usually opposite charges of stabbing or malicious wounding.

Yet Merthyr Tydfil and the towns of what is now called the Rhondda, but was always referred to under the names of its two parishes, Ystradyfodwg and Llanwonno, were markedly more prone to violence. The Glamorgan Midsummer Quarter Sessions of June 1899 heard ten charges of larceny, two of shopbreaking, two of false pretences, one of burglary, seven of wounding, one of assault, one of grievous bodily harm, one of attempted rape, two of indecent assault and one attempted suicide. The Cardiff County Borough Sessions in June 1899 heard twenty-one cases of larceny, six of housebreaking, two of shopbreaking, one of burglary, three of false pretences, one of wounding, one of attempted suicide and one of showing indecent pictures. Earlier in the nineteenth century the difference was more marked, the cases of violence in the valleys sometimes exceeding those of larceny. The valleys also produced the more rural cases of sheep and fowl stealing, poaching and occasional rick-burning. However, the differences should not be exaggerated. In both areas gangs of young toughs (in Merthyr Tydfil usually colliers) raided any place where food, clothes or valuables were kept. Railway stores and depots (especially coal bunkers) were popular targets. Violent industrial action occurred in Cardiff where at the Easter Quarter Sessions, 1891, four seamen including Havelock Ellis, Secretary of the Seamen's Union, got six weeks for rioting, while four more got two weeks. In the Easter Assizes the same year a bus- and a tram-driver were sentenced to two months each for unlawful wounding and damage to tramcars during a riotous assembly of seventy or more. In 1910 and 1911, as we know, industrial violence, rioting and looting moved to the valleys.

How did the Jewish criminals appear in these records? Both from the stereotypes and from the insecurity and partial isolation in which many immigrants and children of immigrants lived, Jewish crime could be expected to follow certain lines. One would expect to find receivers of stolen goods rather than thieves; frauds, forgers and obtainers of goods by false pretences rather than robbers and burglars, fraudulent merchants and petty pilferers among the numerous hawkers and pedlars. And of course they are to be found.

As far back as 1857 John da Costa (usually a Sephardi name), pedlar, was accused in Quarter Sessions of endeavouring to obtain by false pretences one guinea from Elizabeth Rice and one guinea from David Phillips, at Neath. Unfortunately the nature of the false pretences is not revealed, but the prisoner was discharged on sureties. In the Michaelmas Quarter Sessions, October 1875, Kate Isaac, 17, dressmaker, possibly but not certainly a Jewess, pleaded guilty to obtaining 1½ pounds of butter by false pretences. She was sentenced to fourteen days' hard labour and five years in a reformatory. Poor girl; the young were far more heavily punished under the reformatory system than adults. In Quarter Sessions April 1897, Henry Levy, 34, commission agent, was convicted of receiving stolen oxide of cobalt at Landore and sentenced to eighteen months' hard labour in Swansea gaol. In 1883 Hyman Freedman, a Swansea pawnbroker, was sentenced by the Assize Court to penal servitude for five years for receiving stolen watches. At the Winter Assize of February 1881, Jean Goldman, 42, commission agent, was charged with fraudulently concealing goods, shares and mortgages at bankruptcy proceedings to defraud his creditors, but he was found not guilty and discharged. This class of case, in which bankrupts were suspected of concealing their assets, or trading on credit while still undischarged, was not uncommon. In December 1889 William David Israel, 25, hawker, was convicted in Quarter Sessions of obtaining from Nathan Ash one clock, three chairs and an iron stand, the property of John Jacob in Llanwonno. Having two previous convictions for horse stealing he went to Cardiff gaol for twelve months, but was soon after convicted of false pretences again. In 1893 Henry Phillips, dealer, forged a receipt for money, and, it being his eighth conviction for forgery, was sentenced to penal servitude for four years. In 1904 Jacob Bakalov, 23, was sentenced to six months for embezzling small sums from his employer, Joseph Bogod. In October 1914 Joseph Cohen, draper of Tredegar, received four months at Monmouth Quarter Sessions for selling, not for the first time, his own mineral water in the bottles of Thomas and Evans of Porth.

And so it goes on. Occasionally a Jew was found acting as receiver in a mixed gang. In 1908 Benjamin Levinsohn, 19, pawnbroker's assistant, joined with D. Lloyd, haulier, William Bryant, collier, and Price Lloyd, traveller, in breaking and entering the house of Jacob Kransky in Llanwonno, and stealing clothes. Levinsohn and Price Lloyd got twelve months each for receiving the stolen goods. It will be observed that Jews were often the victims of Jewish criminals, not least in breaking and entering cases. The criminal probably knew where the Jewish businesses were, and also how to get into them.

Despite these examples there is no evidence that Jews acted as receivers or forgers or embezzlers or obtained money by false pretences any more often than their non-Jewish associates. There was a steady trickle of receivers who acted as the necessary disposers of stolen goods, and the Jews were a small minority among them. There is no evidence that they organized permanent gangs. The same is true of fraud, embezzlement and false pretences, all of them common crimes. On the other hand, there is plenty of evidence of Jews indulging in simple larceny and house or shopbreaking. Perhaps it is hardly fair to count Louis Slivensky, 10, who with other children and two adults was convicted at Cardiff Quarter Sessions for July 1900 of stealing coal from the Taff Vale Railway Company. The children got one day and the adults two months. As early as 1861 Moses Levy, 24, cab-driver, was convicted with two others of breaking and entering the house of Hezekiah Hughes, Llanwonno, and stealing £4, a silver teaspoon and a sugar tongs, and sentenced to two years in Swansea gaol. He was obviously one of a gang. In an unusual case, William Bernstein, 51, fitter, was bound over at Cardiff Quarter Sessions,

Michaelmas 1909, for breaking and entering a warehouse of the Cardiff Dry Dock Company and stealing a stop valve cover, a spindle and a nut, and other objects peculiar to his trade. In the 1890s there were one or two Jewish horse stealers, but by 1899 Samuel Gottlieb, 18, watchmaker of Cardiff, was stealing bicycles. Cases of stealing and of breaking and entering can be multiplied *ad nauseam*. They reinforce the impression that in crimes against property Jewish criminals were a part, not especially conspicuous, of the local criminal scene. This was true also of the considerable proportion of them who were pedlars, hawkers or travellers. There were many Irish pedlars and hawkers too, some indulging in dishonest activities.

Jews are not noted for sexual crimes, but there were a few Jewish names among those charged with this type of offence. In 1862 David Solomon, 56, was found not guilty of unlawfully knowing a girl aged 10, but in 1894 Morris Jacobs, 36, tailor, received seven years' penal servitude, a very stiff sentence, at the Assizes in Swansea for a similar offence, as did Hyman Rosenthal at Monmouth Assizes in 1904. In 1872 Samuel Marks, tobacconist, was charged with indecently assaulting a girl under thirteen, She said he asked for a kiss and then behaved indecently. He said he just asked for a kiss. The case was dismissed for lack of evidence, but, according to the *Western Mail* the magistrate said to the defendant, 'Get out, you nasty old beast.'[1] An unusual case occurred in 1888 when Simon Freedman, 20, an employee of Isaac Kantorovich, was accused of taking Rachel Kantorovich, aged 14, out of the custody of her mother. Freedman claimed that he was rescuing the girl from her parents who beat her, and also claimed that her father had offered to sell her to him if he waited a year.[2] Although the girl would not support him in the witness box he was found not guilty. When the long lists of unlawful knowing, and even more the gang rapes which appeared before the Assize courts are considered, the Jewish record in this field was not a disgraceful one.

Nor were Jewish offenders often violent, although there were exceptions. There were one or two cases of robbery with violence, usually as part of a gang. In 1854 Moses Lewis (who may or may not have been Jewish) was sentenced at the Assizes to one week for striking Jean Huet on the head with a stone. In 1880 two young pawnbrokers, Jacob and Nathan Tanchan, 15 and 18, were accused of two assaults in one week. The older was fined twenty shillings with costs. Next year they were again in trouble, Jacob being fined at

Bridgend Police Court for damaging a pair of boots pledged with him and then charging more than the legal interest upon them. The following month both were fined for trying to collect a debt, which the debtor had refused to pay on the grounds that the interest was exorbitant, by entering his house, with the bailiff, through a window which they damaged.[3]

If not often violent, Jews were sometimes caught up in militant industrial action. In 1892 Henry Hyman, 30, a painter, was found guilty with five others of intimidating three workmen at Cadoxton near Barry to make them abstain from working for their employer. The Tanchan brothers' debt-collecting activities had attracted a mob, with evident implications for arousing anti-Semitism. The Cadoxton case suggests that in industrial action, as in most crimes, Jews were merely assimilated into the activities and mores of their non-Jewish neighbours.

The south Wales towns and valleys were always haunted by professional thieves and petty criminals who preyed on society. At any one time one or two of these could be of Jewish origin. In the 1860s Merthyr Tydfil was pestered by a pickpocket, Leah Lewis. She appears first in the Glamorgan Michaelmas Quarter Sessions for 1864. She was found not guilty of stealing money and a scarf, but in January 1865 she was convicted of stealing a watch from one William Coleman. In Michaelmas 1866 she was sentenced to two years' hard labour for stealing a purse. Between 1879 and 1885 Henry Singer, a bagman or rag collector, evidently with a horse and cart, stole 30 lb of iron and 100 lb of coal at Maesteg, for which he served five months in gaol. He was lucky to be cleared in 1882 of robbing a warehouse of half a ton of rags.

In the 1890s William David Israel, hawker (already mentioned), haunted the valleys, stealing watches and obtaining articles of clothing by false pretences. But the principal pest in the last two decades of the nineteenth century was Joseph Abraham (or Abrahams). This man, plainly one of nature's inadequates, started his career at the age of sixteen by stealing a pair of boots, for which he received twelve strokes of the birch and fourteen days from Chepstow Petty Sessions. Between 1881 and 1908 he accumulated eighteen convictions in various south Wales towns, almost all for petty thefts of clothing, as well as twenty-three summary convictions for drunkenness and assaults. Yet Abraham was in no way exceptional. The calendars are full of similar cases with similar records, most of them beginning in early youth with a birching and/or sentence to reformatory custody for stealing apples or boots or some small sum of money. Any advocate of the birch or of reform schools (at least as they were conducted in the late nineteenth century) has only to look at these cases to experience doubts about the efficacy of draconian punishment in preventing crime. Moreover, as the nineteenth century wore on the proportion of criminals with long police records rose steadily until the single or occasional offence appeared to be exceptional. Once again the persistent criminal of Jewish origin, whether with an unconquerable addiction to pairs of boots and overcoats or to watches and jewellery was part of a kind of criminal fraternity or subculture. This was no 'respectable' mafia, but a sad throng of recidivists. The persistent petty thief had probably lost his (or her) religious and communal attachment, just as the more frequent Irish criminal had abandoned the discipline of his church. In all the circumstances, and especially in view of the large numbers exposed to the temptations of the hawkers' and pedlars' trades, it is perhaps surprising that there were not more.[4]

In these sorry records of crime and punishment a few special categories of criminal stand out. One is the exceptional offender in an otherwise known and prosperous family. The Tanchan brothers have already been mentioned. In 1861 Nelson Marks, 26, watchmaker (not the convert who became a water-rate collector, but probably a son of Samuel Marks the dyer who had a shop in St Mary Street, Cardiff), was sentenced to two years in Swansea gaol for embezzling 6s.6d. from his master, Bryant Briggs. It was a harsh sentence, but judges were hard on servants who were felt to have betrayed their trust. Four years later he was charged with a similar offence (evidently Briggs had taken him back) but found not guilty. Albert Heitzman, from a well-established immigrant family of watchmakers, became a forger and was found in possession of a die. However the family may have been German and not Jewish.

Another and even rarer category is the frankly dotty, always on the edge of prison or asylum, but not certifiable under the M'Naghten rules.[5] Hyam Jacobs, an elderly jeweller, was in repeated trouble with the law. He was accused of passing false cheques, got two months for lashing out with a stick at some boys who were teasing him, thought he was being spied on, and was apt to commit assaults when drunk. He even tried to pay for a drink with a pork sausage (which he would not eat himself), and having run out of money, told the barman that he 'wanted to pawn his face'. 'That', said the judge, 'is a primitive source of barter introduced by your ancestors'.[6] Anti-Semitic remarks were not uncommon in the lower courts.

By far the most important special category is that of the pawnbrokers.[7] Throughout the late nineteenth and early twentieth centuries Jews had a virtual monopoly of pawnbroking in south Wales. They formed an economically important and indeed wealthy group of considerable social influence. But they probably became more entangled in criminal and civil law than any other category of people in south Wales. If any businessman was beset with temptation to become a receiver of stolen goods it was the pawnbroker. And occasionally he yielded. Greenbone Jacobs, pawnbroker of Swansea, was accused in 1868 Midsummer Quarter Sessions of receiving stolen rope; but the case was dismissed. Hyman Freedman who in 1883 was sentenced to five years' penal servitude for receiving three gold watches has already been mentioned. Most accusations of receiving, however, concerned minor articles of second-hand clothing and cheap jewellery. It was customary for petty thieves immediately to take their loot to a pawnshop where they could get hard cash. When Mary Perryman in 1883 was charged with extensive thefts from her employers a number of Cardiff pawnbrokers were cautioned by the court for accepting articles without question. They included Fanny Freydburg of System Street, Morris Fine of Clifton Street, Abraham Shibko and Montague Barnett, all well-established traders. The pawnbrokers soon became alert to the dangers to themselves and their businesses from the reputation of receiving, especially as thieves frequently stole from one pawnshop and tried to pledge the goods at another, or even the same one. Although a broker — or more probably his inexperienced assistant — sometimes accepted a stolen pledge, more often, as soon as his suspicion was aroused, he sent for the police. Many a thief was caught in this way.

Otherwise the pawnbrokers were brought to court — usually to Petty Sessions — either for causing an obstruction on the pavement, or for accepting a pledge from a child under thirteen, forbidden by the Act of 1872. This Act was a trap since it was very difficult to know whether a child was thirteen or not, and parents sent their children along with their pledge. Nor could the pawnbrokers expect much sympathy from the magistrates, who punished them if they swindled a client but were apt to tell them it was their own fault if they were swindled by a customer.

This leads to the most striking feature emerging from this survey — that Jews were far more often the victims than the perpetrators of crime.

The impression gained from the records is that for one theft or robbery committed by a Jew there were four or five committed against one. Jewish businesses, both in Cardiff and in the valleys, were often of the sort most likely to attract shopbreakers. Pawnbroking was usually associated with the sale of jewellery or clothing or both. Pawnbrokers' shops and houses as well as ordinary jewellers and clothing stores were raided again and again. Sometimes a petty thief like Joseph Abraham filched single articles, and sometimes the shop was cleaned out by professional thieves. Coleman Follick of 40 and 41 Bridge Street, Cardiff, was raided at least nine times between 1890 and 1906. Louis Barnett, a wealthy man with six pawnshops in Cardiff and other towns, suffered depredations on at least seven separate occasions, and there were other records not far short. Of course non-Jewish businesses suffered too. In 1902 William Hamill, 27, engineer, was convicted of stealing three gold pins from H.B. Crouch the goldsmiths, as well as two pairs of gold sleeve links from Julius Hettich, pawnbroker. Some of these robberies were very serious. In 1914 Charles Frederick Lamb, 31, described as labourer, but from his long record a professional criminal, broke and entered the shop of Abraham Shibko, stealing 50 gold watches, 18 watch chains, 25 rings and other articles. Twenty-seven years earlier G.A. Phillips had suffered a similar raid on his jewellery shop in the Wyndham Arcade, which helped to account for his bankruptcy the following year.

This survey of the court calendars produces no very dramatic conclusion. The impression is left of a rather lawless society, in which the work of the law courts was only part of the story. On this stage Jewish criminals played a part, but not a specially prominent one. Nor did they monopolize any special category of crime. Here, as in more constructive activities, they quickly assimilated into the society in which they lived and moved.

Notes to Chapter 3

1. *Western Mail*, 27 January 1872.
2. Ibid., 27 November, 20 December 1888.
3. Ibid., 13 June, 4 July 1881.

4. In 1871, 1,471 pedlars' licences were granted by the police in Glamorgan, and in 1872, 947 were granted. We do not know how many went to Jews, but by this time peddling was becoming an immigrant trade. See 'Return to the House of Commons, March 20th 1872', *Parliamentary Papers* 1872 (291) L, 663. It was said that in 1840 an honest pedlar could average 20 per cent on his outlay, while a dishonest one could make 80–200 per cent by false pretences rather than theft. The profit may have declined as shops became more numerous, and by the end of the nineteenth century the numbers were declining, although there were still Jewish pedlars in south Wales. Cf. Freda Maxfield, 'The Jewish Pedlar in Nineteenth-century Britain', MA course paper in Victorian Studies (Keele University, 1983). I am obliged to Ms Maxfield for the loan of this paper.
5. The rules laid down by the judges following the M'Naghten case in 1843 to distinguish the sane from the insane perpetrator of a criminal act attributed criminal responsibility to any person who (a) knew what he was doing and (b) knew that it was wrong.
6. *Western Mail*, 24 August, 6 September, 21 September, 11 November 1882; 7 February, 20 February, 4 July, 12 July 1883.
7. For pawnbroking see Kenneth Hudson, *Pawnbroking: An Aspect of British Social History* (London, Bodley Head, 1982) and Melanie Tebbutt, *Making Ends Meet: Pawnbroking and Working Class Credit* (London, Methuen, 1983), *passim*. In these two excellent accounts the south Wales pawnbrokers are barely mentioned, no doubt because for some unaccountable reason they scarcely appear in the government enquiries on which the books are based.

4

The Conduct of a Synagogue: Swansea Hebrew Congregation, 1895–1914

URSULA R. Q. HENRIQUES

I

Swansea was an older community than that of Cardiff. Dr Saunders traces the lease of its first burial ground from the Swansea Corporation back to 1768,[1] but it never attained Cardiff's size and importance. This was because by the end of the nineteenth century Swansea had been overtaken by Cardiff as the main coal-exporting port in south Wales, and the provincial Jewish communities depended entirely on the economic opportunities afforded by the towns in which they settled. So the greater communities were to be found in the larger centres of trade and industry. However, unlike Cardiff, Swansea's records have, in part, survived. Three books of synagogue minutes (two from the Goat Street synagogue, starting in 1895 and one from the Beth Hamedrash) remain, along with a letter book containing copies of letters from 1902, most of them written by Hyam Goldberg as President of the Hebrew Congregation. They provide materials for the study of the organization and activities of a provincial synagogue just at the time when the local Jewish population was at its peak. Of course these minutes do not tell the whole story. The actual spiritual life of the individuals whom synagogues are supposed to serve can never be recorded in this way. With regard to community life, many of these records have also disappeared, for example the accounts of the Benevolent Society, which might have thrown more light on the charitable endeavours and attitudes of the time; and a glance at the names in the trade directories of the period suggest that many Jews did not go to the synagogue, or perhaps went only on the high festivals. Undoubtedly some had intermarried with Welsh neighbours and were on their way to total assimilation. None the less the heart of the community was its place of worship, and in any study of it the synagogue cannot be ignored.

Swansea's first large purpose-built synagogue, in Goat Street, was opened by the Chief Rabbi's son, Hermann Adler, on 25 September 1859.[2] It remained the synagogue of the Swansea Hebrew Congregation until its destruction in the air raids of February 1941. When the Minute Book opens in November 1895 the congregation was in full swing under the direction of its wardens, Solomon Lyons, president, and Barnett Goldberg, treasurer. It had some ninety-five paid-up subscribers, mostly heads of families, with a few single women and single men over twenty-one. These included twelve subscribers from outlying towns such as Llanelli, Aberavon, Neath, Bridgend, and Mountain Ash, and one from London. By 1914 this list had grown, by irregular steps, to 147, most of the 'country' members being from Neath, since Llanelli and Aberavon, along with Ystalyfera, had established their own synagogues.

Swansea Hebrew Congregation operated under the terms of its trust as an autonomous republic financed by the subscriptions and donations of its members. Socially it was hierarchical, and politically and constitutionally it was an oligarchy. Its peculiar structure was enshrined in its Book of Rules, which was revised and republished in 1892.

According to the rules, the synagogue seats were divided into six classes, each with its own weekly rental. Presumably the classification accorded with the more or less favourable position of each block of seats in the building in its proximity to the *bima* (reading desk). The occupants of class A seats paid 3s.6d. rental per week, of class B seats 3s., of class C seats 2s.6d., of class D seats 2s., of class E seats 1s.6d., of class F seats 1s. for a married man or 6d. for a single man. Seats in the ladies' gallery were in two classes, 1s. or 6d. The non-resident or occasional attender who showed up only on high festivals was not mentioned in the rules, but the minutes suggest that a subscription of one guinea per year entitled him to occasional seating where available. Others had to take their chance at overflow services. All seatholders were entitled to certain privileges; the right to burial in the Jewish cemetery, the right to buy kosher meat at the licensed butcher, the use of the *mikvah* or ritual bath, the right to send children free to the Hebrew and religion classes, the right to a Jewish marriage ceremony, and the services of the *mohel* in circumcising baby sons. Several of these involved extra expenses, fees as well as offerings for the officiating minister, fees for the *ketubah* or marriage contract, the hire of the *chupah* or wedding canopy, fees for digging a grave. Non-members also had access to these services, but at much greater cost, including fees for *mohel* and tombstone and in most cases a considerable donation or subscription to synagogue funds. The complicated sums to be charged were laid down in the rules, and appear to have been unconnected with seat classification if not with ability to pay. They could be mitigated at the discretion of the Committee of Management, and the Committee minutes are full of individual requests for free or reduced marriages or burials, many of which were granted in whole or in part.

In addition to these religious or ceremonial services members were entitled to political privileges; and these were tightly bound to the seat classification. Class F subscribers paying 1s. rental per week for twelve months, could vote (by ballot) at the election of all paid officials — which would include the minister — and representatives on the Board of Deputies. But voting figures suggest that few if any actually voted, and they had no other political rights. Class E subscribers who had paid 1s.6d. a week for at least thirteen weeks (exclusive of the cost of ladies' seats), and had applied and been elected at a General Meeting, ranked as seatholders entitled to vote at General Meetings. They were known as Privileged Members. The D seatholders who had paid 2s. per week for at least fifty-two weeks could be elected onto the Committee of Management, a sort of executive of seven members responsible to the main body of the General Meeting. Seatholders in classes C to A who had paid at least 2s.6d. per week for two consecutive years were eligible for election as office-holders, that is wardens, consisting of treasurer, president (who had to have served as treasurer), and auditors. Annual elections were held in the autumn at New Year, and the officeholders actually changed at the Eighth Day of Solemn Assembly (Simcha Torah), the last of the great festivals.

The rules could lead to heartache when privileged members fell into arrears or were unable to pay the higher rents but tried to keep their seats. Meantime the connection between seat rents and privileges ensured that the government of the synagogue was effectively in the hands of a small group of prosperous and prominent members, the rules both reflecting and securing the group's political dominance.

That political was backed by social dominance can be confirmed by a glance at the background of those who became president during the period 1895–1914. There were eleven such presidents (some being re-elected for two or even three years). Almost all of their names can be found in the contemporary Kelly's street and trade directories which usually included well-established residents, professional men and substantial manufacturers, shopkeepers and traders. Of the eleven, one (T.D. Owens who was elected but declined to serve) was a dentist, and one, David Seline, who also acted as legal adviser to the congregation, was a solicitor. These could be classed as professionals. Five were pawnbrokers, a striking illustration of the dominant position achieved by successful pawnbrokers in the south Wales Jewish communities, and several other presidents had close relations in the trade. There was also a shipbroker, Hyam Goldberg, a house-furnisher, Michael Jacobs, a draper, Asher Deggotts, and a marine store dealer, Abraham Levy. At least four of the presidents possessed businesses in more than one building, or lived in a residence separate from their business premises, denoting affluence. Two, Michael Jacobs and Hyam Goldberg, became local JPs. Such 'respectability' was only achieved by penniless immigrants after several decades of successful enterprise or over several generations. So office-holders mostly came from families long resident in Swansea or at least in south Wales. It is often difficult to trace with certainty the ancestry of those with the common Jewish names. Michael Jacobs was probably descended from an early-nineteenth-century immigrant clothier and pawn-broker known as Greenbone Jacobs, born in 1796. Abraham Levy was probably descended from another early-nineteenth-century immigrant, a commercial traveller born in Berlin in 1801. Solomon Lyons and Abraham Lyons were part of a cousinry which included Barnett Lyons, another nineteenth-century immigrant, long resident in Cardiff and known as the father of Esther who ran away from home to become a Baptist and became the subject of a famous court case.[3] The brothers Barnett and Hyam Goldberg were the sons of Simon Goldberg, wealthy shipowner and coal exporter and JP. He had been president of the congregation when it first moved to Goat Street in 1859 and again in the 1870s. He was born in Schneidemuhl in 1822 and had lived in Swansea since 1839.[4] The members of the Goldberg family regularly paid higher subscriptions than any one else on the congregation lists as well as donating a series of gifts including a new synagogue schoolroom in 1902, a mortuary and chapel for the burial ground, and a legacy for an annual prize for the best pupil in the Hebrew and religion classes. When the revised synagogue rules were published in 1892 Simon Goldberg was made *Baltifila* (Reader) and

Baltekea (blower of the ram's horn) for as long as he thought fit, and in 1902 he was elected honorary life president. His son Hyam was hardly less powerful than he, and indeed the Goldbergs were a dominant (and highly conservative) force in the government of the congregation throughout the second half of the nineteenth century and the opening years of the twentieth.

The evidence suggests that this was an oligarchy of families, and there was much intermarriage to fortify it. But the oligarchy was not an entirely closed hereditary circle; it could be entered by rising families doing well in the town. The Deggotts family, all drapers, achieved a president, Asher Deggotts, in 1907. The personnel changed slowly with the generations. But the presence of a wealthy established, often British-educated and assimilated group governing the Swansea Hebrew Congregation is evident.

II

The wardens' posts were no sinecure. The treasurer looked after the synagogue finances, collected subscriptions and donations and fees, kept the current accounts which were examined in quarterly meetings of the Management Committee, and drew up and circulated to privileged members the annual detailed balance sheet of all subscriptions and income and expenditure before the autumn Annual General Meeting. He also had the invidious business of allocating synagogue seats, although the dissatisfied could, and did, appeal to the president. The president chaired all the General Meetings including the Special General Meeting called to consider and vote on important matters such as the Management Committee's plans to repair the synagogue or buy a new schoolroom or extend the burial ground, or to alter subscriptions, hire or fire a minister, consider some critical motion advanced by a dissident privileged member etc. He also chaired all the Management Committee meetings, both the regular ones held monthly on Sundays in the synagogue chambers and the numerous special ones which accompanied every crisis. From time to time standing committees were set up, such as the School Committee, also elected at the autumn AGM, and the Burial Ground Committee which came to have its own budget. The president and treasurer formed the constant element when General Meetings were sparsely attended and the numbers in committee meetings sank to three or four. The president also represented the congregation in dealings with the outside world, approved and signed contracts, wrote frequently to the Chief Rabbi in London when there were disputes, and engaged in extensive private correspondence both within and without the congregation on all manner of political and charitable affairs. He had power, but it came through a formidable work load. It was not surprising that there were often difficulties in finding a suitable member who would serve. When found, he was often re-elected for two or three successive years although the latter was contrary to rule 4. This like many other oligarchies was perpetuated at least partly by the small number of those with the wealth, leisure, education and commitment to fulfil the role.

What matters occupied the minds of the privileged members in Committees and General Meetings?

The form and conduct of the synagogue services was obviously important but disputes about these had been fought out earlier in the nineteenth century, and the congregation now followed the lines laid down by the Chief Rabbi in London, without much contention.[5] The struggle for decorum noted in other synagogues had probably been settled (more or less) earlier on. Rule 31 of the 1892 Rule Book stipulated that 'a solemn and reverential silence shall pervade the synagogue. A noisy entering; a congregating of individuals; conversation on any subject whatsoever . . . is to be most strictly prohibited'. No more than an occasional minor 'incident' is recorded, as when Revd Sandheim walked out because the Simcha Torah service was taken by a boy at the behest of the president (Abraham Freedman) without the minister's consent. Most 'honours' such as the position of Chatan Torah and Chatan Bereshit were allocated according to seniority from among privileged members.[6] Remaining complaints of disturbance were caused mainly by undisciplined children who were presumably bored by the services and got out of hand.

Much more interest was generated by the appointment of salaried officers; the minister, the *chazan* or reader, who was also *mohel* and *shochet*, the *shammas* or beadle, and extra teachers for the Hebrew and religion classes. These were elected in General Meetings although the preliminary business of advertising the vacancy, writing to the Chief Rabbi and other officials for references, and choosing which candidates to invite to take a trial service, lay with the Management Committee.

Certain matters, routine but considered important, took an undue amount of time and trouble. Such was the arrangement for the supply of kosher meat, where the licensed butchers were always trying to reduce the rent they paid to the synagogue for the privilege of selling to its members the meat slaughtered on their premises by the *shochet*. But inevitably a major preoccupation, especially of the Management Committee, was money — synagogue revenue and expenditure. The examination of accounts, the fixing of salaries, the utilization of sanctions to enforce the payment of arrears, often by an instalment arrangement, were major preoccupations of the Management Committee. Members grumbled about their subscriptions, refused to pay, protested at threats to deprive them of their privileges or their seats. The trouble was certainly increased by the element of discretion which lay with the Committee, which could, and occasionally did, reduce subscriptions for those who had fallen on bad times, and waive them for those deemed to have earned the gratitude of the congregation. Thus the Revd I. Miron, *chazan* and *shochet*, on retirement through ill health, was granted free seats for himself (with privileges) and his wife, for life. At a humbler level, frequent requests for free burial or marriage at a reduced rate, were received especially from Jews who were not regular subscribers to the congregation and were therefore subject to much higher charges. These might result in a waiver of the congregation's share of the fees. The synagogue wanted money. On the other hand, it could not and would not allow Jews, even wandering pedlars or temporary migrants, to be married in a Christian church or a register office, or buried in a pauper's grave in the municipal cemetery. In this, as in other matters such as religious education, there was a conflict between the congregation's need for cash and its need to prevent Jews from drifting right away from Judaism.

Because of the Swansea Jewish community's rapid growth there were repeated demands for the extension of the burial ground. A special Cemetery Committee with its own account was set up. Hyam Goldberg, president from 1901–4, negotiated extensively with both Swansea Town Clerk and surrounding landowners for the lease of extra ground. His attempts to beat down the Town Corporation's price by threatening to demand that a piece of its own cemetery be reserved specially for Jewish burials free of charge was thwarted when Charles Emanuel, legal adviser to the Board of Deputies in London, advised him that Jews had no right to reserved ground in corporation cemeteries under the Burial Acts.[7] Once the lease was secured Goldberg argued with the Corporation as to who should bear the cost of railing it off, Goldberg maintaining that this was an amenity for the town's public. An argument of another nature developed when the Management Committee decided that the old wall should be kept, that privileged members should be buried inside it and common seatholders buried in the new ground beyond, thus extending the privileges of this life into the hereafter. Resolutions at a General Meeting defeated this plan, but it took several years, on one pretext or another, to remove the wall.[8]

Plans to repair and extend the synagogue building were less controversial, depending largely on voluntary contributions supported by the wealthier members of the congregation. The visit of Chief Rabbi Hermann Adler for the half-centenary celebrations in 1909 provided a good excuse for some extra expenditure on repair and redecoration. More difficulties were encountered in housing the rapidly growing Hebrew and religion school. Hiring the local Board School premises was expensive and unsatisfactory. The synagogue chambers were too small, and a private house which the school committee proposed to buy and convert was deemed unsuitable by the synagogue's architects. There was also the question of what to do about the *mikvah* or ritual bath which unfriendly folk from another congregation, whose members had been charged for its use, declared insanitary, and which the teachers said should not be in the same building as the school.

III

One of the most persistent problems was the management of the Hebrew and religion classes. By 1907 the number of pupils had reached 107. Jewish parents attached great importance to the religious education of their children, perhaps the more so that there was no Jewish Free School in the town, and the children went to the local Board and Grammar schools for their daily education. This led to repeated complaints from the Management Committee that strangers who paid no subscription were sending their children to religion classes without fees and without the permission of the wardens. Here, especially, the want of money was in tension with the fear of losing the younger generation for lack of a Jewish education.

Despite the objections of the parents who did pay their dues it is probable that a blind eye was often turned to the presence in class of an unpaid-for non-member's child.

General Meetings as well as the School and Management Committees were also concerned about indiscipline and lack of progress among the school pupils. In 1908 there were letters of complaint about the children waiting outside to attend the classes. Children ran wild, damaged the synagogue, or disturbed the services. Despite certain amenities — £3 and sometimes £5 was voted most years for a *Chanucah* party or a summer picnic, and prizes for the best pupils (mostly bibles) were available from the Simon Goldberg fund — young people who spent the week at school possibly resented spending weekday evenings or Saturday and Sunday afternoons learning Hebrew. Of course they were not alone; many of their Christian contemporaries spent their sabbath in Sunday schools. But there was persistent criticism of the standards and methods current in the *cheder*. While the older children were taught by the minister, who presumably had had some training as a teacher, the younger ones were allotted to the *chazan* or even to Mr Solomon the *shammas*. The *chazan* was also *mohel* and *shochet*. To the unorthodox it may not be immediately apparent that three evenings a week killing chickens is necessarily the best qualification for teaching small children religion. The *shammas* was not a trained teacher and it was perhaps not to be expected that a person required to do such menial tasks as cleaning the synagogue silver should also be adept at gaining the interest or respect of children, especially when their parents probably regarded him as a kind of upper servant. Not that the synagogue elders were uncaring. Learned and reverend school inspectors possessing university degrees from south Wales or even London, were called in at a fee to inspect the classes, report on the teachers and suggest new methods of instruction. New textbooks were ordered and methods recommended which the junior teachers would not or could not implement. It was resolved repeatedly that the wardens or the members of the School Committee, on a rota basis, should attend the classes (which led on one occasion to the hot-tempered Sandheim calling in a constable, when the president, Abraham Freedman, with whom Sandheim was at loggerheads, attended the school). There were periodical demands for a second fully qualified teacher and several attempts were made to find one. But the appointments seem to have been unsatisfactory and the teachers did not last long. The salary offered — £75 a year for a job which was part-time — failed to attract men of adequate training and calibre. Yet some of the later inspectors' reports were not unfavourable, especially to the teaching of the minister and the standards of the older children. Possibly the concern of the School and Management Committees was not entirely fruitless.

The synagogue was in part a charitable institution. According to the Rule Book (13) it was the duty of the treasurer 'to relieve all poor persons on receipt of a ticket from the President, the amount to be paid is to be stated thereon ... No persons to be again relieved within six months unless under some very special circumstances.' Much time and energy was devoted to considering cases of hardship among the poorer Jews, and the six months clause was generally disregarded, although wardens did try to stipulate that long-term relief cases should be paid by the Benevolent Society. This Society, which was in operation by 1900 was chaired by Mrs Barnett Goldberg. It appears to have shared the support of certain deserving cases with the congregation's funds. The Management Committee usually had two or three poor widows to whom it voted small pensions of 2s.6d. or 3s.6d. per week over the winter months between Yom Kippur and Passover; the money probably paid for their coals. At least one old lady was supported in the Widows' Institution in London. The Rosenberg children, whose mother had died in Swansea, were paid for in an orphanage. In 1902–3 there was trouble over a little orphan girl whose father had deserted her and whom the London Jews' Hospital and Orphan Asylum refused to take since it would not support illegitimate children. The child was consigned to a Poor Law workhouse (where the Chief Rabbi could think of nothing better than to demand she should be visited by a rabbi so that her religious education could be attended to). Fortunately she was rescued by an uncle who lived near Maesteg. Her case gave a lot of work to Hyam Goldberg as president, who was also making persistent but vain attempts to persuade the London Hospital and Orphan Asylum to pay the premium for apprenticing a boy called Myer Finkelbach to a local engraver.[9] In addition to this relief work the distribution of matzos and food to the poor at Passover was left in the hands of the Benevolent Society.

It has been observed that in Manchester and other large centres distinction was made between local resident Jews who for some reason became destitute and had to be supported to keep them off the

Poor Law, and new immigrants whom the local community wanted to get rid of as quickly as possible before they became a permanent burden.[10] Swansea was nowhere near the transmigrant route between the north-eastern ports and Liverpool, and did not have to cope with the streams of penniless Russian refugees trying to get to the New World. But on occasion some such distinction applied, as when money was advanced to send back to Russia an immigrant family whose father could not support them, or to move on another family to Liverpool. There were, of course, disputes between the Management Committee and the Benevolent Society as to who should pay for what; but on the whole the charitable partnership seems to have worked.

IV

One of the most difficult problems in the administration of the synagogue was the management of relations between the wardens and the minister. In this period ministers tended to be welcomed with an enthusiasm which quickly turned sour. Part of the trouble was undoubtedly inadequate pay. The minister in Swansea received £120 a year supplemented by £30 from the Provincial Ministers' Fund in London, which gave that body some say in the appointment. The Management Committee was prepared to pay his removal expenses — and recover them from his first year's salary. There were certain perquisites in the shape of fees for burials, marriages and circumcisions, but they cannot have amounted to much. It was roughly on a level with a Board School master's pay, and teaching was not a greatly respected profession at the time, at least among the British middle classes. Both minister and *chazan* (whose pay was also raised to £150) had to ask the president — who put it to the Management Committee — for leave to go on their annual holiday. This was usually granted when the religion school was closed for two weeks in August, and if they were lucky the Committee granted them £5 or £3 each for their fare. They had to get the president's permission to go away for a weekend, accept an invitation to conduct a wedding or circumcision or to preach in another congregation, or to apply for another post (which was not refused). Such permissions for the minister might be made conditional on his being back in time to take school classes, or for the *chazan* on his being back in time for the evening killing. The times of classes were decided by the School Committee or the School and Management Committees sitting jointly: the money for textbooks had to be voted by the Management Committee. In a row between the minister and a member of the congregation the minister was called before the Management Committee and berated by the president. The latter also told him how many 'lectures' — presumably sermons — he must deliver per month. Unless handled on both sides with the greatest tact, this position must have seemed intolerable to an educated and independent man.

In 1895 the minister at Swansea was the Revd Philip Wolfers. He, however, was appointed minister at Cardiff in April 1899, and hurried away to officiate at a visit of the Chief Rabbi there, to the considerable inconvenience and annoyance of the Swansea elders. By the end of July, after consideration of some other candidates, Revd S. Fyne from Newport was elected at a Special General Meeting by nineteen votes to eight, five not voting.

At first it would seem that all went well. But by the summer of 1903 the School Committee was demanding extra school reports, including the marks gained by each child and comments on the conduct and diligence of those in standard 2. In December 1904 there was trouble (unexplained) about Fyne's failure to conform to the rules of the congregation about honorary offerings. Moreover there was overt dissatisfaction in some quarters with his teaching of Jewish history and religion, and he was accusing the president Hyam Goldberg of obtaining a letter from the Chief Rabbi by fraud. By now the privileged members were divided into pro- and anti-Fyne factions and the minister was being pressed to resign. On refusal he was given six months' notice. After several more months of disagreement and friction he left, and in December 1906 the Revd H.J. Sandheim was elected in his place.

We are told that Sandheim, the British-born son of a dentist and only twenty-three years old on appointment, had ginger hair and a temperament to match.[11] A long story of friction between him and his employers apparently began when he was forbidden, by a narrow vote of the Management Committee, to supplement his income by private teaching. His request for an extra teacher for the synagogue classes was deferred. In June 1907 he applied for a post in Manchester which he did not get. In October 1907 he resigned, saying in his letter,

> I consider that my efforts during the nine months I have been Minister have proved a failure. The conditions which govern my appointment are not those which I anticipated, and I do not feel justified in continuing a work which is out of harmony with my ideas as to the aims of a Jewish minister . . .
>
> After spending ten years in preparation for this calling I realise that there is no scope for achieving any of the teachings which experience or desire would prompt, and I consider it better to abandon the work while I am only at the beginning of my career, than to wait until I have got too far to retract.[12]

A General Meeting, horrified, persuaded the minister to withdraw his resignation, and carried an amendment that,

> In future on all matters of ritual Mr Sandheim be present at meetings . . . and that he be not interfered with during divine services and that it be understood that no radical change be introduced without the approval of a General Meeting.[13]

Although Sandheim evidently had some enthusiasm and talent for teaching, and standards — at least among the older children — improved, the reconciliation was not permanent. In January 1908 he incurred disapproval by asking to be allowed not to read the law in synagogue. He was accused of leaving town without making arrangements for the conduct of the classes, nor leaving the school key. He was hauled before the Management Committee for speaking disrespectfully to the current president, Asher Deggotts, and was again on the verge of resigning. A rapidly deteriorating position was for a time improved by his engagement to be married, on which he was voted a gift of ten guineas as a present from the congregation (which may well have appreciated him more than did the Management Committee). The marriage was performed by the Chief Rabbi Hermann Adler during his half-centenary visit, but the Committee refused to pay his wedding expenses on the ground that it was a personal arrangement between him and Dr Adler. Soon there was renewed trouble when his father-in-law, Mr Neft, asked for privileged seating.

It would be unnecessary and tiresome to follow the tortuous course of Sandheim's relations with the elders of the Swansea Hebrew Congregation. By 1911 the General Meeting was fairly evenly divided between those who wanted to sack him and those who did not, and he was evidently at loggerheads with the president, A. Freedman. Stalemate continued, punctuated with rows, as when the minister criticized a member, Louis Snipper, for letting his son sit a scholarship examination on a Saturday morning. There was continued criticism from the wardens and defiance from the minister. Then, in November 1912 it was suddenly discovered that Sandheim was over £100 in debt, mostly to non-Jews. He was dismissed with £50 in lieu of notice, and the treasurer arranged with Lloyd's Bank for an overdraft of £150 to pay off his creditors. Sandheim left Wales for Canada, changing his name to Revd H.J. Samuels. It was an unedifying story, and one wonders how much of it became public knowledge and whether it did the religious life of the congregation much good. But the strange postscript to Sandheim's term of office in Swansea is that when he died in Montreal in 1924 — still only 41 years old — his body was sent back to Swansea for burial, and interred by the minister of a neighbouring congregation. Possibly it was arranged by his wife's family. Or possibly there was something positive after all in his feelings for Wales, if not for the Swansea Hebrew Congregation.

Sandheim's ministry was followed by a long period of unsuccessful attempts to find a satisfactory minister. It did not end until 1924 with the appointment of Revd H. Fineburg from Poland, who remained until 1946. According to Dr Saunders, he very nearly resigned in 1929. Possibly by his later years the congregation elders had learned to manage this difficult relationship with greater tact and forbearance.

The congregation was luckier in its readers or *chazanim*, Revd Israel Miron and M. Lubner. Possibly because their aspirations were less, they seem to have been more tolerant of the domination of their working lives by the wardens. Miron, in particular, who had served for twenty-five years, was a great favourite with the congregation. When he retired through ill health in March 1900 he was treated with generosity. Instead of a pension he asked for two years' salary to invest in a small business, and was given £300. The congregation incurred an overdraft with Lloyd's Bank which took six months to pay off. He was also given a privileged seat in the synagogue for life, with a seat for his wife. The members subscribed to present him with a purse of gold, a silver *kiddush* cup and a pair of silver candlesticks. When a caterer was required to supply food for the reception of the Chief Rabbi in 1909 Mrs Miron was chosen.

V

The distinctive feature of south Wales Jewry was its division into small scattered communities. These little groups, as they grew in size to form first a *minyan* and then a congregation, needed the help and support of the older, larger communities. In May 1903, Hyam Goldberg as President of Swansea Hebrew Congregation wrote to the President of Merthyr Hebrew Congregation asking him, as Merthyr already had an arrangement with the community at Aberdare, for advice as to an agreement with the new congregation at Llanelli. Llanelli was asking for the services of Swansea's *mohel* and also for land in Swansea's burial ground to bury its dead. No doubt following Merthyr's reply, on 25 May 1903 a General Meeting resolved that Llanelli should be allowed to borrow the minister to celebrate marriages and the *mohel* for circumcisions, and that it could bury its dead in the cemetery. For these privileges Llanelli was to pay £5 a year in quarterly instalments, in addition to all officials' travelling expenses. The arrangement would cover only residents of the town and would last for twelve months.

By the end of 1904 similar arrangements had been made with Aberavon (Port Talbot) and Ystalyfera. They were usually followed by a request for the loan of a *sefer torah* (a scroll of the law of which Swansea possessed a number), during the autumn season of High Festivals. This was normally allowed on condition that the *sefer* was returned immediately after the season ended, in its original good condition. If it was delayed or damaged the loan would not be repeated. Then the new congregation might ask, as did Llanelli, that Swansea's minister, in this case the Revd Fyne, should be allowed to visit monthly to deliver a lecture (presumably a sermon). This was always refused for fear the minister would be distracted from his work in Swansea, but with a proviso that occasional invitations would be accepted. In fact these arrangements were the subject of hard bargaining, designed to avert the danger that the larger congregation's connection with the smaller one would lose it money. When in October 1903, Aberavon, consisting of six families and five unmarried men, offered three guineas a year for privileges which included the use of Swansea's *mikvah*, the Committee of Management proposed to a General Meeting at Swansea that it should be required to pay five guineas in half-yearly instalments — though it did get the loan of a *sefer torah* for a whole year.

These relationships did not always go smoothly. Llanelli probably did not appreciate the addition of individual burial fees of two guineas per adult and one guinea per child to its £5 annual subscription. When the arrangement was renewed there had already been a row between Goldberg and J.D. Rosenberg, secretary of the Aberavon Congregation, about the amount and timing of subscription payments, in the course of which Goldberg demanded payment in advance and extremely regretted 'the tone in which you have thought proper to reply to my letter of Monday last'.[14] But despite the rubs these arrangements must have been valuable in mitigating the sense of isolation of groups of Jews in the small valley towns, and circulating ministers helped to establish links between them. For instance, Fyne was granted permission to go to Merthyr and Abertillery to examine the children in their Hebrew classes. By 1920 proposals were being circulated for a federal constitution for the south Wales congregations. Although this apparently had no outcome the arrangements were evidently significant for the morale if not the survival of the small communities.

VI

The oligarchy of the Swansea Hebrew Congregation never lacked an opposition, whether from without or within. The influx of new migrants, their 'foreignness' and poverty were bound to cause some friction with the comfortable English- or Welsh-born elders of the Swansea Jewish establishment.

The minutes of 1895 open in the middle of a classic row between the wardens of the congregation and immigrants to Swansea and neighbouring towns who were not members of the congregation. The immigrants wanted to buy kosher meat, but the wardens demanded that they should subscribe to the congregation and laid a tax of $2d$ per pound on meat and $3d$ per fowl killed on all non-subscribers. They also used this tax to compel members in arrears to pay their subscriptions. In December 1895 several 'poor foreign workmen' wrote letters of complaint to the Chief Rabbi, and sent a deputation to London to find a *shochet* of their own. Added to this there was trouble about non-subscribers' wives being charged for the use of the *mikvah*, and one, it was alleged, being turned away. This was a not unfamiliar scenario; a split had been narrowly averted in 1871.[15] But it was none the less worrying, and Dr Adler intervened with several letters trying to make peace. To both Adlers, father and son, such rows and the revolts which followed constituted a threat to the central authority of the Chief Rabbinate, and while they undertook conciliation they tended, in the long run, to come down on the side of the settled local establishment. The intervention was in vain, and soon the breakaway group formed what was known as the 'Prince of Wales Road Minyan'. The spokesman of the revolt was David Rutter, a picture-frame maker, who, having been persuaded by Dr Adler not to engage a *shochet* in London returned home and wrote back that 'the present dispute between the English and foreign members . . . has now been settled. The Congregation has no objection whatsoever to our having a *shochet* and teacher for ourselves', and asking permission to engage a Mr Levine, *shochet*, from Penycraig [Pen-y-graig].[16] Adler sent the letter to Solomon Lyons, then President of the Hebrew Congregation, who informed him that there was not a word of truth in Rutter's letter, and persuaded him to refuse permission.[17] But he could not prevent the split. By February 1896 Lyons, with the support of a Special General Meeting, was asking the town clerk to refuse the Minyan's application for a separate Jewish burial ground, at the same time refusing a plot in the Congregation cemetery to any applicant who would not pay 1s. per week subscription.

The policy over burials was evidently part of an attempt by the congregation to retain its hold over the 'foreigners' whom it considered in many cases well able to pay their subscriptions. It would extend its own concession to those who were not. In 1897 the Management Committee granted free burial for the child of a non-member of the congregation. The following autumn, in October 1898, David Rutter made his peace with the Hebrew Congregation.

> I beg to apologise to you of my past behaviour and regret also thereof. Hoping that you gentlemen will accept the above and will kindly renew my membership in the future, offering to pay 1s.6d. per week.

But by this time the new *minyan* was well established. On 20 January 1899 its president, A. Shepherd, wrote to A. Lyons, then president of the Hebrew Congregation.

> Considering the comparatively calm position between your congregation and those to which I belong I have taken the iniative [*sic*]

and convinced our congregation of the advisability of trying to reinstate the former good understanding which had hitherto existed before the establishment of the Foreign Congregation.

Claiming to represent the latter he offered £3 for the privileges of *shochet* and burial ground. But a General Meeting on 16 April resolved that 'the letter from the other Congregation dated 20th January 1898 be not entertained'.

This correspondence reveals the occasion rather than the underlying reasons for the split. It is obvious that the rank and file of the Prince of Wales Road Minyan was 'foreign', of comparatively recent immigration. Probably the newcomers were not at ease with the creeping anglicization of tone and custom in the Goat Street services. Their own synagogue, once established, did not exhibit the decorum the Old Congregation had achieved.[18] In 1912 a General Meeting at Goat Street instructed the minister that the English Bible might be read on Shabbat, provided that it was confined to a portion of the Sidra or the Haphtorah. But there were no fundamental differences of ritual or practice. South Wales was noted for its orthodoxy. There was no Reform movement in Swansea, even though most families of the oligarchy had originated in Germany where Reform was influential. However, the difference between the countries of European origin may have added marginally to the jealousies between new immigrants and old. Such differences were not clear cut. There was no instance of a complete east European village community immigrating as a unit and setting up its own *shul*, as happened in Sunderland.[19]

It is also obvious that the members of the Minyan were comparatively poor. As late as 1910, of twenty-three leading members nine did not make the pages of *Kelly's Directory*. At least for the time being this fostered class differences. It was not surprising that the immigrants did not feel at home with the middle-class grandees, disliked the hierarchy of privilege, and were dissatisfied with their lack of say in the synagogue. Even so, early leaders of the dissidents and many of the rank and file belonged to both congregations. Spokesmen for the Minyan were themselves members of the Swansea social élite, and were content to remain within the Hebrew Congregation and use the split in a power struggle of their own. On the other hand some families were divided by the split, two sons of the Baddiel family becoming wardens in the new congregation while their father remained in the old. The Prince of Wales Minyan was never completely divorced from the Goat Street Congregation, while personal quarrels at the top reinforced more obvious causes of separation at the bottom.

After Rutter's retreat the new spokesman for the Prince of Wales Road Minyan was Abraham Levy, a well-to-do marine store dealer with a separate residence in Eaton Square. Probably descended from one of the old German families, he was a man of some eminence, being at one time president of the Swansea Zionist Society. In January 1902 the monthly Management Committee meeting passed a resolution recording its unqualified disapproval of the conduct of A. Levy who, 'while still a member of this committee promoted and took an active part in a public meeting . . . for the purpose of inspiring hostility against this congregation'. Abraham Levy continued for years to oppose the dominant conservative faction on the Management Committee, on various pretexts and by means of various proposals. However, when in 1909 he actually became president of the Hebrew Congregation his attitude to proposals for change within the congregation became much more conservative.

In 1906 supporters of the Prince of Wales Road Minyan became numerous and wealthy enough to build their own synagogue, the Beth Hamedrash. This development signalled an at least partial reconciliation with the Hebrew Congregation whose relations with it thereafter resembled its relations with the outlying congregations with which it had an 'arrangement'. In June 1906 the Beth Hamedrash Committee was received in audience by the Hebrew Congregation's Management Committee. In September the Hebrew Congregation granted three guineas to the Minyan (the Beth Hamedrash's foundation stone was not actually laid until November) on condition that it might send any poor person it wished to the Minyan festival services. The Revd Fyne, and subsequently Sandheim, were allowed to take services in the Beth Hamedrash on the second days of festivals.

Swansea now had two Hebrew Congregations, and an uneasy cooperation prevailed between them. In 1911 the Beth Hamedrash engaged a Rav from Russia, the Revd Rabbinowitz, who came via Sunderland.[20] As his title denoted he was a very holy man, and the Swansea Hebrew Congregation agreed to pay £25 a year towards his salary. But the Beth Hamedrash could not afford more than £75 a year, including this contribution, and the Rav, seeing no future for himself in the United Kingdom, went home to Russia, accepting

£9.18s., the balance of the Hebrew Congregation's grant, for his fare. In the same year an agreement was made by which the Hebrew Congregation granted the Beth Hamedrash £10 a year and its members the privileges of a 1s. seatholder provided that the Beth Hamedrash submitted periodical lists of its subscribers to the Management Committee at Goat Street who retained the right to veto names. The Management Committee's purpose was evidently to prevent those persons it thought able to pay the Goat Street subscription from obtaining its privileges by paying the lower subscription to the Beth Hamedrash. Of course the arrangement produced friction: but it is a comment on the whole process of communal development that the Beth Hamedrash itself subsequently adopted a system of privileges based on subscription rates.[21]

As well as these agreements there was a certain amount of joint activity across the divide. There was a Chevra Kadisha or joint Burial Society, and in 1911 a joint Schechita (kosher butchering) Board. There were also moves towards a reunion of the two synagogues. But they did not come to anything until after the Second World War, when the Goat Street Synagogue, destroyed in an air raid, was replaced by a new synagogue in Fynnone Street, and the Beth Hamedrash faded out.

The opposition of Rutter and Levy was continued by a prosperous tailor appropriately named Louis Snipper, who was also a member of both congregations. But there was always an opposition within the Hebrew Congregation and it did not necessarily go as far as secession. Much of it was probably due to personal jealousy. When David Seline, a member of another long-standing, prosperous Swansea family, was president in 1908–9 it was safe to snub the powerful Goldbergs. The names of Mrs Hyam and Mrs Barnett Goldberg were rejected at a joint School and Management Committee meeting and Mrs Seline was asked to distribute the prizes. When Mrs Hyam Goldberg tried to get a protégée of hers appointed caretaker she was rejected in favour of a non-Jewish caretaker who, it was said, had given excellent service during a temporary appointment. When Mrs Barnett Goldberg asked for the key of the synagogue to hold a Benevolent Society meeting she was refused. The pomposity and self-conceit of a certain kind of synagogue president was scathingly attacked in an acid 'interview' in an article by the young editor of the *South Wales Jewish Review*.[22]

'I understand Sir, you are President of the local Congregation.'
'I am,' he replied, with a slight but visible expansion of his chest.
'It is a very important position, is it not?' I continued.
'Oh yes, very.'
'And, I suppose, it is only men of great tact who can undertake the responsibility?'
'As a rule. You see, we cannot trust such a delicate post in the hands of anyone who is not sufficiently competent.'
'Just so. But may I ask to whom do you refer as "we"?'
'Why, there is myself and — and — the rest you know.'

The writer went on to hint that the president used his ability to allot the reading of portions of the Law on sabbaths and festivals to pay off old scores. Of course he was careful not to give away whom he was getting at, but the idea of Hyam Goldberg, perhaps unfairly, inevitably comes to mind.

Petty personalities scarcely rank as opposition. More significant were the attempts to invade the top ranks of the hierarchy by widening the area of privilege. These were often promoted by Abraham Levy, but in July 1905 David Seline proposed that all members paying 1s. a week for twelve months should be eligible for election as privileged members with votes at General Meetings. Such motions were invariably lost, but they indicated a ground swell of discontent. In March 1910, at a Special General Meeting, S. Rubinstein proposed a scheme for a Hebrew Educational Board elected by twelve privileged and six non-privileged members, to operate independently of the congregational administration. The Board was set up in the face of opposition reinforced by doubts about its legality; but, evidently having more to do with politics than the improvement of religious education, did not last long.

In 1912 the election of a new Chief Rabbi following the death of Hermann Adler gave Abraham Levy an opportunity to propose that the election conference should be asked to declare that participation in the election would be on the basis of membership rather than of financial contribution. When this was unsuccessful he proposed, in the face of Hyam Goldberg's threat to resign, that the Hebrew Congregation's annual contribution of £5 towards the support of the Chief Rabbinate should be discontinued.

These drives towards democracy and decentralization were not very powerful. The 'foreigners' or 'poor workmen' who might have strengthened them had, in any case, been diverted into their own Beth Hamedrash. The more settled and prosperous members were now joining the privileged ranks in considerable numbers. Nor was the congregation out of phase with other British institutions. While both the House of Commons (although women still had no votes) and local government were by 1910 elected on a wide franchise, the fashion for internal democracy had not spread to schools and other corporate bodies. It was not until 1920 that a General Meeting unanimously resolved to accept no more candidates for non-privileged membership, nor until later that the formal hierarchy of political qualification through seat rents was abolished.

VII

The impression conveyed by the Minute Books of the Swansea Hebrew Congregation is narrow and parochial. The squabbles of a habitually contentious people were fostered by the hothouse atmosphere of a small, inward-looking society. But the impression does not convey the whole truth. As nowadays happens in the modern media, disagreements and sensations tended to get the publicity, agreement and harmony to make less mark. The fiftieth anniversary celebrations in 1909 with the visit of Chief Rabbi Hermann Adler, were undoubtedly occasions of gladness and rejoicing. They appear in the minutes, however, as a series of disputes as to who should be invited, and an attempt by the treasurer to resign over a disagreement about the expenses involved. Also the outside world did intrude. The Russian pogroms of 1905 produced a pledge at the Annual General Meeting to support the fund being raised for the victims, and an appeal to the editor of the *South Wales Daily Post* to co-operate in interesting the Swansea public — co-operation which was freely given. The year before, Hyam Goldberg had been writing to the local MP, Brynmor Jones, trying to extract a pledge that he would oppose the Aliens' Bill in Parliament.[23] Yet the one event which must have been of desperate concern to all the Jews of south Wales, the Tredegar Riots of August 1911, was not mentioned in the synagogue minutes. Possibly this was a deliberate omission in line with the usual Anglo-

Jewish policy of pretending that anti-Semitism did not exist in the UK in the hope that it would go away.

The Swansea Hebrew Congregation was not really isolated. As we have seen there was frequent communication between the scattered Jewish communities of south Wales, which was sometimes extended to include Bristol. There was interchange of preachers, school inspectors, and some joint charitable endeavour between Swansea and Cardiff. London was in reach through the Great Western Railway, and there were contacts with Jewish institutions there, especially with the Chief Rabbi (who, if other congregations consulted him as often about their domestic problems, must have been very busy indeed). There were circulating lecturers who performed at the various literary societies. Swansea, like other towns, had its Jewish Literary Society, which was as much social as literary or intellectual, its Zionist Society, and several participants in freemasonry, which was popular among Jews because it did not exclude them. Contacts with the non-Jewish world were, however, tentative. Both Fyne and Sandheim met the local Christian clergy, and Sandheim preached in the local Unitarian Chapel. The ministers collected annually donations to the Swansea General and Eye Hospital which in return took Jewish members who fell ill. There were business contacts between the congregation and local butchers, architects, builders etc., reasonable relations with the Town Hall, and doubtless individual contacts with people outside the community with which the congregation was not concerned. Jews who contracted mixed marriages or drifted away from the community altogether did not appear in the synagogue records.

VIII

Perhaps the most significant feature of the history of the Swansea Hebrew Congregation was its typicality. South Wales Jewry was unusual only in its scattered geography (dictated by the geography of its host communities) and the economic and social prominence of its pawnbrokers. The hierarchical constitution of Swansea resembled others in Manchester, Sunderland, Leeds, Birmingham and almost certainly Cardiff, indeed probably in every other provincial community.[24] So did its factions and its fissiparous nature. Maurice Dennis has left us an account of the secession which led to the

Edwards Place Synagogue in 1889, with extracts from the now lost Cardiff Minute Book.[25] The resemblance to the disputes from which emerged the Prince of Wales Road Minyan and subsequently the Beth Hamedrash is striking. The Swansea secession was almost a carbon copy except that trouble over marriage fees was added to that over *shochet* and burial ground. There were also the same appeals to and ineffective intervention by the Chief Rabbi. Cardiff, but even more Swansea, were in many ways rather primitive examples of such communities, too small and too remote from the immediate impact of the mainstream immigrations to develop the diversity of synagogues which appeared in, say, Manchester, Leeds or even more, in London. But neither was immune from the trends of nineteenth-century British-Jewish history. The experience and the character of each wave of refugees fleeing from religious and racial persecution and economic repression seemed to repeat themselves. The differences between the 'English' *shul* and the 'Foreign' *shul* which looked superficially like class divisions were differences of generation rather than kind, but augmented by the rapid assimilation of the older immigrants to the customs and standards of their new native country. The anglicization or Welsh assimilation of the early settlers, their mixture of fellow feeling with the newcomers and fear that these outlandish indigents would endanger the hard-won acceptance they had achieved in their cherished country were repeated with each influx. The tension which always grew between the establishment and the newcomers — the impulse of the respectable to discipline in the name of unity those who could not or would not pay subscriptions, or conform to recently hallowed customs, or accord their betters respect — was always held in check by the urge to present a common front to the world outside. Of this the history of the Swansea Hebrew Congregation is but a microcosm.

Notes to Chapter 4

1. N.H. Saunders, *Swansea Hebrew Congregation 1830–1980* (Centenary pamphlet 1980), 209. I am indebted to Dr Saunders' account for the historical background to this chapter, and to Dr Saunders for the loan of the Swansea synagogue records, and for other help in writing this study.
2. There had been an earlier, much smaller building in Waterloo Street since 1818. Saunders, op.cit. 31.

3. Cf. Chap.6, 131 et seq.
4. For Simon Goldberg see Saunders, op.cit., 37, 43. A.E. Einstein, *The South Wales Jewish Review*, 1904, 39 (face).
5. Saunders, op.cit., 33. Dr Saunders says there were disturbances in the synagogue following the introduction of laws and regulations made by Dr Nathan Adler, then Chief Rabbi, in 1847.
6. For Chatan Torah and Chatan Bereshit see glossary of Hebrew words, p. 221. Some difficulties were encountered in arranging the succession of those who carried the scrolls round the synagogue seven times on Simcha Torah.
7. Goldberg to John Thomas Esq., Town Clerk, and to others, 28 March to 8 August 1904; Goldberg to Charles Emanuel, 24 June. Letter Book.
8. It was eventually unanimously voted to remove it at a committee meeting in 1911.
9. Letters of Hyam Goldberg to D. Spero, Jews' Hospital and Orphan Asylum, London, 2, 8, 18, 22 September 1902; 5 February 1903. Letter Book.
10. For more developed even though earlier systems of poor relief see Bill Williams, *The Making of Manchester Jewry 1740–1875* (Manchester University Press, 1976), 290–5.
11. Saunders, op.cit., 49.
12. General Meeting 6 October 1907. Swansea Hebrew Congregation Minute Book.
13. Ibid. The amendment was proposed by the opponents A. Levy and Barnett Goldberg and carried, one member voting against.
14. H. Goldberg to J.D. Rosenberg, Aberavon, 11 November 1903. Letter Book.
15. Saunders, op.cit., 37.
16. Dr Adler to H. Goldberg, 9 December, and correspondence between Dr Adler and Solomon Lyons, 11, 17, 18, 23, 25, 26 December 1895. Minute Book.
17. Solomon Lyons to Dr Adler, 25 December 1895. Minute Book.
18. A meeting of the Beth Hamedrash Committee on 1 February 1914 resolved that letters should be sent to B. Glass and J. Pearlman warning then that they would lose their membership if they continued their usual behaviour. Minute Book of Beth Hamedrash. But note the minutes were taken in English.
19. Arnold Levy, *History of the Sunderland Jewish Community* (London, MacDonald, 1956), 100–67.
20. Ibid., 180–90.
21. Minute Book of Beth Hamedrash. AGM 10 November 1912. A member paying 3d. per week was to be entitled to a seat without vote or other privileges.
22. *South Wales Jewish Review*, no. 6 (June 1904), 92–4. The editor, who wrote under the pseudonym 'Nnamreh' was Alfred Einstein, one of the three brothers who later moved to London and became owners of the Instone Shipping Line and pioneers in commercial aviation. They

changed their name to Instone during the First World War. Alfred Einstein married Hyam Goldberg's daughter.
23. H. Goldberg to Brynmor Jones Esq. KC, MP, 5 May 1904, Letter Book. The Aliens Act 1905 was directed largely against Jewish immigration.
24. Cf. Bill Williams, *The Making of Manchester Jewry, 1740–1875* (Manchester University Press, 1976). Arnold Levy, *History of the Sunderland Jewish Community* (London, MacDonald, 1956), Ernest Krausz, *Leeds Jewry: Its History and Structure* (London, The Jewish Historical Society of England, 1964), R.E. Levy, 'History of the Birmingham Hebrew Congregation', in Zoe Josephs (ed.), *Birmingham Jewry* Vol. II (The Birmingham History Research Group, 1980), *passim*.
25. Cf. G. Alderman, 'Into the Vortex: South Wales Jewry before 1914', note 14, quoting M. Dennis, 'The History of the Cardiff Jewish Community', CAJEX 20 (December 1970), 27. Alderman's account relies largely on Dennis's articles in CAJEX Vols. 19 and 20.

5

The Ministry of the Reverend Simon Fyne in Swansea, 1899–1906

(Reproduced with the kind permission of Indiana University Press.)

LEONARD MARS

I

This study focuses on the Revd Simon Fyne's brief ministry in Swansea from 1899 to 1906. Since he spent such a short period of time in Swansea, why is his ministry worthy of current consideration? I suggest the following three reasons.

> 1. We can gain an understanding of the role of a Jewish minister in a provincial town at the beginning of this century.
> 2. We are able to appreciate the impact of mass immigration by eastern European Jews on already established Jewish communities in Britain, by examining the activities of a minister who served a congregation which embraced both the new immigrants and the established Jews.
> 3. Revd Fyne was a committed Zionist in the formative years of the Zionist movement, so we can grasp the outlook of an early Zionist activist at a time when the Zionist movement had yet to take hold of British Jewry and, indeed, when there was powerful opposition to it from British Jews.

Simon Fyne was born in Kovno, Russia. Unfortunately little is known of his background nor when he came to Britain. This information might have helped to explain the social and political sympathies he displayed in the course of his ministry. However, it is clear that he had an English education, for he was a graduate of Jews' College, London. This bestowed on him the title of minister but not of rabbi which refers to one who had taken *semicha* at a *yeshiva*. He accepted the post of minister to the Swansea Hebrew Congregation in 1899, having transferred from a similar position which he had occupied for a brief period (1897–8) in Newport, south Wales. Before Newport he had been minister since 1883 to Southampton's Hebrew congregation where he had moved from Bath, having served there from 1881.

When Fyne was appointed the Swansea Hebrew Congregation (SHC) numbered some ninety-five members. It was a stratified organization both economically and socially. The linking of seat rents to political privileges ensured that the government was limited to an oligarchy of well-established, comfortably off and respectable men — two were JPs — different in background, religiosity, social philosophy and social class from their east European co-religionists who were coming in increasing numbers to south Wales. Revd Fyne arrived at a turning point in the history of Swansea's Jewish community, and found himself in a position where he had to consider both the privileged members who employed him and the poor new immigrants whose needs, not only religious but also economic and charitable, he served. It would seem from the Minute Book of the SHC and from his letter to Haham Dr Gaster,[1] written at the conclusion of his Swansea ministry, that he had little sympathy for the synagogue élite and much concern for the new immigrants.

From the outset Revd Fyne's career with the SHC caused dissension within the ranks of the privileged members who voted to appoint him by nineteen votes to eight, with five abstentions.[2] Perhaps opposition to his appointment derived from information about his ministry in Southampton where his resignation was 'accepted with pleasure'.[3] He himself was alert to possible conflict with the other salaried official, Revd Miron, employed as *chazan* and *shochet*, since prior to commencing his ministry he sought clarification about the 'proper division' of prayers between them.[4] Revd Fyne's duties included conducting prayers, providing services at *rites de passage* of members and their families and particularly the instruction of children in the rapidly growing Hebrew classes organized by the SHC.[5] In addition, he assumed the role of dispensing charity, of collecting money for the local hospital, of lecturing to non-Jewish organizations, of occasional ministering to Jews in Merthyr, Bridgend and Llanelli, and also of taking services outside the synagogue required by the new immigrants during the High Holidays.

During a minor crisis in April 1901 when the treasurer resigned from the administration of the synagogue, Revd Fyne offered to accept the post of honorary secretary to the SHC. Mr M.L. Marks agreed to become treasurer on condition Revd Fyne's offer be accepted, which it was unanimously.[6] Hence a situation fraught with the possibility of conflict arose in which a salaried minister of the SHC became a member of its administrative committee. Already acting as secretary in October 1901, he was almost elected temporary president and treasurer. In fact, it was decided by the narrowest majority of nine votes to eight 'that in the interests of Mr Fyne, it was not advisable for him to act in the capacity of President'.[7] However, he was elected treasurer on a temporary basis (presumably until another incumbent could be found). In accepting the position, it was reported in the minutes: 'Mr Fyne returned thanks for the honour conferred upon him. Whilst thanking them, for the confidence thus reposed in him he himself could not help but deeply regret the state of things which rendered that step necessary, even temporarily.'

At this time the SHC was riven by factionalism and shortly afterwards, on 20 October 1901, both the new president, Mr A. Shepherd, and the new, temporary treasurer, Revd Fyne, tendered their resignations to be replaced by two members of the establishment, Mr Hyam Goldberg and Mr Ernest Barnett.[8]

From this pinnacle of acceptance and acceptability Revd Fyne descended to often acrimonious discord with the elected leaders of the SHC. In an ambiguous comment on Revd Fyne's report on the Hebrew classes which was to be sent to the Provincial Ministers' Fund the president endorsed it in the following words: 'In the absence of an Independent Examiner I have no reason to doubt the accuracy of Mr Fyne's Report.'[9] From that date the situation between Revd Fyne and the executive of the SHC deteriorated. In June 1902, the minutes report that Revd Fyne objected to the way that offerings to commemorate deceased souls (*Hazkarat Neshamot*) were made to the congregation and asked that the Chief Rabbi's views be sought.[10] In August 1902 it was reported that Revd Fyne had expelled a member's child from the Hebrew classes and the rider was added that 'he be requested to report to the Committee in future before expelling any child'.[11] In October 1902 he was instructed to rewrite his quarterly report on the Hebrew classes and omit reference to the work of the Committee.[12]

The dispute over offerings to the synagogue recurred in December 1904 when the Committee sent a strongly worded note:

> That Mr Fyne be requested to state, in writing, his willingness to conform to the rules, customs and usages of this congregation ... and in the event of no reply being received within 14 days to that effect or his refusal to undertake to make these offerings in future, in the form as customary hitherto, a special meeting of the Committee be convened to further consider the matter.[13]

Revd Fyne's letter of reply was deemed to be 'evasive and unsatisfactory' so that it was resolved to elicit 'in writing, a direct answer "Yes" or "No"'. The second letter received from Revd Fyne was again considered to be unsatisfactory and 'his resignation, to be determined by a General Meeting, would be called unless he agreed to abide by the Chief Rabbi's ruling of 4 June 5662'.[14] In March 1903, Revd Fyne wrote a letter agreeing to comply with that ruling which favoured the president's case. The Committee noted however that Revd Fyne had claimed the Chief Rabbi's ruling had been obtained by fraud and it resolved 'to write to the Chief Rabbi to ascertain if there be any truth in the allegation'.[15] The Chief Rabbi exonerated the president and the Committee agreed that Revd Fyne write a letter withdrawing his allegation. In May 1905 the Committee received a letter from Revd Fyne in which he denied he had ever said that the Chief Rabbi's letter had been obtained by fraud. This reply caused the Committee to comment that it regarded Revd Fyne's denial 'as most unsatisfactory and, having no doubt that the charge complained of was made by him, regrets that he will not see his way to honourably withdraw it'.[16]

In July, as a consequence of the dispute with Revd Fyne, at a Special Committee Meeting the two wardens (president and treasurer) submitted their resignations though the Committee hoped they would change their minds. The Committee agreed to call a General Meeting (of privileged members) 'to receive the resignations of the Wardens, and to consider the following recommendations of the Committee: In view of the resignations of the Wardens and the circumstances which have led to same it is recommended that six months notice be given to the Revd S. Fyne to terminate his engagement.'[17]

A Special General Meeting was convened in August 1905 to discuss the resignations of the wardens and the dismissal of Revd Fyne. From the records of the votes taken, it appears to have been a bitter meeting with the privileged members divided into pro- and anti-Fyne factions. The proposal to accept the resignation of the wardens and the dismissal of Revd Fyne was carried by 17 votes to 14. A second proposal to restore the wardens to office elicited an amendment 'that the resignations of the Wardens be accepted with pleasure on account of the unreasonable manner they have dealt with Mr Fyne'. Twelve members voted for this amendment and twenty for the proposal restoring the wardens to office. In reply the wardens pointedly 'thanked the committee [not the general meeting] for their unanimous vote of confidence' and accordingly agreed to continue in office. The meeting then discussed a proposal which was in fact an ultimatum 'that the Reverend S. Fyne be allowed three days to consider the advisability and also have the opportunity of tendering his resignation by giving this congregation six months notice'. Without recording the votes, the minutes report that the notice was carried.[18]

At the subsequent Committee Meeting a week later the minutes report: 'Letters were read from Mr Fyne declining to resign and accepting six months notice in accordance with the resolution passed at a Special General meeting held on August 20 last'.[19]

Revd Fyne's career in Swansea was coming to a close but even in its final few months it was still eventful. At a Special General Meeting, convened mainly to discuss the future of the other stipendiary official, the Cantor, Revd I. Miron, who had served the congregation for twenty-five years and who was suffering from ill health, the proposal that the Revd Fyne be presented with a testimonial was rejected by twenty-six votes to fourteen in favour of an amendment 'that the matter be deferred six months'.[20] Perhaps, because of Revd Miron's illness, Revd Fyne continued in office after the expiration of his contract on the 4 March[21] since another dispute described as a 'misunderstanding' between him and the treasurer is reported in the minutes of the Committee Meeting held 11 March 1906;[22] however this misunderstanding was subsequently resolved when the honorary treasurer 'expressed regret that any misunderstanding should have been conveyed by his remarks and having emphatically denied any intention of slighting Mr Fyne'. Both Revd Fyne and the treasurer agreed with the Committee that the matter be dropped.[23]

The final reference to Revd Fyne in the Minute Book 13 May 1906 again refers to his defiance of the officers of the Congregation when it records:

> It was reported that Mr Fyne acted as Mohel [ritual circumciser] yesterday to the infant child of Mr B. Sandler, in defiance of the

instructions given by the President to Mr Lubner (successor to Revd Miron who had resigned on grounds of ill-health in March 1906) to perform the operation; the matter was fully discussed by the Committee and, in view of Mr Fyne's early departure from Swansea it was unanimously resolved to take no further action for the present.[24]

Revd Fyne's defiance stemmed from his failure to observe Rule 34 of the Synagogue Constitution which stipulated that a member must first approach and then obtain permission from the president if he required the services of a *mohel*; furthermore the *mohel* was not allowed to offer his services without the consent of the president. It is possible that Fyne may have been approached by Sandler, who was a new immigrant, and who may have wished to exercise what he thought of as parental choice rather than to accept the *mohel* in the employ of the SHC. While it is possible that Sandler may have been unfamiliar with Rule 34 it is highly unlikely that Fyne was ignorant of it and probable that his freelance services were intended as a repudiation of the president's authority.

Revd Fyne's strained relations with the executive of the synagogue may partly be attributed to his personality, which seems to have been less than conciliatory, but since other ministers, both prior to and after him, had their difficulties,[25] it appears that the role of minister itself was subject to considerable strain irrespective of the individual incumbent. Moreover, because of the rapid increase in the Jewish population of Swansea during his ministry, an increase which brought in eastern European Jews whose religious customs and practices[26] were different from those of the established members who controlled the synagogue's executive, the already difficult role of the minister was subject to further strain.

There was in fact a conflict of interest between the anglicized or Welsh lay leaders of the SHC and the east European immigrants, which conflict met in the personage of the minister. As Gouldston points out, the British middle-class Jews sought an English gentleman, hence the foundation of Jews' College in London in 1855 to train ministers for Jewish congregations in the manner of the Anglican Church. However, the immigrants wanted *yiddishkeit* as they knew it in eastern Europe and not in what they called the 'English' *shul*. The Victorian British, Jewish, middle class wanted a rabbi learned in Jewish thought and practice; but they stressed the Englishness rather than the Jewishness of the religious leaders. The status of the Chief Rabbi of Great Britain and the British Empire was alien to the immigrants; his centralized and autocratic control[27] did not conform to the decentralized, non-hierarchical tradition of eastern Europe.

The immigrants also rejected the religious and social leadership of anglicized Jews who were prepared to accept their subscriptions but not to give them any voice in the administration and government of the congregation. These lay readers identified with the Chief Rabbi and enjoyed his support in handling the complaints of what he called Swansea's 'poor, foreign, workmen' (Minutes SHC, 1895).

A good idea of how the Chief Rabbi and the Jewish élite of Britain imagined the model, Victorian, Jewish minister is to be found in the following extract from the *Jewish Chronicle* on the opening of Jews' College:

> The future ministers of the Anglo-Jewish congregation will be men of thorough English feelings and views, as ... conversant with the classics of their own language as with those of the sacred tongue, as acquainted with modern science as versed in ancient lore; men in whom the flow of the burning thought will not be impeded by heaviness of tongue, and whose ardour of enthusiasm will break forth and rouse and kindle with Shakesperian vigour and Miltonian sweetness.[28]

The elders of Anglo-Jewry sought a minister who would be proficient in the secular, scientific field, versed in English and Hebrew literature, who would be primarily an Englishman of the Jewish faith and whose spoken English would bear no trace of a foreign accent. He was to be an English gentleman and scholar who would enjoy the respect of the non-Jewish world into which the newly emancipated British Jews were entering. Whilst the immigrants also wished to gain acceptance in their new country, nevertheless they wished to retain their *yiddishkeit*, which was both religious and ethnic. In short, for the English or Welsh Jew of middle-class status, the question of Jewish identity was purely a matter of religion whereas for the eastern European immigrant Jewishness constituted a twin identity based on ethnicity and religion. This different perception of the nature of Jewish identity lay at the heart of the conflict between the leaders of the SHC and their immigrant congregants.

From the minutes it appears that Revd Fyne enjoyed the support of the new immigrants and of the faction among the privileged members who were opposed to the leadership of the Goldbergs, Selines and Barnetts. The support he enjoyed of the poorer members of the

Jewish community, especially the immigrants, was based on several criteria. Firstly, it may have stemmed from his own immigrant background, but more so from the practical assistance he gave them from the distribution of welfare payments that were channelled through him by the SHC; secondly, his teaching of their children with which they expressed satisfaction; thirdly, his leading of prayers at overflow services, since the synagogue in Goat Street had a limited capacity of just over 200;[29] and fourthly his commitment to Zionism that had an appeal to the immigrants and was unpopular with the middle-class, anglicized Jews. In short Fyne was a champion of the newer and poorer members of the SHC and I think it no coincidence that his departure hastened rather than caused the establishment in 1906 of the rival congregation known as the Beth Hamedrash.[30]

II

When Revd Fyne assumed his ministerial duties in Swansea he was already a Zionist, but when exactly he joined the Zionist movement I do not know. What is certain is that during his brief ministry in Newport he was involved in the movement since, at a meeting of the newly formed English Zionist Federation[31] held at the Central Hotel Cardiff on 21 October 1900, he was described as the delegate for Newport.[32] On the evening of the same day 'at a large public meeting held under the auspices of the English Zionist Federation in the Cardiff Synagogue, Cathedral Road',[33] Revd Fyne proposed the following resolution:

> This meeting pledges itself to do all in its power to further the Zionist movement in the United Kingdom by endeavouring to obtain increased support for the English Zionist Federation.[34]

What is significant here is that the official meeting of the English Zionist Federation was held in a hotel, a non-Jewish venue, whereas a fringe meeting was held in the synagogue. The British synagogues as formal religious organizations were largely hostile to Zionism[35] and so, too, were two powerful British Jewish institutions, the *Jewish Chronicle* and the Chief Rabbi. Other powerful bodies of Anglo-Jewry were also hostile to Zionism, such as the Anglo-Jewish Association, the Board of Deputies and the Jewish Board of Guardians. For Cardiff's new and prestigious synagogue, which opened in 1897, to host such a Zionist meeting, albeit unofficial, was an exception, possibly explained by the lingering influence of its founder Col. A. E. W. Goldsmid, but it constituted a breakthrough for the Zionist movement; hence the significance of Fyne's resolution proposed and passed in the synagogue.

Fyne himself recognized this breakthrough in a long letter to the *Jewish Chronicle* in which he remarked:

> I rejoice that Zionism is being at last admitted into the Synagogue — and the English Synagogue. Admitted into the Synagogue! How strange it sounds! Is Zionism a proselyte, a kind of Gentile fad that has to be authoritatively admitted into the Synagogue? To our shame, be it confessed that such is the case![36]

and he continued, after comparing the claims of the Church and of the Synagogue to the land of Palestine, with praise of the Cardiff synagogue:

> The authorities of the Cathedral Road Synagogue are to be congratulated upon being (to my knowledge) the first English synagogue to open its portals to the Zionist movement, to invite it to take its stand upon consecrated ground — its proper place.

Fyne concludes his letter with an attack upon the editor of the *Jewish Chronicle* for his journal's anti-Zionist stance and suggests that had he been present in the synagogue he might have changed his position.

At the Cardiff meeting Simon Fyne first met the Haham, Dr Moses Gaster,[37] and within days wrote to him about his letter to the *Jewish Chronicle*.

> You must have thought me rather bold to have lectured the 'Chronicle' on its uncompromising attitude towards the movement. But a spirit of satire came over me as I left the meeting, and felt, as I never did before, the ridiculousness of the position taken up by our Orthodox opponents and so I gave vent to it.[38]

Commenting on his reason for praising the Cathedral Road Synagogue he observes:

> My object in giving prominence to the action of the authorities of the Cardiff Synagogue is such that *you* [Fyne's emphasis] will appreciate — to act as a precedent, as an example for Synagogue Wardens in other

towns to do the same. For not until 'Zionism' and the Synagogue become thoroughly united, can we hope for any real success, for any adequate result of the labour in the field of Zion.

In May 1905 Fyne again wrote to Dr Gaster about the Zionist movement,[39] this time on the issue of the Uganda Proposal.[40] Fyne praises Dr Gaster for his opposition to the Uganda Proposal:

> I have read through your vigorous masterly speech carefully noting every point and can only say I (also as a Zionist as opposed to Africandist) am in complete agremeent with you. It will be, perhaps, a revelation to you, that I have opposed the nomadic scheme ab initio.
> On the 13th September 1903 — soon after the Congress [Zionist Congress] I addressed here a public meeting in condemnation of East Africa. I remember bringing my address to a close with these words ... it is not *now* for *us*, to look out for a land, when *God* had already done so and did so before even the *birth* of the Jew. A land we have — the trouble is only as to the best and legitimate way to get into it. It is not for us to choose *Africa* when God has chosen *Asia*.

Asserting his own Zionist activism he urges the Haham to assume leadership of the Zionist movement and to oust those who favour the Uganda Proposal:

> As one who has written and spoken as a Zionist from the very beginning, allow me to thank you for your speech. We require a defender of the breached rampart[41] when renegades take the lead and have the brazen facedness to speak in the name of the people whom they have insulted and outraged. Arise, for it is incumbent upon you.[42] You are the man to take the lead; and if you only fight long enough, energetic enough and consistent enough you will succeed. God willing you will succeed.[43]

On the 9 December 1905, eight years after the first Zionist congress in Basle, and six years after the formation of the English Zionist Federation, Revd Simon Fyne who was then serving out his notice to SHC, gave a lecture at the Swansea Public Library entitled 'Zionism'. *The South Wales Daily Post* in its report,[44] a few days later, which described him as a 'Jewish rabbi', noted that he discoursed to a large audience and observed 'that by special request the lecture will be printed'.[45] Revd Fyne, who described himself in his lecture 'as a Jew and a Zionist'[46] considered that the realization of Zionism's aims would depend 'not only upon the sympathy and goodwill of the public, but even upon its active participation and practical support'. Accordingly, he saw it as his duty both to inform and to convince the non-Jewish world of the case for Zionism and he sought to accomplish these goals by asking a series of questions each of which constituted a separate section, seven in all, of his lecture:

> Now, what is 'Zionism'? What does it aim at — to begin with; and what does it seek to accomplish? Is there any need for it? Is it desirable? Is it practicable? Will it benefit the world — render it more humane, more moral, more religious, and more peaceful when accomplished?[47]

Revd Fyne defines Zionism as Jewish nationalism and points out that as such it is an ancient phenomenon since Jews had lived in Palestine as a nation for many centuries until expelled by the Romans; he argues that Jewish nationalism had not been expunged by dispersion, but had remained dormant, in his words, 'in a state of suspended animation'[48] and that it was Zionism's task to act the physician and awake it from its trance.[49] Fyne saw Zionism's first task in ambitious terms 'to make all Jews Zionists'.[50] He recognized that this would be no easy matter but considered that if Jews were to return as a nation to their own land then they would need to be united as Zionists in order to convince the rest of the world of the rightness of their case:

> The Jewish people must wish for it (the return to its own land) first, before anything can be done in the matter. Neither the World nor Providence will consider the matter at all, until the Jews themselves have expressed that desire and expressed it unequivocally, clearly, and unmistakably.[51]

The initial goal, then, of Zionism was to stimulate the national consciousness of the Jews, so that as a united people not only the rest of the world, but also God himself, would heed their appeal.[52] After achieving that initial goal, Zionism's aim was 'to secure a legally assured home for the Jewish people in Palestine, guaranteed by all the powers of Europe (Asia and America) as Belgium or Switzerland'.[53] Invoking scriptural authority Fyne argues that Jews have a stronger claim to Palestine than its then current inhabitants:

> The Arabs and Turks can no more be regarded as Palestinean [sic] than the English element in India can be called Hindus. Palestine has no *real* [emphasis in original] native population now, and has not had any for the last 18 centuries.

As proof of the lack of true belonging to Palestine by the Arabs and Turks he shows how unsuccessfully they had managed the land which 'can hardly support' a sparse population of 600,000,[54] whereas by his reckoning 'at the time of David and Solomon, Palestine ... sustained a population of about 7 millions in ease and affluence.'[55]

In a phrase that may have gained acceptance in Zionist circles at the time he remarks that 'Zionism seeks to restore the people without a country to the country without a people'.[56] However, the restoration of the Jewish people to the land of Palestine was not to be achieved by force of arms as under Moses or Joshua, nor as vassals of a single foreign power as was the case when Persia restored the Jews after an earlier exile, but rather 'they would enter it as the protégés of all the powers of Europe, Asia and America, all of whom would guarantee Jewish independencies'.[57] He considered that the European powers in particular had a special moral responsibility for the restoration of the Jews to Palestine since, 'was it not Rome — a *European* [emphasis in original] power that dispossessed us of it?'[58]

In his discussion of the question about the need for Zionism, Fyne embarks on an analysis of the predicament of the Jews, especially in Russia, which according to him contained the majority of the Jewish people, about six million; he discusses the deep-rooted anti-Semitism of the Russians which characterized the Czar, his bureaucracy, the Church and the peasants and was manifest in officially inspired pogroms; nor was he optimistic about improvements in the position of Russian Jewry in the event of any political reform since he thought anti-Semitism too deeply ingrained and concludes:

> There is no home for the Jews in Russia — for this century at all events.[59]

One answer to the solution of the problems of the Russian Jews was emigration but Fyne considered that the rest of the world was either unwilling to accept them or unsuitable for their settlement. He points out that earlier in the year the Anti-Alien Bill had been passed in England (*sic*) and this bill was directed 'to our shame'[60] at Jewish aliens; irrespective of that piece of legislation England was too densely populated and the UK could at most absorb 100,000[61] leaving 5,900,000 with an emigration problem; North America had reached saturation point since it had imposed restrictions on immigration;[62] South America, especially Argentina, he ruled out, since Jews already there had formed Zionist organisations; Australia was reluctant to admit immigrants and he cited as evidence the failure of General Booth's emigration scheme; he scathingly rejected Africa on the grounds that 'the coastlands are full, and the interior is fit only for savages'. By a process of elimination, he explains and exclaims that

> the finger of providence would seem to point towards no other land for the solution of the Jewish Question but Palestine![63]

On the question of the desirability of Zionism, his opinion was that national renewal in Palestine was of mutual interest to both Jews and Gentiles since what he termed 'racial nationalism' was resurgent, 'with the inevitable result, that sooner or later, Israel will have to go from Europe'.[64] In his view, even if Jews sought assimilation it would not be granted because of the opposition of European nationalism which would insist on the Jews forming their own homeland, a sentiment which he shared:

> Jew, as I am, I say that to a very large extent they are quite right.[65]

Pointing out that small countries such as Belgium, Switzerland and Romania had achieved independent status he asked rhetorically why Israel with a population of twelve million could not also become independent. He opined that the Jewish question was too big a problem to be settled by individual European powers and that it required an international solution involving the co-operation of Europe and America to resolve the Jewish question by restoring 'Palestine to the Jews and the Jews to Palestine'.[66]

Because Zionist aspirations seemed a utopian dream[67] Fyne addressed himself to the practicability of achieving an independent Jewish state in Palestine. He considered that a conference of European powers which would unanimously decide for 'neutralising Palestine as the legally secured home for the Jewish people'[68] would be able to coerce Turkey into relinquishing its hold on Palestine. He was convinced that Turkey believed that ultimately it would have to yield the territory to the Jews and would do so rather than see Palestine occupied by a European power. Moreover, he considered that the

European powers would rather yield it to the Jews than allow any one of their own number to control it.[69] He recognized that the solution to that problem would be to make them extra-territorial,[70] though he waspishly observed that if they could be entrusted to the 'non-Christian Turk' then equally they could be vouchsafed to 'the Jew, the brother of Jesus, according to the flesh'.[71]

Fyne concluded his lecture with an examination of the various benefits that Zionism would bring to the world at large. He suggested four such benefits — economic, moral, religious and political. Economically, he believed that the emigration from Europe, America and Africa would reduce population pressure in those continents, reduce competition and relieve the economic depression; in addition, the development of Palestine would provide economic opportunities for industrial countries. Morally, the benefits would be indirect, namely that with the departure of Jews from Europe, anti-Semitism would disappear since there would be no Jews to hate, and the Russian government in particular would have no need to sponsor massacres perpetrated by the masses. In religious terms the restoration of Jews to their land would enhance the status of the Bible and its prophetic statements and trigger a universal, religious revival; the kingdom of heaven would be established on earth. Politically the restoration of Jews to Palestine would create what Fyne termed an 'International Arbitration Bureau'[72] (inverted commas in original) since Jews from a variety of nations would settle there yet simultaneously retain their sympathies to their countries of origin and hence protect the interests of their natal countries; in fact they would be representative in Palestine of their countries of origin and would arbitrate impartially disputes which foreign countries would refer to the new state in its role as an Arbitration Bureau. The adoption of the role of International Arbitration Bureau by the new nation would reduce the number of wars and increase peace throughout the world.

Fyne's lecture indicates aspects of both his English experience and of his eastern European origins. The English element is manifest in his prejudices about Africa as a place where 'the coastlands are full' possibly with European colonists, 'and the interior fit only for savages';[73] in his reference to Wales subsumed under England (and that to a Welsh audience!);[74] in his language when he described the Russian peasantry as 'the lower orders'.[75] Stylistically, too, there is an attempt to employ what may be charitably called a form of rhyming couplet and, less charitably, crude doggerel which I suspect he penned himself;[76] the text, too, indicates that he was a reader of *The Times* since it refers to a letter that appeared in that paper one day prior to his lecture.

The eastern European background features in terms of his preoccupation with Russian Jewry. This preoccupation he justifies because of Russia's large Jewish population and its vulnerability to state sponsored anti-Semitism. It is true that he refers to Jews living in North and South America and Africa but his emphasis is firmly on the plight of Russian Jewry.[77] From his comments on the predicament of Russian Jewry, it seems unlikely that he at least, as a Russian Jew, would have sympathy and support for Russian state interests once settled in Palestine. It seems probable that he saw himself more as an English Jew, especially when one considers his remark about 'our shame' in the context of the Aliens Act of 1905.[78]

Overall Fyne's lecture reveals the viewpoint of a religiously-committed Zionist, not that of a secular nationalist Zionist. In some ways he was prescient; for example, he recognized that radical or evolutionary change in Russia would not ameliorate the Jewish condition in that country in the twentieth century and that European nationalism would threaten western and central European Jewry. He was utopian in his belief that the world would benefit from the creation of a Jewish homeland and over-optimistic about the messianic, millenarian impact of the return of the Jews to Palestine.

A year after his lecture on Zionism, Simon Fyne wrote a third and final letter from Swansea[79] to the Revd Dr Gaster, when he was no longer in the employ of the SHC. Its contents were not about Zionism but rather about employment. Now unemployed, and embittered by his ministerial experience of at least four small provincial congregations, he requested the Haham to intercede on his behalf for a vacant position at Montefiore College, Ramsgate, of which Dr Gaster had been principal from 1891 to 1896.

> . . . the position of a Jewish minister in the small provincial congregation is extremely unsatisfactory. The moneylender who, by his wealth or his family connections, becomes Parnes [community leader] rules with a high hand, showing respect neither for learning nor for principle, and reduces the position of Minister to that of a slave — seeing therefore this vacancy advertised I made up my mind to apply for it. Here I would devote my time to study, and feel happy.

> Now, you Sir, as the Haham [written in Hebrew], and knowing me, you can do much more I should say to help me secure the appointment, if you will but interest yourself in my candidature.
> Would you be good enough to give me a recommendation, or better still, perhaps to write direct to the Chairman of that Committee and otherwise to put a word or two in on my behalf?

Although he had already been replaced as minister to the Swansea Hebrew Congregation he signed his letter to the Haham as the incumbent of that post.

In a diplomatic rejection of Fyne's supplication, in which he outlined his constitutional position vis-à-vis Montefiore College, the Haham remarked that he was unable to comply with the request.[80]

This letter must have been one of the last that Revd Fyne wrote from Swansea since he next appears in The Jewish Year Book with an address in Dalston, London, described as 'ex-Minister Swansea Synagogue'.[81] For six years there is no trace of him in The Jewish Year Book until he reappears as minister to a congregation in Ottawa, the United Hebrew Brethren Synagogue of King Street (founded 1902).[82] From 1912 to 1920 he was minister to the Adath Yeshurun Synagogue of King Edward Avenue, Ottawa, from which post he resigned to go to Palestine.[83]

I do not know how long Revd Fyne spent in Palestine, nor in what capacity he was there, whether as a pilgrim or as an immigrant, but from the 1920s until at least December 1934 he was minister to the Ohel Jacob congregation in Philadelphia, Pennsylvania.[84] Both in Ottawa and in Philadelphia Revd Fyne was held in higher esteem than in England and Wales where, as we have seen, in Southampton his resignation was 'accepted with pleasure' and in Swansea he was dismissed. In Ottawa his resignation was accepted with 'considerable regret'.[85] Whilst age and experience may have matured Revd Fyne and improved his diplomatic skills, it seems more likely that the social composition of his North American congregations, composed of recent immigrants from eastern Europe who lacked the class structure of British society, made his position as minister more tolerable and manageable and less prone to conflict.

Notes to Chapter 5

1. Letter dated 26 December 1906 in the Gaster Papers located at the Mocatta (now Jewish Studies) Library, University College, London.
2. Indeed, he was not the first choice of wardens Seline and Sol Barnett, but their own candidate was rejected by 22 to 10 so that they then proposed Revd Fyne rather than re-advertise the post. Minutes of the Swansea Hebrew Congregation (hereafter SHC) 30 July 1899.
3. Minutes of Southampton Hebrew Congregation 1897 quoted in letter from Mr Sydney Weintroub.
4. Minutes of SHC, 1 August 1899, 7 September 1899.
5. In May 1902 60 children were on the roll. In December 1902 102 children were on the roll.
6. Minutes of Special General Meeting, 13 October 1901.
7. Ibid.
8. Minutes of General Meeting, 20 October 1901. The invitation to Mr Hyam Goldberg to become chairman was couched in fulsome, apologetic, supplicating terms, viz. 'that the meeting of the Swansea Hebrew Congregation deeply regrets the action of its members some four years ago by which Mr Hyam Goldberg had cause for grievance in consequence of which he withheld his practical interest in congregational affairs; and that the representative meeting, now assembled, cordially invite him to allow himself to be nominated for the office of President'.
9. Minutes of SHC, 23 March 1902.
10. Minutes of SHC, 1 June 1902.
11. Minutes of SHC, 17 August 1902.
12. Minutes of SHC, 5 October 1902.
13. Minutes of SHC, 11 December 1904.
14. Minutes of SHC, 5 February 1905. (NB: the use of both the Roman and the Hebrew calendar, 5662 being equivalent to 1902.)
15. Minutes of SHC, 5 March 1905.
16. Minutes of SHC, 7 May 1905.
17. Minutes of SHC, 27 July 1905.
18. Minutes of Special Meeting, 20 August 1905.
19. Minutes of Committee of SHC, 27 August 1905.
20. Minutes of Special General Meeting, 15 October 1905.
21. Minutes of Committee Meeting, 28 January 1906.
22. Minutes of Committee Meeting, 11 March 1906.
23. Minutes of Special Committee Meeting, 18 March 1906.
24. Minutes of Joint Management and School Committee Meeting, 13 May 1906.
25. E.g. his predecessor Revd Wolfers and his successor Revd Sandheim, cf. 96–8 above. Note, too, that in North America Revd Fyne was held in higher esteem. There he enjoyed the title of Rabbi.
26. E.g. their request for segregated seats in the *cheder* (minutes of SHC, 25 January 1903) which was defeated in a vote and also the prayers for the deceased souls.

27. Described as 'Adler's pontifical regime' in S.A. Cohen, 'The Reception of Political Zionism in England: Patterns of Alignment among the Clergy and Rabbinate 1895–1904', *Jewish Journal of Sociology*, XVI (1974), 177.
28. A.M. Hyams, *Jews' College, London, 1855–1955* (London, Jews' College, 1955), 24–5.
29. B. Goldblum's 'Swansea' (Proceedings of Conference on Provincial Jewry in Victorian Britain, 6 July 1975), 1–11.
30. N. Saunders, op.cit., 9.
31. The English Zionist Federation was formed in January 1899 at the Trocadero Restaurant in London, P. Goldman, *Zionism in England 1899–1949* (London, Zionist Federation of Great Britain and Ireland, 1949), 20.
32. *Jewish Chronicle*, no.1647, 26 October 1900, 25–6.
33. Ibid.
34. Ibid.
35. SHC included. Thus the President of SHC, Mr Hyam Goldberg, wrote to the President of the Swansea Zionist Association, Mr A. Levy, and refused him permission to put up notices of Zionist meetings in the Hall of the Synagogue (SHC Letter Book 31/1/02). However in 1905 when the Committee of the SHC received a request from the Zionist Association to use synagogue premises for meetings, permission was granted (minutes SHC, 19 November 1905). Sir Samuel Montagu, MP and President of the Federation of Synagogues, opposed Zionism (a) as unpatriotic for an English Jew and (b) as irresponsible for a religious Jew (S.A. Cohen, 'The Reception of Political Zionism in England . . .' *Jewish Journal of Sociology* (1974), 177).
36. *Jewish Chronicle* (see no.32), 9.
37. Dr Moses Gaster (1856–1939), head of the English Sephardi Synagogue, born in Bucharest, Lecturer in Romanian Language and Literature at Bucharest University, later a Lecturer in Slavonic Literature at Oxford, and an early member of the Zionist Movement.
38. Letter 28 October 5661 (1900) in Gaster Papers no.123A/138 held in the Mocatta Library (now Jewish Studies Library), University College, London. I am grateful to Mrs Trudi Levi, cataloguer of the Gaster Letters, for her assistance with this correspondence.
39. Letter of Simon Fyne to Moses Gaster (21/193 Gaster Papers).
40. Uganda Proposal — an offer made in 1903 by the British Government to Dr Herzl to establish a Jewish colony in East Africa under British sovereignty. Herzl was in favour of acceptance but was opposed by a large number of Zionists who eventually rejected the offer.
41. 'A defender of the breached rampart', Fyne writes in Hebrew 'Goder Gader v'omed b'aparetz'.
42. 'Arise, for it is incumbent upon you', Fyne writes in Hebrew 'Kum kee alecha hadavar'.
43. 'God willing you will succeed', Fyne writes in Hebrew 'Vehefetz Adonai b'yadcha yitzlach'.

44. *South Wales Daily Post*, Tuesday 12 December 1905. This title of Rabbi, which Revd Fyne seems to have bestowed on himself since he was not a qualified rabbi, appears, albeit in brackets, after his name on the front cover of the lecture.
45. Most of this section is based on that lecture, a copy of which was made available to me by Mr Oscar Benjamin of Swansea. The publication of the lecture may have been financed by M Jacobs and Co., cabinet makers and upholsterers, since an advertisement for this firm forms the back cover of the lecture.
46. Ibid., p.2.
47. Ibid., p.2.
48. Ibid., p.3.
49. Ibid., p.3.
50. Ibid., p.4.
51. Ibid., p.4.
52. Ibid., p.4.
53. Ibid., p.5.
54. Ibid., pp. 5 and 6.
55. Ibid., pp. 5 and 6.
56. Ibid., p. 6. B. Lewis, *Society and Anti-Semitism* (London, Weidenfeld and Nicolson, 1986) 172, observes 'the phrase is attributed to the Anglo-Jewish novelist Israel Zangwill, who in an article published in 1901 remarked "Palestine is a country without a people, the Jews are a people without a country. The regeneration of the soil would bring the regeneration of the people"' (175). Footnote 9 of B. Lewis, 269, n.9, cites the reference 'The Return to Palestine' in *New Liberal Review* (London), 11 December 1901, 627. Lewis acknowledges Professor Michael Curtis for drawing his attention to this reference.
57. Ibid., 6.
58. Ibid., 7.
59. Ibid., 9.
60. Ibid., 9.
61. Ibid., 9. NB: the switch from 'England' to 'the U.K.' perhaps reflecting his awareness of Celtic Britain.
62. In fact Fyne was wrong since in the decade 1900–9 immigration reached a figure of 8.2m in the USA of whom 952,767 were Jews and until 1914 USA immigration remained high, cf. P.R. Mendes Flohr and J. Reinharz, *The Jew in the Modern World* (Oxford University Press, 1908), 530.
63. Ibid., 10.
64. Ibid., 10.
65. Ibid., 11.
66. Ibid., 11.
67. Ibid., 11.
68. Ibid., 11.
69. Ibid., 12.
70. Ibid., 12.
71. Ibid., 12.

72. Ibid., 14.
73. Ibid., 10.
74. Ibid., 9.
75. Ibid., 13. 'When the lower orders will become automatically more humane, more moral, in spite even of themselves.' This moral transformation would result from Jewish emigration from Russia.
76. My colleagues in the Department of English at University College Swansea have been unable to identify these couplets, though perhaps other scholars may detect their provenance. For example describing the Roman occupation of Palestine he writes 'until Rome, the rapacious eagle swooped down on the country and seized it as a prey, leaving the Jews to wander whither they may' (ibid., 3); also in describing Palestine in 1900 as 'She looks, even now, as bereft as on the day the Jews have left' (ibid., 6). Certainly they lack the 'Shakespearian vigour' and 'Miltonian sweetness' expected of graduates from Jews' College.
77. Fyne was involved in raising money in Swansea to alleviate the victims of the Kishinev pogroms of 1903, cf. Minutes of SHC, 7 June 1903.
78. Ibid., 9.
79. Letter from Revd Fyne to Dr Gaster 26 December 1906, in Gaster Papers.
80. Letter from Dr Gaster to Revd Fyne 28 December 1906, in Gaster Papers (Letter No. 451).
81. Jewish Year Book 1906–1907, 340.
82. Jewish Year Book 1913, 142.
83. The Jewish Year Books report him as being in Ottawa from 1914–32. These dates are inaccurate and reveal that we should be sceptical about the reliability of the Jewish Year Book as a source. The archivist of the Ottawa Jewish Historical Society, Shirley Berman, informs me (letter of 8/2/88) that Revd Fyne was minister to Ottawa's congregation from 1912–20 and that he resigned to go to Palestine.
84. Letter 9 May, 1988 from the Archivist, Lily G. Schwartz, of the Philadelphia Jewish Archives Center, which letter contained a copy of a letter to Rabbi Simon Fyne, 11 December 1934.
85. Diamond Jubilee Bulletin of the Adath Jeshurun Congregation (c. 1964), 12.

6

Lyons versus Thomas:
The Jewess Abduction Case
1867–8

URSULA R. Q. HENRIQUES

I

On the evening of 23 March 1868, Esther Lyons, accompanied by two young women of about her own age, knocked on the door of Croome Villa, Roath, the home of the Revd Nathaniel Thomas, minister of the Baptist Tabernacle, Cardiff. The Revd Thomas was out for the day, but his wife, Laura Emily Ann Thomas, well known for her religious work among children and young people, was at home. But this was not a routine visit, for Esther, aged eighteen, was an orthodox Jewess, and she was running away from her family. It was the start of a *cause célèbre* which was to shake the town of Cardiff, make headlines in the national press, and exercise a baneful influence on relations between the Jews of south Wales and the powerful Welsh Baptist community for generations to come.

The Lyons case, or the Jewess Abduction Case, as most of the press called it, is not unknown to historians. The story was told under the title 'The Abduction of Esther Lyons', by Raymond Woolfe (CAJEX, July 1952, Vol.2, No.3, pp.14–23). However, a careful reading of Woolfe's article shows it to be incomplete, resting almost entirely on the reports and correspondence published in the *Cardiff and Merthyr Guardian* for 1868. The detailed accounts of the Assize court trial of July 1869 in the same paper have barely been tapped, the later legal proceedings and other sources not at all. Evidently there is more to be revealed about the Lyons Case. With the valuable assistance of Miss Katherine Doyle I have tried to discover some more about this intriguing, if in some respects still obscure, affair.

Barnett Lyons, originally an immigrant from Poland, but long resident in Cardiff, lived with his wife and growing family at his pawnbroker's shop, 11 Mount Stuart Square, near the docks. Esther was his eldest daughter. She had an elder brother, Reuben, and five younger sisters and brothers; and after the habit of Victorian families her mother was expecting yet again in March 1868. Having left school at sixteen, Esther was now expected to help her parents. In May 1867 her father had opened another pawnshop in Castle Road, Roath, as an endowment for Reuben, who was engaged to be married. Esther was required to work for her father there. From September to December of that year she shared the work with a non-Jewish hired shop-assistant, Sarah Carver, from Newport. The two girls slept in the shop during the week and came home to Mount Stuart Square from Friday to Sunday nights. However, in December Esther was summoned home to help her mother look after the younger children. Sarah left the shop on 24 December but she remained in Cardiff, and she and Esther continued to meet. Esther was also 'keeping company' with a young man, Theodore Goodman, son of a Jewish family from Pontypridd who were close friends of the Lyons's, although there is no evidence that she was particularly attached to him. Whatever conflict over the nature of Esther's family relations was to emerge later, the impression remains that, as a daughter at home, she felt that little attention was paid to her wishes or prospects. As with many Jewish girls at the time, even her religious education was perfunctory. Rabbi Nathan Jacobs of the East Terrace Synagogue came two or three times a week to teach the children Hebrew, but it transpired that Esther could read Hebrew words but did not know what they meant. Reuben, who must have celebrated his *Barmitzvah* in the traditional way, would have been more seriously educated. Nor was her standing in the family very high. Barnett (but it was after the event) called her 'dull and nervous', and, unlike the other children, not inclined to respect nor obey her parents. But he claimed that she was cherished all the more for this reason.[1]

The truth was that Esther did not get on with her mother. Whether, as she later claimed, her mother starved her, kept her indoors, pinched her, throttled her and beat her with a chair leg, a hairbrush and the fire irons is a matter for doubt. In any case Mrs Lyons was in poor health and constantly pregnant, so powerful physical violence would have been unlikely. It was admitted that she objected to Esther's preference for reading newspapers and novels to doing the housework, and she certainly resorted to nagging and slapping. Her father, of whom she was fond, evidently did not interfere effectively.

The family failed to take Esther's discontent seriously until the crisis was upon them.

The crisis was probably precipitated (though she later denied it) by the finding in Esther's room, by her sister Rachel, of a new purse with a half sovereign in it. Rachel gave it to Reuben, who promptly took it to his mother, a piece of 'sneaking' which cannot have endeared him to Esther. It is not clear whether she was frightened of being accused of stealing, or of accepting a bribe from the Baptists; but without pausing to pack any spare clothes she left home. First she went to see Sarah Carver, who was staying with a friend, Janet Green. But Sarah, who was on bad terms with her own father, could offer her no refuge in Newport. So they decided to call on the Thomas family at Croome Villa, where they arrived late at night, asking for refuge for Esther.

So far the facts are not in doubt, but the subsequent Assize trial was to turn on the question of whether Esther went to Croome Villa spontaneously, or whether she was enticed there. Barnett Lyons stoutly maintained that Esther went as a result of a deep-laid plot to abduct his children and convert them to evangelical Christianity. It did indeed emerge that Esther, while at Roath, had been under the eye of Mrs Blagdon, mother of Mrs Laura Thomas, who lived with her other daughter opposite the Roath shop. Mrs Thomas was already acquainted with Esther's cousin, Dinah Lyons, whom she was trying to convert, but who turned out to be too 'indecisive'; in other words she baulked at being baptized. Dinah and Esther, out walking a month or two before, had heard music coming from Tredegarville Chapel, out of curiosity had gone in to investigate, had watched acolytes being baptized, and had been recognized. It would seem that serious conversion attempts had begun with this event. Dinah was given a New Testament to pass on to Esther, though she denied that she had delivered it. In any case, the Thomases were already known to Esther, or she would hardly have been willing to go to them. But no evidence ever emerged that she was urged, or even invited to do so. Mrs Thomas stoutly maintained that she tried in vain that evening to persuade the young woman to go home. Whether Mrs Thomas's word could be relied upon the reader must decide.

Esther Lyons stayed at Croome Villa one night, with the reluctant acquiescence of the Revd Nathaniel Thomas, when he came home. Next day she was taken by a Mrs Alice Arthur to 20 Canal Street. Sarah Carver, who came the following afternoon, saw her there with some religious books on the table. She was told to say goodbye to her, and shortly after Esther left in a cab, Sarah being required to stay in the house so that she could not see which way they went. In fact they went to 1 Brighton Terrace, to a small school kept by a Mrs Sleeman, wife of another minister. Next door, at 2 Brighton Terrace, lived a Mrs Hollyer, a friend of Mrs Thomas, who had already been implicated in the attempt to convert Dinah. Esther stayed there under the name of Jane Barton until the end of April. A bedstead was brought in for her and she was given some of Mrs Hollyer's daughter's spare clothes, and the process of converting and educating her went on apace. She was said to be doing sums, and was allowed to play croquet in Mrs Sleeman's garden, but when her father came enquiring for her she was helped over the garden wall into Mrs Hollyer's premises. Towards the end of April, Mrs Hollyer's sister, Mrs Keep, came from London. Esther was taken to Chepstow, avoiding the policemen watching for her on Cardiff Station platform, who she said ignored her. She stayed there a week, and then moved on to Stroud, where Mrs Keep came to fetch her to stay at her home in Finchley Road, St John's Wood, London. Meantime, Sarah Carver, renamed Elizabeth Wood, had been placed in a 'situation' in Bristol. It was evidently desired to prevent her from having any contact with Esther's family. Although she disliked the 'situation' and grumbled about it angrily in her correspondence with Mrs Hollyer, she was firmly kept there and used as a go-between in forwarding letters from Esther to her parents.

When Esther disappeared on the night of 23 March her father and Reuben went out to search the streets. Finding nothing they alerted the police, and after a week's agonizing search, as a result of police enquiries Barnett Lyons went to Croome Villa to see the Revd Nathaniel Thomas. Mr Thomas told him his suspicions were groundless, but a later interview with Mrs Thomas was slightly more fruitful. Mrs Thomas admitted that Esther had slept at Croome Villa on the night of 23 March but denied any knowledge of her present whereabouts, saying 'you ask me too strong questions'.[2] At a later interview she admitted that she had sent Esther to Brighton Terrace, but denied all knowledge of her subsequent movements. At least by now Barnett Lyons knew that his daughter was in the hands of conversionists, and not in the Victorian underworld. On 25 May, when Esther was safely in London, in response to one of his appeals, Mrs Thomas wrote Lyons a long letter. She denied telling any falsehoods; she had told the police she was *wilfully* ignorant of

Esther's whereabouts. She had had to protect Esther, who had come to her for refuge from a *very wretched* home, and would never betray her. Her conscience was clear, she would do the same again, and was not afraid of any punishment he could inflict.

> I am a FRIEND and no ENEMY of yourself and family; and would not harm a hair of your heads, and would do and *suffer* a very great deal for your salvation, and pray (oh! how fervently) that the veil may be removed, and that with joy you may see and adore the blessed Messiah who died for you on Calvary, and look upon Him whom you have pierced, and mourne and bathe in the Fountain opened for sin and for uncleanliness, and be saved!

She added that she could find out Esther's whereabouts, and bring her to Cardiff, but would need travelling expenses and repayment of money spent on her clothes. She suggested a sum of £10, the balance to be returned. Finally she wrote that Esther was dearly loved by all who had to do with her. 'What a *mine* of *wealth* in her loving heart her mother has lost.' If Mr Lyons would send the £10 and give a pledge to leave Esther's decision to her own desire, Mrs Thomas would find her out and have the plan laid before her.[3]

This letter was probably a blunder. It allowed Barnett Lyons to claim that his daughter was being held for the purpose of making money (which was certainly not true, the cost of her keep being far higher than any expenses claimed from her parents). He had it published in the newspapers, and cited as a proof of 'refined cruelty' and hypocrisy on the part of the minister's wife, who 'flings her poisoned arrow into the bereaved mother's breast'. Further negotiations followed, in the course of which Lyons signed a paper of conditions for the interview. But the interview was cancelled, for, according to a letter written by Mrs Thomas on 3 June, Esther refused to come to it. Shortly after, Lyons received an undated, unaddressed letter from his daughter, saying that she had left home of her own free will, and had embraced Christianity.[4] Neither this letter nor subsequent ones seemed to Lyons to be genuine. The spelling and the grammar were altogether too perfect, and the language (as Mr Justice Blackburn was to comment) was that of a preacher rather than a half-educated young woman.

Lyons now resorted to the law. He went to London and consulted Messrs Sampson Samuel and Emanuel, solicitors to the Board of Deputies of British Jews, who briefed a counsel, Mr Oppenheim, to apply to Mr Justice Blackburn in the Court of Queen's Bench for a writ of habeas corpus to produce Esther in court. Mrs Thomas thereupon declared that she would 'stand to be whipped to death' rather than restore the girl. Oppenheim produced Esther's undated letter to her father as proof that she was being coerced. Blackburn could find no proof that Esther was being detained against her will that was sufficient to justify a writ of habeas corpus, but he considered that the letter, rather than being genuine, was a composition of the Baptists, and he granted a summons against Mr and Mrs Thomas to show reason why a writ of habeas corpus should not issue. The Thomases responded with an affidavit (sworn statement) saying that they did not know where Esther was. Barnett Lyons's friend, David Goodman, now revealed that he had been to Thomas's chapel and heard him telling his congregation that he would have to go to London to produce Esther Lyons in court, and appealing for sympathy and assistance.[5] Thomas replied that he had not used these words, and that Goodman, a foreign Jew, could not have understood his remarks which were in Welsh. He denied any wish to interfere with parental authority, and claimed he was being persecuted. He had received a letter signed: 'A Jew who hates the imposter and swindler Jesus Christ'. If he consulted the flesh he 'would never again help the helpless or succour the oppressed'.[6] The letter about Christ was angrily repudiated by Lyons and other correspondents as a scurrilous invention, while it was pointed out that Goodman had lived in Pontypridd for twenty-seven years and understood Welsh very well. Mr Justice Blackburn said he did not believe the Thomas's affidavit, and if he had been a Lord Chancellor, he would have sent them to prison for contempt of court. But he still could not issue a writ.[7] At this juncture Esther (or her representative) wrote to the *Cardiff and Merthyr Guardian* denying that she had left home under any coercion whatever. She was quite ready to meet her father in the presence of witnesses, and to tell him what he already knew, that 'Of my own accord I left his house, and that I have found in Jesus of Nazareth the saviour of my soul and have been baptized in His name.'[8]

Meantime, what was Esther doing? She spent some two months in Finchley Road as companion to Mrs Keep, and then moved to a school for Jewish converts kept at Tottenham by a Dr Lazarone, and a Dr Schwartz, minister of a Presbyterian chapel, who were both converted Jews. She was baptized on 23 June by the Revd Sleeman at Mr Stott's chapel, Abbey Road, London, as 'Anna'.[9] She was now in the hands of professional conversionists, and in touch with more formidable (if not more confident) intellects than those of Messrs Thomas, Hollyer and Keep. Dr Schwartz became her adviser, and 'helped' her to write her letters. He also convinced the Baptist ladies, and eventually Esther herself, that she must submit to an interview with her father.

During the summer negotiations proceeded between Mr Lyons's and Dr Schwartz's solicitors for an interview between Esther and her father. Meantime Barnett and Reuben were still searching for Esther, coming up to London, and possibly even engaging a detective. Esther's friends redoubled their efforts at concealment. Letters from her to her family arrived with Bridgend postmarks. One even sported a postmark from Neuchâtel, and contained a rather vague reference to Swiss scenery. At last, late in August, Barnett received a letter from Schwartz's solicitors, Messrs Norris and Allen, proposing an interview between himself and his daughter at the office of Messrs Sampson Samuel and Emanuel on 1 September. Esther would be accompanied by a lady and a gentleman. She would see her father privately, and then, in the presence of her father's solicitor, but not of her father, would declare whether she would return with her father or stay with those with whom she now was.[10] Lyons hastily agreed, but the meeting was postponed. It emerged later that when Schwartz accompanied Mr Allen on a visit to Sampson Samuel, wearing a white necktie, the mark of a minister, Samuel sent him out of the room and would speak only to Allen. This caused a furious quarrel in which Lyons wrote to Norris and Allen saying their behaviour was unworthy of their profession, and only withdrew the letter when threatened with a total cancellation of the interview. Schwartz called Sampson a 'bigoted Jew', and Lyons later called Schwartz a 'Meshummad' or apostate.[11]

The interview between Barnett Lyons and his daughter took place on 2 September in the offices of Messrs Norris and Allen, 20 Bedford Row. Barnett came with Reuben, a brother-in-law (Esther's uncle), and his solicitor. He was taken alone into a back room, and after nearly an hour Esther was shown in. 'When she left my house and protection she was in a robust state of health, happy and contented looking. I found her now trembling and nervous, and Oh! so fearfully emaciated and haggard, that my heart ached for my poor misguided offspring.' Asked by what means she had been induced to leave them, she began a long statement and said she had 'suffered a perfect martyrdom', but suddenly interrupted, and 'trembling all over, became so terrified she could proceed no further'. When asked to go with him she said: 'How can I, I have taken . . . I have been baptized'. 'I said, "Never mind, I will forget and forgive all that." She gave no reply but wept and dropped her head as though perfectly bewildered.' When he begged her on his knees to return to him, 'She appeared to be labouring under some powerful influence, and exclaimed "I shall go mad, I shall go mad."' He entreated her to consider the subject for a week and let him know the result. She said, 'I cannot do that, I must ask my friend whether I may do so.' After half an hour Allen, who had been watching them intently through a window, came in. Reuben and the uncle and solicitor were then called in, but Barnett was excluded. When Reuben and the uncle, after kissing Esther, tried to speak to her, Allen sent them out and declared the interview at an end.[12]

This, of course, was Barnett Lyons's account of the interview. Schwartz's, at the subsequent trial, was different; he said the interview had lasted at least an hour. He said that Lyons had apologized to him for writing against him in the papers and asked for his help in arranging a second interview with his daughter, and in letting her come home for a week. In return he had told Lyons that if Esther had been under his control he should have seen her immediately, and she would never have been baptized before the interview. But she could not go home, 'because she was a Christian, and they would despise Jesus whom she would praise'.[13]

Esther herself at the trial gave an account of the interview very different from her father's. She said her father had threatened to disinherit her, had tried to get her to sign a document, and when she refused without her solicitor had said that his mother would 'rise from her grave and cry out for revenge'. When her father had asked her to take a week to think it over she had told him her determination was already made. She admitted that her letters were partly written for her, but insisted that she agreed with everything in them. 'The thoughts were her own.'[14]

After the interview Esther returned to Mrs Keep for a month, where she was told that the Jews were 'much enraged' and would 'tear her to pieces if they caught her'. 'She read in the newspapers that the Jews would crucify her as they'd done her Saviour.'[15] After moving about for a few days while somebody tried to break into Mrs Keep's house, she was sent off to a place with the unlikely name of Pancarnarvon, in Prussia. There she remained for nine months at Mrs

Keep's expense, learning German with the Pastor of Stroube, and only returned to Britain for the trial. Or so she said; but one must wonder whether she ever went abroad at all.

Barnett Lyons returned to Cardiff, uncertain what to do but determined not to give up. At law he was in a weak position. He had already failed to get a writ of habeas corpus. Young persons over sixteen had a right (as Mrs Thomas had been careful to ascertain) to live where they pleased. Nor was there anything illegal in trying to convert someone to another religion, providing they were not coerced nor detained against their will, and it was now apparent that Esther would not support any such allegation. Lyons had spent a lot of money, and was quarrelling with his solicitors about whether or not he had agreed to abide by his daughter's decision.[16] Strenuous attempts to get up a fighting fund on his behalf had failed. By the spring of 1869 it seemed as though the case would peter out. But by the summer he had acquired a new and enthusiastic solicitor, Mr Joel Emanuel, who, on consulting eminent counsel, Mr Michael and Mr Chitty of King's Bench Walk, had been advised that the plaintiff had good grounds for action. While the object of the action would be not so much to recover damages as to restore Miss Lyons to her family, there was every possibility that the exposure and expense of a trial would have 'the beneficial effect of causing conversionists to hesitate before again resorting to similar means to obtain converts to Christianity'.[17] Barnett Lyons would sue the Thomases and others for enticing away his servant (who was also his daughter) from his service to his financial detriment in the sum of £2,000. If he could not get his daughter back he could at least punish his enemies.

Barnett Lyons v. *Revd N. Thomas and Others* (The Jewess Abduction Case) was heard at the Assizes in Cardiff Town Hall from Monday 26 July to Saturday 31 July 1869. Joel Emanuel had instructed Mr Hardinge Giffard QC, later to become the famous judge Lord Halsbury, and Mr Michael. The defendants were represented by Mr Grove, soon to become a High Court judge. The Assize judge was Baron Channell.[18] The defendants were the two Thomases, J.E. Hollyer and his wife, and Ellen Keep. The jury was carefully vetted to exclude Baptists and Jews. Cardiff Town Hall was thronged day after day with eager spectators, mostly females in their best attire, including many Jewesses. Such excitement was rarely available in the dull provincial life of mid-Victorian Britain, and hundreds who could not squeeze into the Town Hall stood about outside waiting for juicy pieces of sensation and scandal to emerge.

In the course of the trial the events between the crucial dates of 23 March and 3 September 1868 were fully investigated. In every aspect of the story the two sides adduced conflicting statements, on oath. Esther herself dwelt on her cruel treatment at home, saying she had resolved to run away twelve months before, but her mother had locked up her out-of-door clothes. She was supported by three servant girls formerly in the employment of the Lyonses, but contradicted by other servants, all her own family, and their friends the Goodmans. The attempts of Mrs Blagdon and her other daughter to convert Dinah, and also to approach one of Esther's younger sisters (who ran away), were revealed. Mrs Thomas had, with forethought, destroyed all her letters, but correspondence between the sisters, Mrs Hollyer and Mrs Keep, had (how is not known) fallen into the hands of Lyons's lawyers. These revealed in detail the stratagems employed by that remarkable group of ladies to conceal Esther's whereabouts from her family. They also revealed some of the spite which underlay their pious professions of religious love. Mrs Keep had written to her sister on 2 June 1868 that the mother (Mrs Lyons) was near confinement and not unlikely to die: 'I say of mortified rage, they say of grief'. The Jews were in a great rage just now, and if 'Cissie' wrote 'All's well, good night', it would be sufficient notice that all was well. Any letter from Mrs Sleeman should be in handwriting different from that of herself, or Esther or Mrs Thomas.[19] That letter was to attract much comment. During the trial several women used the conventional weapons in their Victorian armoury. Mrs Lyons established herself in the courtroom immediately opposite the witness box, and when Esther was brought in, fainted away. The judge, saying he did not want the witness unnerved or intimidated by her family, had Mrs Lyons removed from the court. Both Sarah Carver (now Mrs Sarah Jones) and Esther fainted when cross-examination got too hot for them. Esther, who seemed 'very feeble' and was accommodated with a chair at the judge's direction, had to be sent home with the keeper of Cardiff Gaol, and returned next day much restored. The townswomen enjoyed it all, and the press had a field day.

Baron Channell's summing up was not on the whole favourable to the plaintiffs. The questions at issue were, firstly, whether Esther's departure from her father's house had been voluntary, and secondly, whether the defendants had 'harboured' her while she was still a servant. The answer to the first of these, on the evidence, must have been 'Yes'. It was not very clear what 'harbouring' meant in this context, but the answer to the second appeared to be not proven. However, the jury, while exonerating the Hollyers and Mrs Keep, brought in a verdict of guilty against the Thomases, and awarded Mr Lyons £50 damages. The judge thereupon gave the Thomases leave to appeal.[20]

The following Sunday Mr Thomas went before his chapel congregation and offered to resign. But his audience announced their warm support, and set up a fund to finance the appeal.[21]

Encouraged by his court victory, Barnett Lyons now tried to get Esther made a ward in Chancery, with Reuben as her official guardian (for fear that there would be objections to himself). But the move backfired disastrously. Mrs Keep and Dr Schwartz put in a counter-application for the guardianship. Vice-Chancellor James summoned Esther, who was living with Mrs Keep in St John's Wood, for a long personal interview in chambers, and as a result refused to nominate a Jewish guardian. Lyons appealed to Lord Justice Giffard in court, who refused to alter the verdict. Vice-Chancellor James, he said, had seen the young lady and was satisfied that she was a genuine convert to Christianity. She had been baptized, would be twenty next February, and appeared to be of a most nervous temperament. 'To compel her to return to her father's house would be most prejudicial to her health.'[22] But her guardians were required to allow her father to see her at any time he chose to apply.

The Thomases' appeal against the Cardiff Assize Court judgement was not taken until June 1870, when it was heard in the Queen's Bench before Justices Blackburn, Mellor and Lush. Legal argument went on for a day and a half, centring largely on precedent. Finally the judges, by a majority verdict, overturned the Assize Court judgement and found for the defendants on two grounds: that there was insufficient evidence of enticement, and even if there had been, Esther was not under any contract of service to her father. Blackburn (who had originally cast doubt on the veracity of the Thomases' affidavit) disagreed, saying there was sufficient evidence of enticement; but he was overruled. The judges cancelled the £50 damages, and awarded costs to the Thomases.[23]

Barnett Lyons now threatened to take the case to the Court of Appeal, and the Thomases, to avoid further trouble, agreed to forgo their costs. This did not deter Lyons from bringing a criminal action against them in the Cardiff police court for perjury. He based it on Mr Justice Blackburn's comment in Chancery chambers in July 1868 that he did not believe the Thomases' affidavit that they did not know where Esther was and had used every endeavour to find out. During December 1870 much of the old evidence was gone through again. Mrs Hollyer was closely cross-examined (Mrs Keep had died). But the magistrates were unwilling to charge Mrs Hollyer, a Crown witness, with perjury. Lyons, on his lawyer's advice, declined to be bound over to prefer a bill of indictment against the Thomases in Assizes. As the *Cardiff and Merthyr Guardian* put it, 'The case is now finally closed'.[24]

The abundance of detailed but conflicting evidence in the Lyons case raises almost as many questions as it answers. Was Esther's really a cruel and violent home? We shall never know. What was Esther really like? Was this one more case of the Victorian girl of superior natural abilities denied the opportunity to develop her capacities? Probably not. There are no indications of special intelligence; rather the reverse. At the trial she was described as 'a small, child-like looking girl, with no striking marks of her race on her features'. Yet she had mounted a very effective teenage rebellion. Doubtless she suffered for it. She had been fond of her father, and had wept when she was hiding at Mrs Sleeman's and he passed by the window. But she bore furious witness against her family, and in the end the quarrel became irreconcilable. It is unlikely that the change made her happy. All who saw her, including the Chancery judge, testified to her nervousness. She did not need to believe the legends told her about Jewish revenge to realize that she could not live at home as a Christian. And however much she was under the influence of the conversionists, and indebted to them for the sanctimonious and provocative letters sent home in her name, there is no reason to doubt that her conversion was sincere, nor that her own determination made it impossible for her father to get her back or to win his lawsuits. What happened to her afterwards? Did she ever marry? How did she fare? Alas, after 1870 she vanishes into thin air.

Barnett Lyons was obviously torn by grief at the loss of his daughter, as well as by shame that she should be a 'Meshummad'. In the eyes of orthodox Jews this was the ultimate sin, even though more assimilated families such as the Marks, first Jewish settlers in Cardiff, regularly lost members to baptism in each generation. As it became increasingly clear that his daughter would not return, his motives shifted towards revenge: 'The Jewish community may at some future time (with the help of the God of our fathers)', he wrote to the *Jewish Chronicle* in March 1869, 'see how a Jewish father can strive to repair, or if not, avenge the atrocious wrong committed on him by these bigoted and unprincipled zealots.'[25] It is difficult to blame him.

Mrs Laura Thomas was described in court as 'a lady whose firmness and decision are marked in her countenance, her keen look and compressed lips betokening no small degree of energy and self-possession'. She was probably the leader of this strange knot of fanatical women — the *Jewish Chronicle* called them 'very odd Lydias and Dorcases'[26] — who did not hesitate to employ deception for the purpose of making converts, and whose religious anti-Semitism bubbled beneath the surface of their professions of Christian love. The two most sacred tenets of mid-Victorian morality were truthfulness and the sanctity of the family. Mrs Thomas broke the first freely; her willingness to break the second was probably accounted for by her own history. Born Miss Blagdon, the eldest daughter of the squire of Boddington Manor, Gloucestershire, she had when quite young undergone some sort of religious conversion experience. Thereafter she had become dissatisfied with the state of piety in her local Anglican church. Quarrelling with her father over his preference for moderate religion and high living, she had finally left home, taking her mother and sister with her. 'Guided' to go to remote Carmarthen, she had sampled various Nonconformist chapels, had been rebaptized by the Revd Nathaniel Thomas, and subsequently married him.[27] Her husband was working-class, Welsh-speaking, and had started down the mines at the age of seven, losing an eye in an accident.[28] Although he became a leading and respected Baptist minister, moving to Cardiff in 1856, the world would consider that she had married disastrously beneath her. They had no children, and their opponents, of course, suggested this was an added inducement to break up the families of those who had. Certainly she wore the trousers, and having divided her father's family did not seem to balk at dividing someone else's in the cause of conversion. Defiantly she proclaimed that she expected her reward in Heaven.

II

Public opinion as revealed in the press generally condemned the 'abduction' of Esther Lyons. The *Jewish Chronicle*, leading organ of Anglo-Jewry, was, not surprisingly, outraged. It perceived the Cardiff case against a background of increasingly aggressive conversionism arising from current evangelical movements. For instance, Dr Schwartz was one of a group of ministers (several of them converted Jews) who in the East End of London regularly supplied feasts of bread and butter, tea and coffee to destitute glaziers from central Europe, accompanying them with readings from conversionist literature in Hebrew. To their 'surprise' these charitable endeavours had been condemned by the Chief Rabbi, Dr Adler. The London Society for Promoting Christianity among the Jews was quarrelling with its junior partner, the Society for Propagating the Gospel among the Jews, the former going so far as to deny publicly any knowledge of, or connection with, the Lyons Case. The *Jewish Chronicle* called them 'The Great Gull Societies' because, it said, they were always shrieking and dabbling in murky waters. It deplored all conversionists, associated and individual. In its sympathy with Barnett Lyons it went even beyond the Victorian doctrine of the sanctity of the family, appealing to the overriding authority of the parent as justified by the fifth commandment: 'Honour thy Father and thy Mother'.[29] During the winter of 1868–9 its editor tried to organize a defence fund for Lyons. But after a meeting in the Borough Synagogue, Walworth Road, to which hardly anybody came, the attempt broke down. A number of individuals in the provinces — and Hebrew congregations led by Lyons's friends in Cardiff, Swansea, Merthyr Tydfil and Pontypridd — sent in subscriptions. But the total was trivial, and eventually they were returned to the senders, or devoted to the relief of Russian Jews. Lyons was left to pay his legal expenses largely out of his own pocket, assisted by Joel Emanuel, who gave his legal services free. The trouble was that the Board of Deputies of British Jews and the Ecclesiastical Board would do nothing. The Board of Deputies, currently chaired by J.M. Montefiore, nephew of Sir Moses Montefiore, was too busy fighting the cause of oppressed Jews in Romania and Russia to worry over much about a case of doubtful legal validity in Cardiff. It did not respond to the *Chronicle*'s criticisms (which fell short of attacking Sir Moses himself). The wealthy Anglo-Jewish establishment in London was always timid about denouncing anti-Semitic manifestations in Great Britain, and preferred to keep a 'low profile'.[30] In contrast, the Welsh Baptists got up generous subscriptions for the Thomases.

Most liberal and Nonconformist papers, both religious and secular, agreed in principle with the *Jewish Chronicle*. The *Nonconformist* believed Esther's testimony that she had left home because of her mother's cruel treatment, but bitterly blamed Mr Thomas for not informing her father of her whereabouts. 'What is not human cannot be Christian, and all the apparent conversions in the world will not justify a departure from the most exact and open truth.' Even *The Freeman*, the leading Baptist weekly, exhibited embarrassment when the story first broke, taking quite a different stand from that of some of its correspondents. Under the heading 'A Strange Story', its editor commented: 'Suppose the facts are at all as represented, what can be thought of the fanaticism which could regard the claims and affections of a father and mother as nothing when there was a chance of making the girl a proselyte?' But at their annual conference in August 1868 the Welsh Baptists unanimously passed a long resolution regretting the proceedings against their much beloved brother the Revd Nathaniel Thomas, because of his humanely sheltering for one night a young person who left her home because of alleged cruelty, and especially his persecution by certain parts of the press. The conference declared its unwavering confidence in Mr Thomas as 'an upright man, an exemplary Christian, and a devout minister of the Lord Jesus'.[31] As the months passed *The Freeman* swung round. After the trial of July 1869 it published long extracts from the evidence of Esther and the two Thomases, omitting all the rest.[32] It had come to accept the Welsh Baptists' line, that the Thomases had simply rescued a poor girl from cruel parents, ignoring all evidence of conversionist purposes.

The secular papers did not mince their words. The *Cardiff and Merthyr Guardian*, in a leader of 29 August 1868, denounced the melancholy want of sincerity and candour in Croome Villa, and the Thomases' pride, callousness and defiant temper. It greeted Mrs Thomas's demand for £10 towards the cost of bringing Esther to Cardiff for an interview with her father with the words, 'Talk of Shylock, his pound of flesh after this!'[33] To the *Standard*, which reported the case in detail, the question was simply 'Whether the zeal of religious proselytism can or cannot with immunity override all the restraints of social duty, and violate rights anterior and superior to all differences of creed'.³⁴ The editor considered that while Lyons did not appear in a very amiable or dignified light, Mr Thomas had forfeited respect 'by a disregard of truth and a system of evasion and equivocation worthy of a jesuit'. The weekly *Cardiff Times* published on 9 August 1868 a long, detailed and powerful leader. It agreed that there was insufficient evidence to conclude that Esther had been enticed away from her family, and prophesied, correctly, that the verdict would be overturned. It thought that the jury had wanted to demonstrate 'their reprobation for the uncompromising zeal for proselytism which led Mr and Mrs Thomas to disregard the sacredness of the family relation'. Esther may or may not have been cruelly treated, but the Thomases had no business to conceal her from her father for the purpose of conversion inaugurating 'the system of evasion and deceit, suppression of truth and acted if not spoken lies which an attempt to hide a wrong and indefensible action always involves'. At a meeting to support Mr Thomas's defence, several gentlemen who had subscribed liberally condemned the entire proceedings with regard to Esther Lyons, and were only stretching forth a helping hand to an earnest and sincere fellow Christian who had given passive consent to the schemes of his active wife and her uncompromising friend Mrs Hollyer, and was placed in a painful and embarrassing position. As a body, said the leader-writer, the Nonconformists utterly repudiated the Thomases' conduct, and ought not to share the odium it had so rightly incurred.

Several papers wanted to know how the public would have reacted if Mr Thomas had been a Roman Catholic priest and Esther a member of the Church of England, appealing in this way to popular anti-Catholic prejudice. From all sides analogies were made with the Mortara case, now ten years old, in which the infant son of an Italian Jew had been secretly baptized by a priest at the instance of his nurse, and subsequently kidnapped and sent to a monastery. Neither the international outcry nor even an attempt by Sir Moses Montefiore to interview Pope Pius IX had restored him to his parents. But as Schwartz pointed out, the cases were not analogous, since Edgar Mortara was a small child, while Esther had to be considered a responsible and consenting adult.³⁵

Condemnation of the Thomases did not necessitate praise for the Lyonses. Esther, in particular, attracted very little sympathy. The *Jewish Chronicle*, while condoling with Barnett, thought the Jewish community well rid of Esther,³⁶ although one or two of its correspondents raised a demand for better religious education of Jewish girls. The *Standard* thought Esther 'pert and wilful' and did not doubt that 'she got her ears boxed now and then, or that she deserved it'.[37] *The Times* believed that she had left home on well-founded calculations of advantage.[38] The Tory papers had little affection for Jews in general and Jewish pawnbrokers in particular, but all of them baulked at a proselytism which violated the sanctity of the family.

Tory press attitudes illustrated a curious inversion of usual political partisanship in the Lyons case. The Lyonses' counsel in 1869, Hardinge Giffard, already a well-known Tory controversialist, had been a Conservative candidate for Cardiff in the general election of 1868. Nathaniel Thomas had been a member of the selection committee of Colonel Stuart, the victorious Liberal. The Baptists along with other Nonconformists supported the Liberals in the name of religious liberty. They demanded the disestablishment of the Church of England, and when Gladstone disestablished the Anglican Church in Ireland in 1869 this seemed to be coming near. The Tories were not sorry to be able to point out the hollowness of the professions of tolerance among some of their more fanatical religious and political opponents. At the same time the 1860s were, in some ways, the peak period of religious liberalism in many sections of British public opinion (the late nineteenth century with its flood of central European refugees saw a revival of anti-Semitism, though mainly of an economic and social kind). Most Victorians of all denominations thought the kind of proselytism practised by the Thomases and their friends a betrayal of genuine Christianity.

The Lyons case did not, as readers of the *Jewish Chronicle* feared, encourage the conversionists to further efforts of the same kind. The trouble and animosity incurred by the Thomases and their allies seem to have been something of a lesson. But the effects of that case did not end in 1870. Biographies or rather hagiographies of the Revd Nathaniel Thomas and his wife were published by two Baptist ministers at the turn of the century.[39] By their biased, and indeed factually inaccurate accounts of the Lyons case, as well as by their snide comments, it was obvious that ill feeling against the Jews lingered on, at least in south Wales. Was there any connection with the anti-Jewish riots which broke out in Tredegar and the upper Welsh mining valleys in 1911? It is difficult to establish such a link although it might be legitimate to look for it in some of the revivalist preaching in the valleys. One can only make the obvious generalization that fanaticism and intolerance leave an evil legacy behind them.

Notes to Chapter 6

1. Letter from Barnett Lyons in the *Jewish Chronicle*, 7 August 1868, p.5. Most of the information about Esther's relations with her parents comes from the detailed transcript of the Assize Court trial held in Cardiff Town Hall in July and published in the *Cardiff and Merthyr Guardian* on Saturday 31 July and 7 August 1869.
2. Quoted in a long letter from Barnett Lyons to the *Cardiff and Merthyr Guardian* dated 3 August 1868, published on 8 August, 6.
3. Ibid.
4. Ibid.
5. Ibid. This, of course, was Barnett Lyons's account of the events, including Blackburn's remarks.
6. Letter from Nathaniel Thomas, published in the *Cardiff and Merthyr Guardian* on 15 August, 5.
7. Letter from Barnett Lyons to the *Cardiff and Merthyr Guardian*, 22 August 1868, 6.
8. Letter from Miss Lyons to the *Cardiff and Merthyr Guardian*, 22 August 1868, 6.
9. Evidence of Esther Lyons at the Assize Court trial. *Cardiff and Merthyr Guardian*, 31 July 1869, 7.
10. Letter from Barnett Lyons to the *Cardiff and Merthyr Guardian*, published 12 September 1868, 6.
11. Letter from C. Schwartz DD, dated 21 September, published in the *Cardiff and Merthyr Guardian*, 26 September 1868, 6.
12. Letter from Barnett Lyons to the *Cardiff and Merthyr Guardian*, 12 September 1868, 6.
13. Evidence of Dr Schwartz, *Cardiff and Merthyr Guardian*, 31 July 1869, 8.
14. Evidence of Esther Lyons. Ibid. 7.
15. Ibid.
16. Ibid.
17. Letter from Joel Emanuel dated 25 June, published in *JC*, 2 July 1869, 3.
18. 'Baron' is an archaic title for an Exchequer Court judge.
19. Letter of Mrs Keep to Mrs Hollyer read out in court by Giffard in his opening speech. Report of Trial in the *Cardiff and Merthyr Guardian*, 31 July 1869, 6.
20. Report of Trial, ibid., 7 August 1869, 6.
21. *Cardiff Times*, 7 August 1869, 3.
22. *Cardiff and Merthyr Guardian*, 24 December 1869, 5.
23. Ibid., 2 July 1870, 8.
24. Ibid., 10 December 1870, 8; 17 December 1870, 8; 24 December 1870, 8.

25. *JC*, 12 March 1869.
26. Ibid., 13 August 1868, 6.
27. Revd David Davies, *Christ Magnified. The Life of Mrs N. Thomas of Cardiff* (London, 1884), *passim*.
28. Thomas Morgan, *Cofiant y Parch. Nathaniel Thomas, Caerdyff* (Llangollen, 1900). I am greatly indebted to Mr Brian James MA of the Humanities Library, University College, Cardiff, for translating parts of this work into English for me.
29. 'Let Conversion Societies and unattached Conversionists learn that parental authority is vindicated by the majesty of the law and the Decalogue is set on high as a guiding code of conscience in enjoining a tribute of honour from child to parent.' *JC,* 6 August 1868, 5.
30. *JC*, 1869–70, *passim*.
31. *The Freeman*, 28 August 1868, 658.
32. Ibid., 6 August 1869, 627, 633.
33. *Cardiff and Merthyr Guardian*, 29 August 1868, 5.
34. Reported in *Cardiff Times*, 7 August 1869, 3.
35. *The Freeman*, 11 September 1868, 737.
36. *JC*, 14 August 1868, 4.
37. Reported in the *Cardiff Times*, 7 August 1869, 3.
38. Reported in the *Cardiff and Merthyr Guardian*, 7 August 1869, 6.
39. See notes 27 and 28 above.

7

The Tredegar Riots of August 1911

ANTHONY GLASER

I

Since the readmission of the Jews to Britain by Cromwell in 1656, anti-Semitic violence in this country has been a rare occurrence. The Jew Bill riots of 1753 and the Fascist-inspired disturbances of the 1930s are the most notable instances. In both cases, however, there is evidence that popular anti-Semitism was stirred up by disgruntled politicians for their own ends.[1] Moreover, both these events centred on London where the majority of British Jews were concentrated. No doubt, for the same reasons, the anti-Jewish and anti-foreign agitation of the 1880s and 1890s which led to the setting up of the Royal Commission on Alien Immigration and the passing of the Aliens Act of 1905, was mainly concerned with the situation in the capital. In 1911, the year of the riots, when the total Jewish population was about 240,000, approximately 150,000 lived in and around London.[2] Provincial anti-Semitic mob violence was, in fact, unusual although in the eighteenth century Jews were sometimes subjected to sporadic harassment such as that following the Chelsea robbery and murder case of June 1771. Despite pervasive undercurrents of anti-Semitism, between the Jew Bill riots and the Fascist era the Tredegar Riots of 1911 stand out as the sole example of serious anti-Jewish outbreaks.

In the course of the nineteenth century the Jews of south Wales had dispersed throughout the principality. In their small groups and communities, after an initial period as pedlars and petty traders they had, for the most part, settled down as shopkeepers. Numerous adverse references in the local press to court cases involving Jewish pawnbrokers suggest that they were not particularly popular figures in the valley towns.³ But this does not explain why the whole community was the main target of the mob violence which erupted at Tredegar and the surrounding towns in the summer of 1911.

To begin to understand this we must first examine the contemporary climate of general social and economic unrest. In doing so we are not suggesting that the Jews were simply made the scapegoats for the problems which the Tredegar workforce were experiencing during the coal and rail strikes, although this is the essential drift of Dr Alderman's essay on the riots.⁴ The argument must be accorded serious consideration; the problem is to decide how much weight to give it as an explanation for the violence.

II

> July and August 1911 . . . witnessed the onset of the gravest strike movement that till then the century had known.⁵

A succession of events had contributed to creating an atmosphere of social and economic unrest. There had been anti-trade union and anti-working-class judgments handed down by the courts. These included the Taff Vale decision of 1901 and the Osborne Case of 1908, and they helped to create a current of opinion within the Labour movement which seriously questioned the parliamentary system as the principal means of improving the position of working-class people. In the 1910 general election, for instance, Labour lost a quarter of the seats won in 1906. That year (1910) also saw the rejection by the House of Lords of the 'people's budget', in which Lloyd George had attempted to introduce a number of social welfare measures. The cumulative effect of these disappointments encouraged Labour to look towards direct industrial action as a means of gaining their objectives; syndicalism assumed an increasing importance in working-class ideology after 1910. Static or falling real wages and rising prices provided further stimulus to the widespread feeling of discontent.

In July 1910 a rail strike took place at Newcastle which, although lasting only four days, was particularly bitter. In September the Lancashire cotton industry narrowly avoided a general lockout. A few weeks later a lockout of the boiler-makers on the north-east coast did take place and lasted fourteen weeks. It cost the union £100,000 in strike pay — all to no avail; it ended with their defeat. South Wales miners employed by the Cambrian Trust struck in November and remained out until August the following year. At Tonypandy colliers attacked the pithead seriously damaging ventilating machinery, 'And thereupon a riotous mob looted and terrorised the place for three days'.[6] Swansea and Bristol police were brought in by the authorities in an attempt to restore order but they proved ineffective. Thereupon Glamorgan's Chief Constable contacted the Home Office and asked for troops to be sent to the town. Two companies of infantry and two hundred hussars were dispatched from Salisbury Plain but were stopped at Swindon by Winston Churchill, the Home Secretary. They were on their way to south Wales again the following day and patrolling the streets of Tonypandy and the neighbouring valley towns from the early hours of 9 November.

What attracted so much national attention at the time was not the strike itself but the violent outburst of lawlessness during which the town's commercial high street was all but wrecked. It was this lawlessness which, at a time of industrial tension elsewhere in the coalfield, singled out Tonypandy and brought in the troops.[7] There is little doubt that their presence and the manner in which they and the police seemed to be supporting the colliery owners in their efforts to break the strike, augmented the feelings of bitterness among the striking miners and their supporters.

David Smith in an interesting if somewhat partisan article on the Tonypandy disturbances insists that the riots

> should be seen as evidence of social fracture as much as of industrial dispute. The crisis occurred within the framework of conventional labour relations; the crowd's response, in both strike and riot, was strictly that of an already industrialised society; but they also chose targets symbolic of their discontent.[8]

The language is oblique, but by targets the author obviously means the shops, no doubt the symbols of capitalism and respectability. This, he seems to think was the mob's intention; to attack and destroy the bastions of capitalism. The looting was incidental! Churchill, writing to King George V on 10 November 1910 had, according to Smith, clearly misinterpreted the events and was simply retailing the popular, police-inspired explanation of the insensate action of the rioters in wrecking shops in the town of Tonypandy against which they had not the slightest cause for animosity, when they had been foiled in their attack on the colliery.[9]

Whilst not wishing to draw a simple parallel between the acts of lawlessness which occurred at Tonypandy in November 1910 and those at Tredegar in August 1911, we should at least note their proximity in time and place. We should also note that the targets of violence and looting were, in both instances, the local shopkeepers. That the traders under attack at Tredegar were all Jewish, which was not the case at Tonypandy, will clearly require further investigation and explanation.

For the next six months there was a lull in the overt discontent, but then a dispute occurred which appears to have sparked off others. On 10 June the seamen of the British merchant fleet struck for higher wages. They were generally regarded as the most helpless of organized workers; nevertheless, on 24 June the Southampton shipping magnates surprisingly acceded to their demands. The effect on restless workers in other trades was marked. Sporadic strikes followed among labourers in the engineering industry and in the docks, where on 1 August 200,000 port workers struck. Their demands were also conceded. Meanwhile the London Carmen's Union brought its members out amid much violence. This dispute was quickly settled, in time for Asquith's government to countermand an order sending troops into London. At the same time there were dock strikes at Manchester and Liverpool where savage rioting resulted in troops being summoned. They fired into the crowd and two men were killed. A group of Liverpool railway workers struck in support of the dockers and by mid-August the four main rail unions had taken the decision to call out all their members. In spite of Asquith's attempted intervention the strike went ahead and the country found itself in the throes of a general rail strike. Industrial Britain was paralysed.

Soldiers were employed in an attempt to overawe the strikers and prevent civil disorder. The ploy did not work at Llanelli, where rioting broke out and shops and a train were looted. Two men were killed when, as at Liverpool, troops fired on the crowd. Five men also perished as a goods wagon they were attacking exploded. On Saturday 19 August the *Cardiff Times* printed the following editorial:

Riot and Revolution?

As we write, troops are being moved about the country just as if the nation were in the throes of a bloody revolution. The object is anticipatory — the fear of trouble, not to meet active trouble in the majority of cases but as a precautionary measure. Those in charge of the peace are apparently becoming nervous and the very means of precaution are spreading panic among the people ... So far Liverpool has proved the black spot of the country ... where the military have fired on the mob [news of the trouble at Llanelli that day had obviously not yet reached the newspaper.] Here the offenders have not been the strikers but the worst elements in the city just as we saw in the Cardiff streets and docks ... the trouble extends and the whole country is threatened.[10]

The allusion to Cardiff refers to the dock strike then gripping the city, where seamen of all nationalities, except a few Greeks and Chinese, united against the employers. In the House of Commons, Keir Hardie questioned the Home Secretary on the justification for sending troops to Cardiff. Churchill answered: 'Those in authority have requested 500 infantry and we are meeting reasonable requests by local authorities. It does not follow that the troops will be used.'

On Saturday 19 August the rail strike was finally settled. That night a crowd, later estimated at several thousand, roamed through the streets of Tredegar and began attacking Jewish shops.

III

The town of Tredegar, known until just after the end of the Napoleonic Wars as Tredegar Iron Works, was named in honour of Sir Charles Morgan of Tredegar House, Newport, who had leased the land on which both the works and the town were situated. Even a brief survey of its history reveals that it was no stranger to crowd violence. Evan Powell, its native-born historian, described in 1884 the troubles which followed the lean times of 1801,[11] and broke out again in the depression after the end of the Napoleonic Wars.[12]

There were further disturbances in 1882. This time the rioters found a target in the Irish. The *Western Mail* reported the disturbances on 10 July:

Fights between Irish and Welsh — Despatch of Troops from Cardiff.

> Nearly every house in Red Lion Square, which is the stronghold of the Irish wrecked ... In East Lane two houses were nearly fired, beds and furniture thrown into the street.

The following night it was reported that the rioters were

> burning the goods of the Irish residents ... scenes of the most heart-rending nature.

At 8 p.m. Major Herbert, the Chief Constable of Monmouthshire, arrived and took charge of the volunteers and special constables who were guarding the armoury. In the course of the riot the Welsh made a determined attack on the furnaces of the iron works where the Irish had taken refuge:

> Their purpose was to exterminate them, but the rioters were repelled by Captain Parker and his staff of men.[13]

The next day the *Western Mail* printed an editorial which contained the following passage:

> The feelings between the Welsh and Irish populations of the great industrial centres of south Wales have always run high, but such an outbreak has rarely been witnessed ... it is scandalous that at times like these such scenes should be possible, they would be unknown but for the existence of a prejudice born of ignorance.

The disturbances rumbled on. Parnell, leader of the Irish Nationalists, in a question to the Home Secretary in Parliament, referred to the 'persecution of innocent people'.[14] Attempts were made by the press to get at the cause of the lawlessness. It was discovered that an Irish Catholic had recently been converted by the Salvation Army, which had arranged for a meeting in the town for the erstwhile Catholic to narrate the marvellous experience of his conversion. There was a violent reaction from the Irish community which, though numbering several hundred, was heavily outnumbered by the native Welsh and thoroughly beaten in the ensuing fighting.

By 12 July the Welsh ring-leaders had been rounded up and brought before the magistrates. That same day the *Western Mail* reported disturbances against the Irish at Abergavenny and the threat of disturbances in Ferndale. There were references in the newspapers to rumours of an 'exodus of the Irish from Wales' and of 'Irish people fleeing Tredegar and seeking refuge in Merthyr and Cardiff'.

As the news emerged that two Irishmen had been killed, declarations of shame and regret appeared in the local press, hedged about in some reports with excuses for the violent behaviour of the Welsh. 'Morien' (the pen name of a regular contributor to the *Western Mail*) wrote thus:

> Such deeds bring the name of our Wales into discredit. The Welsh blood is terrible once roused but to give expression to its fierceness by deeds of vengeance upon a helpless multitude is disgraceful in the extreme.[15]

Sympathy for the plight of the unfortunate Irish found practical expression in the setting up of a public subscription.[16] Among the subscribers appeared the names of at least three Jews, Louis Barnett, S. Blaiberg and Barnett Jacobs.

Significantly there was also considerable public sympathy for the accused. They had been removed to Usk to await trial and while they were in prison a public collection was made in Tredegar and in a number of the adjacent towns, to provide them with meals. Before the trial took place a letter appeared in the *Western Mail* entitled 'A Defence of the Welsh'. The correspondent demanded to know why the 'Irish perpetrators (of the riots) had not been charged?' He went on to assert that alien Roman Catholicism was the underlying cause of the trouble at Tredegar.[17] The next day a reply was printed challenging this xenophobic view, but the sentiments expressed in the original letter undoubtedly had support in some Nonconformist circles. Similar expressions of local sympathy and support would be heard for those accused of looting and riot in 1911. Evidently there were common factors in the local support for the rioters on both occasions, in religious solidarity, class solidarity and xenophobia. But there were differences too. There was, for instance, no complaint of Jews accepting lower wages than the native Welsh for employment at the iron works, a charge levelled with some justification against the Irish in Wales during the latter half of the nineteenth century. Jews and Welsh rarely competed with each other in the same labour market.

By 1911 the xenophobic feelings of the citizens of Tredegar had found a new target. A.M. Weiner, a Russian immigrant who spent his childhood in Nant-y-glo and later emerged to become a lecturer in Modern History at King's College, London, writing on the 1911 riots, observed that:

> Tredegar had always been hostile to alien elements in its midst. On an earlier occasion (July 1882) the population had expelled their Irish fellow citizens from the town, when they came to seek work in the collieries and iron works. Now it was the turn of the Jews.[18]

Once again attempts would be made by the local press and others to lay the blame for rioting and looting on small groups of drunken strangers. But it is beyond dispute that local townspeople were involved, mostly, as the subsequent trials showed, members of the 'respectable working class'. As David Smith points out,

> the accusation against 'strangers', like that against 'youths', seems common to the aftermath of most riots as a way of pinning guilt to those with no real stake in what is considered the day to day reality of local life.[19]

What special features guided the outburst of 1911 against the Jews? Their role in the economy of the town was, typically, the provision of clothing, furniture and pawnbroking services to the colliers and their families, and they had been successfully fulfilling this role for forty years. From the evidence of Fred Hopkins's narrative of the events of 1911, relationships between the Welsh and Jewish communities had generally been amicable. Instances of harmonious coexistence can be given. In 1904 S. Wolfson, a local trader, was elected vice-president of the Tredegar Chamber of Trade. Louis Harris, a pawnbroker, was appointed as one of the superintendents of examinations for the local school board and subsequently invited to become vice-president of the Tredegar Men's Literary and Library Society, the only non-Jewish institution in Wales to subscribe to the Jewish Encyclopaedia. From 1904 Jewish members of the Workmen's Literary Institute could compete for scholarships to the Intermediate School. The first successful Jewish candidate was Lionel Rosenbaum, son of a shopkeeper who proudly displayed the sign above his shop 'Established 1861'. Hopkins considered it significant that the Workmen's Literary and Library Institute had opened its membership to Jews, and observed that Jewish newspapers were always to be found on the stands of the Institute's reading room, on the wall of which hung a portrait of Israel Zangwill. He recalls being told that the town's senior rugby club had tried, on a number of occasions, to persuade the father of Gershwin Rosenbaum to allow his son to play for the team. The attempts were unsuccessful as club matches were, of course, played on Saturday. Hopkins considered that in the life of a Welsh valley community an invitation to a Jewish boy to play for the town's rugby team constituted a significant degree of acceptance. On the other hand, he shrewdly points out that a group of people from whom the Jews were unlikely to receive a wholehearted welcome were the local gentile shopkeepers who probably regarded the Jewish shops as unnecessary competition.[20] Abraham Weiner, however, suggests that relations were not as amicable, at least on some levels, as Hopkins believes. He says, 'Apart from the necessities of business, they had little contact with the non-Jewish population in whose midst they lived.'[21] But he adds that this did not apply to the younger, British-born generation.

There were, then, some evident causes for the souring relations between the Jews and their neighbours in Tredegar. Business rivalry increased in hard times, while flourishing pawnbrokers served to the labouring classes as serviceable 'symbols of Capitalism', much more accessible than the rich coal-owners and Lord Tredegar in his sumptuous mansion outside Newport. If official correspondence during the riots is to be believed, there was in the town at least one Jewish landlord, of unsavoury reputation, indulging in extortionate raising of rents. Equally serious were some ideological factors. The Labour Party at the time was infested with anti-Semitism, some of it expressed in Blatchford's popular *Clarion* newspaper. The great Nonconformist revival which swept Wales in the early twentieth century had an anti-Semitic edge. Since the Lyons Case of 1867 there had been signs of hostility on the part of the powerful Welsh Baptists towards the Jews.[22] In 1904 some converted Jews had been brought to Llanelli to preach in furtherance of the revivalist campaign, and this coincided with an attack on *shechita* (ritual slaughter).[23] The year before there had been an unpleasant disturbance at Pontypridd involving the age-old and ever-renewed blood libel.[24] The Monmouthshire Welsh Baptist Association, meeting within a week of the 1911 riots, would refuse to pass a resolution expressing sympathy with the Jews who had suffered in the disturbances.

Whatever the signs and portents, it is unlikely that Tredegar's Jews could have anticipated the ferocity of the attacks that overwhelmed them and their businesses on the Saturday night of 19 August 1911.

IV

The main news in the 19 August evening edition of the *South Wales Argus* was the settlement of the national railway strike. The previous day the newspaper had reported that railway stations in the valley towns of Monmouthshire were deserted; Tredegar was specifically mentioned. Nothing moved in or out of the town. The famous Pochin Colliers train, reputed to be the longest in the world, was at a standstill, and Tredegar workmen made no attempt to get to work by other means. Perhaps it was their way of showing sympathy with the railway men.[25] The stop press section of the newspaper contained a short account of the rioting at Llanelli earlier that day. Troops of the Lancashire Fusiliers had fired on the crowd, killing two men. Further deaths had occurred when a railway wagon carrying calcium carbide had come under attack by the mob, had been set on fire and exploded. There was no hint of trouble at Tredegar.

The Tuesday evening edition of the *Argus* again gave front-page prominence to the rioting at Llanelli, disturbances at Tredegar appearing under a much smaller heading. The report stated that rioting in Tredegar had begun with an attack on Jewish-owned shops in Salisbury Street, the shops' contents being looted and the premises destroyed. A man had been seen running away from one of the Jews' shops with a bowler hat full of watches.[26] The reaction of the police was immediate and violent. Fifteen people required treatment for injuries at the Tredegar cottage hospital, nine of whom were resident in the town. Among the injured was a thirteen-year-old boy from Charles Street. The *Argus* reporter asked one of the townspeople why the riot had started and received the reply that it was an attack on 'the rent-grabbing Jews'.[27]

The Jewish press confirmed the reports of the local newspapers. The *Jewish Chronicle* wrote:

> Shortly before Saturday midnight a band of about 200 young fellows began a tour of Tredegar, attacking Jewish shops and singing 'several favourite Welsh Hymn tunes'. The shops were wrecked and the contents looted.[28]

Police reinforcements were summoned and arrived from Ebbw Vale but were not sufficient to control the rioters. Accordingly, on Sunday afternoon the local magistrates met and a decision was taken to ask for military help. Troops of the Worcester Regiment arrived from Cardiff on Monday afternoon just in time to deal with fresh disturbances. Already, however, there were rumours circulating that the rioters planned to march over the mountains and attack Jews in other towns. They were well-founded, for on Monday night and on Tuesday Jewish shops in Ebbw Vale and Rhymney were looted. During Tuesday the lawlessness spread to Victoria, Cwm, Waunllwyd, Abertyswg and Brynmawr. By midweek troops had been deployed to the main areas of disturbance, which were now quiet. However, on Wednesday night, premises were attacked at Bargoed in Glamorgan; soldiers did not arrive there until next day. Throughout Friday and Saturday large numbers of rioters became involved in running fights with troops and police in the town. Meanwhile two Jewish shops were set on fire at Senghennydd. That weekend, quite suddenly, the disturbances ceased.[29]

Understandably, right from the outset, those in authority took an extremely serious view of the events. This much is clear from the letters and telegrams which passed between Tredegar, Abergavenny (the HQ of the Chief Constable) and the Home Office in London. It is equally evident that Winston Churchill, the Home Secretary, was also very much concerned about the developing situation.

Home Office documents reveal that the initial response of the authorities to the events of Saturday night was a telegram from Victor Bosanquet, the Chief Constable, to the Home Secretary, dispatched in the early hours of Sunday morning.

> Serious attack on Jews at Tredegar last night, eighteen shops looted threatened fire premises police hopelessly outnumbered threats similar mischief tonight likely extend neighbouring colliery towns no police available to reinforce suggesting requiring military. Chief Constable.[30]

The Under Secretary at the Home Office responded:

> In reply to your telegram Secretary of State replies that no Metropolitan Police can be spared at present stop. Colonel Freeth if applied to will be able to furnish other military aid and to direct some police assistance from Glamorganshire.[31]

Several hundred troops had been stationed in various parts of south Wales as part of the precautions taken by the government against industrial unrest. Colonel Freeth commanded them from Cardiff.

A separate appeal for help was sent to London on Sunday by the chairman of the Tredegar magistrates, Mr A.S. Tallis, a director of the Tredegar Iron and Coal Company and the town's largest employer. The Home Office reply was sent not to Tallis but to the Chief Constable, with a copy to the Officer Commanding the military at Llanelli.

> Home Secretary has received reports of disturbances that have occurred in Tredegar and other places. He requests that you will keep in close touch with Lieut. Col. Freeth who commands the troops in south Wales and will keep him informed of all that is happening and apply to him if any further military aid is required.[32]

Telegrams continued to pass between south Wales and London. E.H. Davies, Clerk to the local Justices of the Peace, informed the Home Office on Monday morning that further looting had taken place and the police had been stoned. 'The magistrates felt compelled to read the Riot Act, and call out the troops.'

On receiving this news the Home Secretary instructed the Chief Constable and the Chairman of the Magistrates to forward full reports on the disturbances to the Home Office, and it was in these reports that the first official references were made to the alleged antisocial behaviour of some Jewish businessmen. Assuming that the allegations were believed throughout the town they would explain why Jews were the particular targets for hostility during the riots. They would also provide, if needed, a convenient justification for anti-Jewish activity.

In his report requested by the Home Office, Tallis stated that the violence was directed specifically against the Jews, then proceeded to comment:

> There being a number of this nationality in the Town, some of whom during the last few years have been purchasing slum dwellings and, it is freely rumoured, considerably raising the rents for the same. I know of no other reason other than this which would give rise to the feeling against the Jews many of whom are respectable citizens and who have been in business in Tredegar for very many years.[33]

The same day Monmouthshire's Chief Constable also sent in his report to the Home Secretary, expressing similar opinions.

> I have the honour to report that in all the Colliery districts in this County, Jews come to settle down. Though they usually arrive apparently without means, they soon establish themselves in business and acquire house property. As soon as they become landlords they raise rents very high, and, I am told, make their tenants deal at their shops. There is in consequence a very strong feeling against them. This is the case in Tredegar and there is a determination expressed by the inhabitants to get rid of them.[34]

Two months later Bosanquet was requested to furnish a further report. Sufficient time had elapsed for him to reflect on the events of August, perhaps to discuss them with colleagues, but his opinions remained unchanged.

> Ill feeling has long existed against the Jews settled in the colliery districts in this County. Many Jews acquire house property, generally of the worst description. They forthwith raise the rents to an exorbitant extent and are bad landlords.[35]

The charges are explicit and can lead only to the conclusion that the underlying cause of the violence was the intense resentment and discontent generated by unfair rent increases and truck arrangements enforced by a number of Jewish property owners. Once under way the violence then got out of hand and led to a general attack on Jewish interests. This is the explanation advanced by the authorities, and it suggests that the Jews had only themselves to blame for the misfortunes which befell them. But whatever they thought, the authorities could not permit lawlessness, destruction and looting to run unchecked in the streets. The law had to be upheld and order imposed.

Although Tallis was not, the Chief Constable was well aware that the causes of the unrest were several and complex. He wrote:

> The present state of general unrest is too favourable an opportunity to be missed for attacking the Jews. The advance in prices owing to the Railway Strike has also caused ill feeling.[36]

The question then arises; were these charges of rack renting and bad landlordism true and justified?

A clue may be found in the report of Arthur L. Dixon, a Home Office official, of a conversation between himself and Joseph Cohen of Tredegar at the Home Office on 23 August, which also gives a vivid account of the riots.

> One of the Jewish refugees from Tredegar, Mr Joseph Cohen (103 High Street, Tredegar) called here today and gave me an account (which impressed me very much) of the terrible nature of the riots which have occurred. Mr Cohen himself is a mineral water manufacturer employing several hands. He has a brother, also living in Tredegar, Mr Michael Cohen of 15 Commercial Road, who keeps (or, rather, kept) a drapery shop. Mr Cohen told me that the Jews of Tredegar had had some inkling that trouble was coming from the roughs; he himself had mentioned their fears to the Police who made light of them. On Saturday the attack on the shops of the Jews commenced in a small way by one or two boys throwing stones at windows. The bystanders began laughing and jeering, and gradually as the crowd collected the spirit of disorder grew until what at first seemed a small matter developed into a serious riot and attack on the shops and houses of Jewish residents. Mr Michael Cohen's shop was looted so thoroughly that he could not find a change of garments for his children when he had to flee. Mr Joseph Cohen's English neighbours banded together and protected his house on Saturday, but on Sunday the crowd became so menacing that he fled to the house of a friendly neighbour, taking his wife (who had recently been confined) and child and invalid mother with him. His sisters found refuge in another house and were so terrified that they spent Sunday in the cellar. Yesterday Mr Cohen brought his family to London but was so much in fear that he had not ventured to go to his house to change from his working clothes before he came. His house, he understands, has been ransacked from top to bottom, he does not know what has come to his factory but he presumes that has suffered too. The loss which Mr Cohen has suffered, including the damage to his house and property and to his factory, which he had recently rebuilt and installed with fresh machinery, and also the interruption of his business, will, he says, have quite ruined him, and there are many other Jews — for instance, those who have larger families — who are in worse plight even than he. All the Jews, he says, have fled from the neighbourhood and a good many English residents are fleeing too . . .

The importance of this account is enhanced by the comments which Dixon added in his own hand:

The above was Mr Cohen's story.

> The Supt. of Police, to whom I have since spoken, adds that this Mr Cohen is the man who, in his opinion, is, more than any other Jew, the cause of the anti Jewish feeling. He has been buying up old house property and raising the rent etc. He does not appear to have exaggerated the violence of the rioters: the Police offered to afford him protection, with military aid, to go to his house and bring away any valuables, but he did not accept the offer. His house has not, however, been ransacked. It is very likely that he will put in a substantial claim against the Police Authority. The Board of Jewish Deputies are arranging, through the Jewish Guardians for Mr Cohen's pauper accommodation for the time being.[37]

The *South Wales Argus* paid particular interest to Mr Cohen, hinting that his business activities were at the root of the anti-Jewish feeling.[38] In January 1911 his application to convert a house in Red Lion Square into two flats had been refused by the Tredegar Town Council.[39] Abraham Weiner discusses the accusations levelled against Joseph Cohen and dismisses them.[40] However, the Chief Constable had no doubts about Cohen's culpability although he was more charitable in his opinion of the other members of the community.

> The Jew in Tredegar who was the chief cause of the ill-feeling was not a shopkeeper, and so could not be injured through his property, but the mob once started, attacked all the Jewish shops without discriminating between those against whom a grievance existed and those who had been useful members of society, and were entitled to the gratitude of the community for many acts of generosity.[41]

The Chief Constable was wrong in suggesting that Joseph Cohen could not be injured through his property since he did have a shop and his factory could have been laid waste. However, what emerges from his comments is that one Jew or possibly one family of Jews in Tredegar had been behaving in an injudicious and probably disgraceful manner, and had pulled down vengeance on the heads of all the rest. Of course there is no proof of Cohen's malpractices which were not strictly illegal. However, credibility as to his lack of scruple is reinforced by the fact that three years later he was tried and jailed for four months for selling mineral water from his factory in the bottles of the much better-known firm of Thomas and Evans of Porth.[42]

Bosanquet's report of 25 October also expressed certainty that the disturbances were not as spontaneous as some of the newspapers had suggested.

> The young hooligans of Tredegar planned the attack on the Jews and chose the time of the railway strike as a suitable opportunity. Saturday (pay) night, with the streets crowded, was all in their favour. The older people were no doubt cognisant of the scheme and supported it . . . many people previously considered respectable took part in stealing all they could lay hands on.[43]

Fred Hopkins's uncle, a butcher's salesman, was an eyewitness of the riots, and his recollections support the Chief Constable's view that violence against the Jews was premeditated. This is Fred Hopkins's account of his uncle's conversation:

> We had suspected something to happen, as all the week there had been talk of this meeting which this bunch of chaps who were trying to get this petition up to get the Jews moved out of the town . . . The conversation on the Monday was about the coming railway strike, as this was expected to take place on the Wednesday . . . By the Thursday night all the conversation was about the Jews buying-up all the Groceries in the shops. I can remember one of the blokes saying that he had heard that some of the Cohens had had big boxes of stuff delivered to their places . . . This started another argument regarding the Jews buying up the houses in Red Lion Square and in other streets then dividing them into two houses and charging higher rents.[44]

Thus did gossip inflate rumour, and vice versa.

Press reflection and comment on the riots varied. The Jewish press reacted initially with unequivocal condemnation. In its edition of 21–26 August the *Jewish World* ran a headline — 'An All British Pogrom in south Wales' under which was printed:

> Our memory goes back in vain in search of a parallel for such anti-Jewish excesses in modern England. We can only compare the terrible events in the attacks made on our people in the time of the Crusades or more appropriately to the pogroms with which the pages of Russian latter day history have been besmirched.

A week later the paper had radically changed its view on the nature of the riots and informed its readers that:

> Rioting and looting would have taken place, Jews or no Jews. There happened to be unoffending Jews as well as unscrupulous hooligans, and the fact that Jews have been the victims must not . . . lead us into the error of unduly magnifying the Jewish aspect of what has occurred.[45]

The inclination to deny an explicit anti-Semitic content to the riots was perhaps fuelled by the fears of anglicized Jews that the mass immigration from central Europe could undermine their position as ordinary British citizens. They did not want to acknowledge the existence of anti-Semitism in British society. Thus the *Jewish World* quoted the *Daily News* which reported an unidentified Jewish MP as saying:

> It is not a religious movement . . . We do not associate this outbreak with any hostile spirit against Jews as Jews.[46]

Another Jewish MP, Stuart Samuel, concluded that his co-religionists in Monmouthshire had become 'the outlet of the lust of criminals and the vulgar'. This view was encouraged by attempts to write off the rioters as 'young hooligans' and 'roughs', terms employed by the *South Wales Argus* among others, and repeated in some of the national newspapers.[47]

Many of the Welsh papers were also eager to promote the view that the outrages were not primarily directed against the Jews. Both the *Western Mail* and the *Cardiff Times* carried vivid accounts of the troubles while refuting all accusations that the people of the valleys were anti-Semitic. They were helped by the contributions of two Jewish correspondents, one of whom, I. Davidson, wrote as follows to the *Western Mail*:

> . . . Members of the Hebrew faith do not believe for a moment that anti-semitic feelings account for the looting and plundering of which so many co-religionists have been victims . . . Wales, sir, need not feel ashamed of 'cowardly attacks on the Jews'. She cannot be held responsible . . . No Sir, Dame Wales is to be congratulated upon the fact that her sympathy is at the present moment with the Jews and that she has lost no time in giving expression, both in pulpit and the press to the abhorrence of the evils committed by an irresponsible body on a law-abiding and peace-loving section of the community.[48]

A much longer and apparently more carefully reasoned letter to the *South Wales Argus* from Bertram Jacobs, a barrister and member of the Jewish Board of Deputies, extended this line of argument. It was evidently contributed with the intention of dispelling any comparison between the Tredegar riots and the Russian pogroms, and of calming emotions and reducing the temperature of debate. He disclaims to be acting as an official spokesman for the Board of Deputies. The letter sets forth the position of those who saw no advantage for Welshman or Jew in publicly exposing the shortcomings of either community. On the contrary, he has fulsome praise for both, blames unruly and unrepresentative elements for the disorder and takes to task those metropolitan Jews who lived too far from the area of conflict to have an informed understanding of the situation.

> It is important that there should be a balanced consideration of the causes of the riots in south Wales and Monmouthshire . . . The widespread belief among the Jewish communities is that the riots were anti semetic (*sic*) in their origin or else violently tinged with the colour . . . A charge of anti semitism is, however, a serious charge to bring, both for those who prosecute it and against those whom it is alleged. Injustice by strange paradox will breed injustice and nothing could be imagined more likely to embitter the relations between the Jewish inhabitants of south Wales and Monmouthshire and their Christian neighbours than an allegation against the latter of anti semitism which does not exist. The hypothesis is that the outbreaks . . . were bottomed in anti semitism and had come on essence with the pogroms against the Jews in South Russia . . . On the appearance of things the hypothesis was provisionally justified and perhaps inevitable, but I hope that a fuller consideration of the facts . . . will enable all those who have adopted the anti semetic explanation to discard it. With the facts and circumstances I think I may claim to some intimacy . . . I would mention that I was born and brought up in the affected area . . . I was in the near neighbourhood of the actual riots during the whole of the contingency. Some of the sufferers are my intimate friends. The conclusion I would press upon those interested is that the events were in no real sense religious, anti semetic or anti jewish (*sic*). In support I solicit consideration of the following points:- (1) The attacks were not confined to Jewish shops in any one place . . . (2) No Jew was attacked in person, although some think they would have been if there had been the opportunity. In fact there were ample opportunities . . . (3) No private house of any Jew attacked. (4) No attempt was made on any synagogue . . . (5) In several cases the attacks did not eminate (*sic*) in the town itself but were carried out by a gang of young men who drove

up in brakes. (6) All classes of the non-Jewish populace showed the utmost sympathy with the Jews. In several cases townsfolk risked their own persons to save Jewish shops. (7) The risings at Tredegar and the neighbourhood must be considered in connection with those at Cardiff and elsewhere. At Cardiff the attack was on the Chinese. At Lannelly a few weeks back, it was upon the Railway Goods Store. A day or so ago it was directed to the firing of a farm. At Tonypandy it was not suggested that any distinction was observed between Jewish or non-Jewish shops. It may be mentioned that this is not the first occasion on which destructive rioting has taken place at Tredegar.

Many will remember those of thirty years back where the principal sufferers were the Irish inhabitants, (8) The attacks were not accompanied by any cry's of 'Down with the Jews' . . . at the utmost the suggestion was 'Let's have a go at the Jews' shops', a wholly different thing in its significance. The destruction was not wanton but was directed to the obtaining of loot . . . The Jews . . . are reputed to be wealthier than their neighbours and therefore, likely to have more loot and lootable goods . . .

While I desire, that south Wales and Monmouthshire shall be acquitted of the charges of intolerance or anti-semitism, I would also repudiate the suggestion that those Jews in these districts have given cause for feelings against them on the part of their non-Jewish neighbours. There is nobody less fairly open to it. The Jews of south Wales and Monmouthshire contain the smallest appreciable proportion of black sheep. They identify themselves thoroughly with the non-Jewish inhabitants . . . The Welsh are the most tolerant and kind hearted of peoples. In no part of the world have the Jews met with better treatment than in Wales.[49]

Mr Jacobs's letter is a plea, doubtless written with the best intentions, rather than a critical analysis of events. Several points could be challenged, including those in the final paragraph, which is more an entreaty for a state of affairs that should exist than a description of one that did. Possibly the writer was attempting to counter the impression created by Lord Rothschild who, when asked in the midst of the riots by Dr Hyamson to approach his contacts in the government on behalf of the threatened Tredegar community, exclaimed, 'They are a bad lot and probably deserve what they are getting.'[50]

An examination of the minutes of the Monmouthshire County Council also raises some doubts regarding Jacobs's claim that 'the Welsh are the most tolerant and kind hearted of peoples'. There is no word of sympathy in the minutes for those attacked, nor of condemnation of the rioters. In fact the only direct reference to the riots appears in the entry of 30 August, when Councillor Jim Winstone, a Miners' Federation sponsored representative, complained that the police had been unnecessarily brutal in the use of their batons and had struck members of the public who were merely onlookers. However, there was mention in the minutes of the anticipated level of compensation claims and a sum of £12,000 was set aside to cover them. Mr Hunt of Newland, Davies and Hunt, auctioneers of Newport, was appointed as assessor to receive, examine and negotiate the claims.[51]

At a further meeting of the council held in early September, Mr Hunt reported that the total settlement was likely to be in the order of £16,000.[52] Compensation was discussed at every subsequent meeting, until on 8 November a figure of £15,547 was presented. The council, however, decided that the original figure of £12,000 should be the final offer to the claimants. After discussion this was revised to £12,500 and an increase in the county rate of 2*d*. proposed to cover it.

In the event the claims for compensation at Tredegar approved and presented by Mr Hunt totalled (to the nearest £1) £7,156, of which £5,596 was actually paid. A large proportion of the claims were for comparatively small sums for replacing broken windows, which were paid in full. The list shows clearly that while shop windows in Commercial Street, Church Street and Bridge Street — the town's shopping centre — were smashed indiscriminately the Jewish shops had been looted. Also, the looters were not after groceries, but were stealing valuables from jewellers, furnishers and drapers. The larger claims, for loss of stock, were generally reduced by a quarter to one-third. The highest of these was from Joseph Cohen, for approximately £1,087, of which he received £837.

Similar phenomena appear at Ebbw Vale where, surprisingly, the total claim was higher than that for Tredegar — £7,447, of which £5,988 was paid in compensation. The difference was largely accounted for by two very big claims, from Lyons & Co, outfitters and pawnbrokers, for £1,699 and Simon Sidle, jeweller, for £1,120, which were settled by payments of £1,618 and £1,015 respectively.[53]

These scales of compensation appear, on the whole, to have given satisfaction. Fred Hopkins tells us that the money paid to the shopkeepers of Tredegar — and of the other towns — 'transformed these establishments from small shops into modern business premises'. A good deal of malicious comment circulated to the effect that some shopowners had done very well out of the riots — perhaps the sort of remark to be expected from people who were jealous of the local traders. But the point, if exaggerated, was supported by one of Fred Hopkins's Jewish correspondents, who as a young girl was present with her family at the riots: 'The people who lost all their belongings were amply compensated and one of them said on receiving his compensation, "They were not rioters, they were angels!"'[54] Perhaps Jewish shopkeepers, originally from eastern Europe, were not accustomed to being compensated for pogroms by the authorities.

This young girl also drew attention to the kindness of her non-Jewish neighbours.

> On the Sunday night the police expected more trouble. Our very kind neighbours insisted on us going to their house and would not allow us to go home until the early hours of the morning ... it is impossible to describe the kindness and sympathy of our gentile friends.[55]

Her comments are supported by the recollections of an old lady, Mrs Marie Davies, who wrote about her childhood memories of the riot at Tredegar in *Gwent Local History*.[56] She was taken to sympathize with the Jewish families; with Mr Bernstein who had had his windows broken, with the Samuels, 'A lovely family' of which one daughter was a teacher and another a talented pianist, with the Harrises, the Brodies and the Fines. She had a remarkable story about a Cohen baby, newly born, which was cared for by the Penberthy family until its own family, who had fled in a hired horse and trap, returned.

Such sympathy was, as we have seen, less conspicuous at the official level. The exception was the Rhymney District Council where a resolution was unanimously passed condemning all citizens who had been involved and expressing sympathy with the victims.[57] The council members were predominantly colliery owners, professional people and independent shopkeepers. From this group were also selected the magistrates. In Tredegar, Jews constituted about one-quarter of the shopkeepers, yet there were no Jewish councillors nor magistrates. In Rhymney, Israel Fine had been a town councillor for several years, and was, at the time of the riots, a Justice of the Peace. But the compensation lists also show that in Rhymney the rioters had attacked and looted non-Jewish shops as well as those owned by Jews.

Despite the immediate sympathy of good gentile neighbours, as time went on popular feeling swung over to the side of those who had been charged and sentenced for taking part in the disturbances. The majority of those found guilty received prison terms. On 15 September, for instance, of fifteen rioters charged thirteen were imprisoned for periods ranging from twenty-eight days to six months.[58] Mrs Marie Davies records that the magistrates became very harsh in the punishment of suspected rioters. 'Also the police were raiding the houses of innocent people and there was danger of trouble as a result.'[59] Her father, Ebenezer Thomas, with the support of two friends including a Methodist minister, called a meeting on the recreation ground at which 3,000 people attended (Fred Hopkins gives the number as 7,000) to protest against the severe sentences. They complained that scant consideration was being given to the youth and respectable home backgrounds of the accused, and that the sentences were exacerbating local tensions. A petition requesting their reduction was organized and sent to the Home Secretary, followed two days later by a similar letter to the Home Office from the Tredegar Workmen's Emergency Committee. But Churchill refused to intervene in the matter.

V

Industrial unrest did not end in 1911. The strike impulse which had contributed so much to violence continued throughout the following years, and up to the outbreak of war in 1914. It is well documented in George Dangerfield's *The Strange Death of Liberal England* (Paladin, 1970). At home the suffragettes were contributing their vociferous agitation, while abroad the Agadir crisis had erupted.

But what, in a small part of south Wales alone, nudged this tendency in the direction of an anti-Jewish outbreak which appears to have taken most of the population by surprise, not least those good and kindly neighbours who were far from hostile towards the local Jews? Dr Alderman considered that the Jews were made scapegoats for the economic and social ills of south Wales at the time of the coal and railway strikes; but surely it was not as simple as that.

The answer may lie, at least partly, in certain special features of the locality. The element of religious anti-Semitism has already been mentioned. On 6 September the Baptist Association met at

Blackwood. A resolution expressing sympathy with the Jews was proposed. Several ministers took exception, one delegate arguing that resolutions did more harm than good, and encouraged the Jews. He pointed out that there were about one hundred Jews in Tredegar now, and if they had many more resolutions they would have five hundred there. The resolution was dropped.[60]

The element of economic anti-Semitism was generally more prominent. Dr Alderman points out that stories of Jewish financial skulduggery and rack renting, though lacking real substance, were widely believed in the riot areas.[61] The evidence does not completely bear out the contention that they lacked real substance. Lord Rothschild's dismissive remark is at least as telling as the long arguments of I. Davidson and Bertram Jacobs — although only Lord Rothschild would have dared to make it.[62] The Chief Constable's reports (which were not anti-Semitic in tone) and the statements of witnesses that one or two families were bad landlords and greedy shopkeepers have to be taken seriously. A rate book for Tredegar for the year 1914 survives in the Gwent County Record Office in Cwmbrân (the earlier books are lost).[63] This reveals that the majority of Jews in the town were owner-occupiers of their own house and shop, quite often possessing one or two extra houses which were let off to a tenant, frequently another Jew. Of those who, it appears, made a business of letting property, by far the biggest (by 1914) was Michael Cohen, who owned four named, and evidently substantial houses in Beaufort Street. David Cohen owned two houses each divided into two, in Church Street; Aaron Cohen and L.L. Fine each owned a row of five low-rated houses, probably slum property, Fine's cottages being divided, apparently back to back. (He had two others.) By far the largest owners were, cumulatively, the various Cohen families (there were at least four) who possessed some twenty-four properties between them. All this was extremely small beer. There was no comparison with the main landlords of the town, who owned whole streets of houses. And if the Jewish landlords in one or two cases had divided cottages into two small flats, they were not the only ones to do so. It appears, then, that if one or two Jewish families may have merited a bad reputation as landlords, an anti-Semitic element emerged in extending this to smear the whole community. This form of 'rich Jew' anti-Semitism is typical of its kind. There is sometimes an element of truth in stereotypes, but their consequence is to turn the anger generated by the shortcomings of one into an unreasoning attack on all.

The full reasons for the Tredegar Riots have yet to emerge. They remain something of an enigma wrapped in a mystery. Anti-Semitism, mostly of a mild kind, undoubtedly existed in the industrial valleys of south Wales in the early years of the twentieth century. It was active at a time when the many diverse people who had immigrated into the industrial areas had had time to blend into small cohesive groups of a specialized character, forged by the hardships and comradeships of labour in heavy industry. They were faced with a continuing infiltration of refugees from central Europe. Inevitably in times of stress and violence, hostility grew. Considering the conditions prevailing in the mining valleys the existence of a hooligan element is not surprising. It is remarkable that the anti-Jewish riots of Tredegar and the Monmouth valleys were not repeated elsewhere in south Wales, nor in the United Kingdom.

Notes to Chapter 7

1. G. Alderman, 'The Anti-Jewish Riots of August 1911 in South Wales', *Welsh History Review*, 6 (1972), 190.
2. Jewish Year Book 1911, 267, 273 4. Quoted Alderman, op.cit., 190.
3. G. Alderman, 'The Jew as Scapegoat? The Settlement and Reception of Jews in South Wales before 1914', *Transactions of the Jewish Historical Society of England*, XXVI (1974), 62–70 *passim*. For the Chelsea case and its consequences see Todd M. Endelman, *The Jews of Georgian England 1740–1830* (The Jewish Publication Society of America, Philadelphia, 1977) 198-201.
4. Alderman, op.cit.
5. R.C.K. Ensor, *England 1870–1914* (Oxford History of England, Oxford, Clarendon Press, 1987 edition) 437–44.
6. Ibid., 439.
7. Martin Barclay, 'The Slaves of the Lamp — the Aberdare Miners' Strike 1910', *Llafur*, 2 No.3 (1978), 24.
8. David Smith, 'Tonypandy 1910: Definitions of Community', *Past and Present*, 87 (May 1960), 162.
9. Ibid., 162. Smith was quoting from Randolph Churchill, *Winston Churchill, Young Statesman 1901–1914*, II, 375.
10. *Cardiff Times*, 19 August 1911, 6 col.2.
11. Evan Powell, *History of Tredegar* (revd edn. 1902, Newport, South Wales Argus Ltd.), 27.
12. Ibid., 37.
13. *Western Mail*, 11 July 1882.

14. Ibid., 11 July 1882.
15. Ibid., 12 July 1882.
16. Ibid. 17 July 1882.
17. Ibid., 17 July 1882.
18. A.M. Weiner, 'The Tredegar Riots', CAJEX, 26 No.1 (April 1976), 19.
19. David Smith, op.cit., 167-8.
20. Fred Hopkins, 'The Riots at Tredegar in 1911' (unpublished narrative or article) 23. Hopkins is a most useful source of eye-witness accounts. He had an impressive memory for names and places, and he was able to obtain from the Home Office copies of official documents which are extremely informative source materials.
21. A.M. Weiner, op.cit., 18.
22. Cf. p.147.
23. *South Wales Daily News*, 24 November 1904, 6.
24. *South Wales Argus*, 18 August 1911, quoted by Fred Hopkins, op.cit., 11.
25. Fred Hopkins, op.cit., 12.
26. Fred Hopkins quoting the *South Wales Argus*, op.cit., 34.
27. *South Wales Argus*, 21 August 1911; from G. Alderman, 'The Anti-Jewish Riots', *Welsh History Review*, 6 (1972) 195. Fred Hopkins, op.cit., 34.
28. G. Alderman, 'The Anti-Jewish Riots', *Welsh History Review*, 6 (1972), 192, quoting the *Jewish Chronicle*, 25 August 1911.
29. A.M. Weiner, op.cit. 19–22, and local newspapers.
30. PRO H.O. 144 1160/212987/1, quoted by Fred Hopkins, op.cit., 43.
31. Ibid., 43.
32. Ibid., 44.
33. PRO H.O. 144 1160/212987/2. Tallis to Churchill, 21 August 1911, quoted in Colin Holmes, 'The Tredegar Riots of 1911: Anti-Jewish Disturbances in South Wales', *Welsh History Review*, 11 (December 1982), 218.
34. PRO H.O. 144 1160/212987/3. Bosanquet to Churchill, quoted in Holmes, op.cit., 219.
35. PRO H.O. 144 1160/212987/3. Bosanquet to Churchill, quoted in Holmes, op.cit., 219.
36. PRO H.O. 144 1160/212987/3. Bosanquet to Churchill, quoted in Holmes, op.cit., 220.
37. PRO H.O. 144 1160/29987/3 and 3a. Holmes, op.cit., 220-21.
38. *South Wales Argus*, 21 August 1911, quoted by G. Alderman, 'The Anti-Jewish Riots of August 1911', op.cit., 195.
39. Tredegar Council Minutes, January 1911, referred to by Fred Hopkins, op.cit., 63.
40. A.M. Weiner, op.cit., 22.
41. PRO H.O. 144/1161/212987/13 quoted by Fred Hopkins.
42. Cf. p.77.
43. PRO H.O. 144/1161/212987/13 quoted by Fred Hopkins.
44. Fred Hopkins, op.cit., 27.

45. *Jewish World*, 1 September 1911, quoted in Alderman, 'The Anti-Jewish Riots of August 1911 in South Wales', *Welsh History Review* (1972), 194.
46. *Daily News*, 28 August 1911, quoted in Alderman, op.cit., 193.
47. Alderman, op.cit., 193–4.
48. *Western Mail*, 29 August 1911, quoted by Fred Hopkins, op.cit., 57–8.
49. *South Wales Argus*, 2 September 1911, quoted by Fred Hopkins, op.cit., 59–60.
50. A.M. Weiner, op.cit., 24.
51. Monmouthshire County Council Minutes, 30 August 1911, Gwent County Record Office, Cwmbran.
52. Ibid., 9 September 1911.
53. Report and Valuation of Riot Claims at Tredegar, Ebbw Vale, New Tredegar, Cwm and Rhymney, October 1911. Cc. 9 Gwent County Record office.
54. Mrs Jessie Hamilton to Fred Hopkins and Fred Hopkins, op.cit.
55. Ibid.
56. Marie Davies, 'Childhood Memories', *Gwent Local History*, 63 (Autumn 1987), 32–3.
57. Rhymney District Council Minutes, 4 September 1911, quoted by Fred Hopkins, op.cit., 56.
58. Extracts from Petty Sessions Records, Tredegar Police Court, 4 Sept.–5 Oct. 1911, Gwent County Record Office.
59. Marie Davies, op.cit., 32.
60. *Jewish Chronicle*, 8 September 1911, *The Times*, 7 September 1911, quoted in Alderman, 'The Anti-Jewish Riots of August 1911, op.cit., 192.
61. G. Alderman, 'The Jew as Scapegoat? . . .', *Transactions of the Jewish Historical Society of England*, XXXVI (1974–8), 66.
62. An eye-witness who was seven years old at the time of the riots, distantly related to the family concerned and who now lives near Cardiff, agrees with Lord Rothschild's opinion.
63. A 350 R.B.1 Gwent County Record Office.

8

Jewish Refugees and Jewish Refugee Industries

ANTHONY GLASER

I

The appearance of Jewish refugees in Britain after 1933, the year Hitler came to power, was a consequence of events in central Europe. The numbers of refugees and what happened to them were also deeply affected by the political and economic conditions which prevailed in this country. However, before dealing with these matters in detail it will be instructive to compare the refugee immigration of the 1930s with the wave of immigration which took place between 1880 and 1914. Both their similarities and differences are important.

The method of counting immigrants at the turn of the century and before was haphazard and the resulting statistics are consequently unreliable. The government's main source of information was an Act of 1836 which required the master of every ship entering a British port to submit to the Board of Trade a list of all aliens carried, with details of their trades and occupations. These data eventually appeared as the monthly and annual aliens lists. Attempts were made to distinguish between passengers *en route* to destinations other than Britain and those who planned to settle in this country. Unfortunately the criterion for being *en route* elsewhere was the possession of a transatlantic ticket which thousands of persons did not purchase until they reached the UK. Thus the figures of immigrants were inaccurate and exaggerated. One result of this was that the monthly and yearly returns proved a fertile ground for those sections of British society who were opposed to the admission of aliens and who wished to exaggerate the volume of immigration. The Board of Trade returns for 1904, for example, recorded that 95,724 aliens were described on the lists as 'not en route'. This was seized on by the *Daily Mail*, a newspaper noted for its anti-immigrant sentiments, and the following alarmist headline soon appeared: '95,000 More Aliens Admitted'. A similar headline appeared in the *Daily Express*.[1]

Despite the difficulty of obtaining reliable immigration statistics Lloyd Gartner has calculated that between the years 1880 and 1914 some 120,000 Jews entered Britain although this figure may be an underestimate of their number.[2] While government statistics made no attempt to classify immigrants by religion, Jewish and non-Jewish sources were in general agreement that in the period before the Aliens Act of 1905 the overwhelming majority of immigrants described in official documents as aliens were Jews. The number of German and Austrian Jews entering Britain between 1933 and 1939 has been estimated at 55,000, and the total from all European countries at around 80,000, over half of the earlier influx if we accept Gartner's estimate, and just about half if we accept V.D. Lipman's upper figure which he gives in his book *A Social History of the Jews in England, 1850–1950*.[3] Of these, according to Marion Berghahn, some 30,000 were transmigrants on their way elsewhere, who were caught in England by the outbreak of war.[4] By the 1950s some had resumed migration. About 50,000 remained in Britain.[5]

Most of the earlier immigrants were poor and in some cases destitute. However, unlike their gentile neighbours, many of whom also took part in the great westward movement, they were not peasants nor farm labourers but people with some experience of urban life gained either from an eastern European city ghetto or, more commonly, a *stetl* (the typical small town in the Russian Pale of Settlement). They had not assimilated, but had preserved their own language (Yiddish), their own customs and trades. They were also, for the most part, traditional orthodox Jews. As immigrants they concentrated in the East End of London, in Manchester, Leeds, Birmingham, Glasgow and other urban areas, although a number settled in the industrialized towns and villages of Durham and south Wales.

By the end of the nineteenth century alarm, hostility and anti-Semitism directed at the flood of central European immigrants were growing in sections of the British public. In 1882 a Select Committee of the House of Commons, investigating the problems of sweated labour and overcrowding, reported that there was no need for restrictive legislation on immigrants.[6] However, in 1902 the government set up a Royal Commission on Alien Immigration. From its report in 1903 it appeared that the Jewish immigrants were accused of being impoverished, destitute, dirty and of insanitary habits and liable to spread infectious diseases. They became a burden on the rates. They congregated in limited localities, causing the native inhabitants to be dispossessed by overcrowding, by driving up rents and driving down wages. They refused to intermarry and assimilate and formed solid and distinct colonies. Their influence, in large numbers, interfered with observance of the Christian sabbath. Most of these charges were confuted or weakened by the actual evidence in the report, and the Commission contented itself with recommending the establishment of an Immigration Department with officers at the ports to intercept undesirable immigrants, criminals, prostitutes, idiots and lunatics, persons of notorious bad character and those likely to become a charge on the rates.[7]

The upshot of the Royal Commission was the Aliens Act of 1905. This provided for immigration officers at each port empowered to exclude 'undesirable aliens', defined as persons without the means of support for themselves and their families, lunatics, idiots, sick persons likely to become a charge on rates or detrimental to the public; or convicted criminals from a country with which Britain had an extradition treaty. There were also provisions for expelling alien felons, prostitutes, tramps, and those living in insanitary conditions due to overcrowding. But a clause specifically exempted political and religious refugees in danger of persecution.

The Act, which caused much apprehension in the Jewish community, was less draconian than it seemed. The Liberal governments which took office after 1906 administered it without rigour, and it did not prevent another 45,000 or so immigrants gaining entry before the outbreak of war in August 1914.[8] Yet it was the first serious government interference with Jewish immigration into Britain.

In the face of these reactions from sections of the British public and government the long-established and anglicized Jews were alarmed, fearing that the huge influx of refugees, who seemed to some of them as alien as they did to their gentile compatriots, would undermine their hard-won position of respect and acceptance. The Jewish Board of Guardians adopted a tough policy of refusing assistance during the first six months after immigration, and persuading newcomers to settle in non-Jewish areas. With the help of the Poor Jews' Temporary Shelter at London Docks, they assisted immigrants to emigrate elsewhere, or to return home.⁹ A big Jewish 'settlement' in the East End provided clubs, English games and education for the children of immigrants, instilling British middle-class morality and attitudes into the young immigrants, and helping many of them to find their feet in the new society.¹⁰ Despite the enormous subscriptions collected for the victims of the Russian pogroms, the reactions of the Anglo-Jewish establishment appeared ambiguous.

The rise of Hitler was probably an even greater shock to the anglicized middle-class Jews than the East European pogroms. It was nearer home; Germany since the war had seemed to become a democratic, tolerant state. The German Jews and those from Austria and Czechoslovakia who made up the bulk of the new immigration, although not particularly popular — they were felt to be too didactic and humourless, in fact too German — resembled in many ways the more prosperous British ones. An appreciable proportion of them had held professional posts or had been manufacturers or businessmen on their own account. They tended to be secular in outlook or, if religious, attracted to some branch of Reform Judaism rather than orthodoxy. Their background was generally well-to-do, and before the Hitler era they had been, by European standards, a privileged group.

This time British Jewry took swift action, quickly establishing a committee to help the refugees. Many British Jews opened their homes to refugee guests, or advanced money for sponsoring immigrants. But the Committee gave an undertaking to the government that:

> All expenses, whether in respect of temporary or permanent accommodation or maintenance will be borne by the Jewish community without charge to the state.¹¹

The British government was to hold the community to this undertaking even when after 1938 it became clear that the refugee problem was assuming proportions unforeseen when it was given, and the rest of the world was closing its gates to the Jews trapped on the continent. The government, with the precedent of 1905 behind it, was far quicker to take restrictive action than its predecessors partly, no doubt, because the upper reaches of the establishment were riddled with Fascist sympathizers. The basic principles of British policy, formulated in the early months of Nazi rule, were that Britain's interests should predominate over all other considerations, and that she should obtain the maximum benefit from any refugees fortunate enough to be admitted.

It would be in the public interest to try to secure for this country prominent Jews who were being expelled from Germany and who had achieved distinction whether in pure science, applied science such as medicine or technical industry, music or art. This would not only obtain for this country the advantage of their knowledge and experience, but would also create a very favourable impression in the world, particularly if our hospitality were offered with some warmth.[12]

The self-regarding restrictionism inherent in this principle was reinforced, for different reasons, by the jealousy of middle-class professionals who, in a period of middle-class unemployment, feared the competition of refugees for their jobs. The academics who formed an Academic Assistance Council to seek out and invite German Jewish scholars to teaching or research posts in British universities were an honourable exception. In particular, the British Medical Association fought tooth and nail to keep out refugee doctors, and forced those who came in, however experienced, to pass the British medical qualifying examinations, in English, before they were allowed to practice.

As the Nazi persecution intensified and the numbers of those seeking asylum increased, so obstacles to their entry were augmented. After the Kristallnacht violence of November 1938 the government required visas for entry as well as a deposit of between £50 and £100 from the sponsor of each refugee admitted. Work permits were denied except for trainees in factories, domestic servants (of which there was a shortage) or agricultural labour. Under pressure the 'Kinder Transports' or rescue of unaccompanied children was permitted. More important for the purposes of this study, refugees, while not permitted to take up employment save in exceptional cases, were allowed to become partners in British firms, or to set up their own business employing British workers.

Such restrictions were in tune with quite large sections of public opinion. In Parliament attitudes did not follow party lines; those for and against a more liberal immigration policy were on both sides of the House. On 9 March 1933 Mr E. Doron (Unionist, Tottenham) asked the Home Secretary if he would take steps to prevent any alien Jew entering this country from Germany, and went on to state:

> Hundreds of thousands of Jews are now leaving Germany and are scurrying from there to this country... are we prepared to allow aliens to come here from every country while we have 3 million unemployed? If you are asking for a von Hitler [sic] in this country we will soon get one.[13]

In the less responsible press there was a constant tendency to exaggerate numbers. This was especially so in the *Daily Mail* and *Daily Express*, prominent in opposition to refugee entry, as they had been before 1905. The liberal papers the *News Chronicle* and the *Manchester Guardiàn* generally championed the refugee cause. The new arrivals had tended to settle in or around London but in this climate of confusion, in which hostility to Jewish immigrants was important, if not predominant, the government had no difficulty in directing them to parts of the country away from the big towns. Such a policy of dispersal had been suggested by the Royal Commission on Aliens of 1902 but not embodied in the Aliens Act of 1905. Men with capital (although most of this had been seized by the Nazis, leaving its former owners destitute) or with special business skills could come to Britain provided they settled, not in the areas of denser Jewish population, but in the remoter 'distressed areas' of heavy industry where unemployment was rife.

II

Unemployment in Britain had been increasing rapidly in the 1930s and by 1935 had reached over two million of the insured population. It was a serious economic and social problem in all the advanced industrial states. While in Britain it did not reach the level of Germany during its worst period, in certain areas it was higher, especially in the older regions of traditional heavy industry among which were south Wales, west Cumberland, the north-east of England, and parts of Scotland. Unemployment there remained high even when other affected areas began to recover, and only showed some signs of improvement when Britain started to rearm after 1935. Against this background the government was extremely reluctant to accept additional burdens in the form of refugees who (although some economists argued otherwise) they believed would swell the unemployed total and worsen what was already regarded as an intractable problem.

South Wales, along with the other depressed areas, suffered the effects of a twofold economic crisis. Firstly, there was the steady decline in the region's traditional industries of coalmining and metal production, which had begun after the First World War and continued throughout the 1920s. The decline was seen by orthodox economists as simply one of the downward phases of the trade cycle, but in reality it was a different matter. It had continued for more than a decade and was the result of changes in the pattern of world trade and in technology, for example, the substitution of oil-burning boilers for coal furnaces in ships. Therefore the expected upturn of the trade cycle, whenever it came, could not bring employment levels in south Wales, nor in the other distressed areas, back to where they had been immediately before the general trade slump. Secondly, there was the world-wide business recession of 1929–33 which adversely affected all the industrialized world.

The government's response to the growing unemployment was to set up the Industrial Transference Board in 1928, under which workers were removed from the coalfields to parts of Britain where jobs which depended on the use of electric power, such as chemicals and the growing motor industry, were more plentiful. In this way the Midlands and the new industrial growth points strung out along the Great West Road to the west of London became the new homes of many Welsh families. But coalmining in Britain, which had employed well over a million workers in 1923, by 1938 employed some 701,000, while the iron and steel industries had also reduced their workforce by at least 8 per cent.[14] Increase in the distribution, building, printing and electrical trades and the Welsh migration eastward had made little dent in the unemployment in the heavy industrial areas.

By 1934 the National Government led by Ramsay MacDonald had concluded that exceptional measures were required to tackle the problems of the depressed areas. It was also realized that the solution could not be left entirely to the unassisted efforts of private enterprise, at least not with a parliamentary election due shortly. Accordingly, special investigators were appointed in April 1934 and instructed to report on the state of these areas. Their report was available for the government in the autumn, and by the end of the year the first of the Special Areas Acts had passed through Parliament. The Act provided for the appointment of two Commissioners, one for England and Wales and one for Scotland. They were to co-ordinate all activities in pursuit of solutions to the problems, and their powers of action were wide. Initially they concentrated on short-term measures of relief, but eventually a long-term strategy evolved, namely the provision of government-financed factories on trading estates. The employment on these estates was in industries new to the area and quite different from those on which it had formerly depended. Furthermore the trading estates introduced advanced concepts of factory lay-out and made attempts to landscape factory surroundings. The overall effect helped to change the image of the Depressed Areas, making them more attractive as industrial locations. Additional legislation was introduced in 1939 which initiated the principle of offering financial inducements to firms to settle or expand in the Special Areas (as they were now called).

The Commission considered two possible locations for trading estate sites in south Wales, one at Pontypool on the northern rim of the coalfield and the other at Treforest. The latter, situated a mile or so south of Pontypridd, was finally selected. Some idea of the magnitude of the region's unemployment problem is conveyed by the following figures extracted from the *Report on the South Wales Trading Estate* prepared, at the request of the Commission, by Sir Alexander Gibb and Partners.[15] The statistics show by district the number of registered unemployed living within a ten-mile radius of the Treforest site in 1936. Its purpose was to demonstrate the availability of local labour for the proposed factories.

Table 1: Registered unemployed within ten-mile radius of Treforest, 1936

Office	Insured Population	Unemployed	Percentage Unemployed
Pontypridd	12,320	6,535	53
Taffs Well	1,830	574	31
Porth	8,790	3,691	42
Tonypandy	11,020	5,615	51
Treorchy	16,570	4,736	28
Pontyclun	3,090	742	24
Caerphilly	9,790	3,615	37
Mountain Ash	9,920	2,117	31
Total	73,330	27,625	Average 38

With an average of 38 per cent of the insured population unemployed the need for a remedy was obvious and pressing. However, there were special problems in establishing a successful trading estate in south Wales. These were set out forcibly by Hugh Beaver who wrote and presented the report for the Sir Alexander Gibb partnership. His opinions and judgement carried some weight as he had already submitted a report, the recommendations of which had been adopted, on the feasibility of setting up a trading estate at Team Valley. He stated his reservations thus:

> On the whole therefore, it seems to us that for several reasons the position in South Wales is more difficult than that on the North East coast... and a different type of industry may be required for the South Wales Trading Estate. Moreover it must be realised that in the general view there seems to be an even more impenetrable gloom lying over South Wales than the North East, which together with the prejudice in the mind of the ordinary business man in London regarding the type of labour to be obtained in Wales, hampers every effort to persuade the industry to move west. Our own experience and recent enquiries have fully convinced us that such a prejudice exists. And there is the feeling that South Wales is much more remote from London than is the North East coast . . . Apart from this, there is the unfortunate fact that communication across the Severn is so extremely bad. We expressed the view in reporting to the North East Trading Estate Company . . . that the primary consideration is road transport. For that reason it is to be hoped that communication across the Severn will be improved, and particularly that the long debated Severn Bridge will be built.
>
> We have somewhat emphasized the difficulties . . . in establishing a Trading Estate, since if we are correct the policy of the government and your Board will need to take note of those special difficulties and obstacles, and counter balancing inducements must be found to hold out.[16]

Presumably the reference to the prejudice in the minds of businessmen regarding the type of labour in Wales was an allusion to the propensity of Welsh miners to strike. If the opinions expressed in Hugh Beaver's report were shared by the business community, the reluctance of British businessmen to move to the area, even if tempted by inducements, can be readily understood. But for the industrialists among the threatened Jews of central Europe, the trading estates which were being built in this country came just in time. As there was a marked unwillingness on the part of British firms to go to the Special Areas, the authorities began to show an interest in finding refugee businessmen who would agree to settle there and to start up businesses in the waiting empty factories.

The contribution of these immigrants to solving the problems of south Wales promised to be significant. Many brought with them new manufacturing skills, new products and processes and sometimes capital if they had been able to leave the continent early enough. Some had been able to channel money out of Europe through sales organizations or branch offices which had been established in this country before the advent of the Nazis. Others had simply abandoned successful businesses when they had been forced to leave their homes, and it is likely that such men felt that having saved the lives of themselves and their families they had little to lose and much to gain by starting again, especially as the authorities in their adopted country appeared willing to provide generous assistance. One may also speculate that the initiative and drive which would motivate people to emigrate under threatening circumstances would also express itself in a spirit of enterprise. (Usually the most vigorous and enterprising are the first to emigrate.)

Although the door was closed to the general run of refugees, it could be opened to those willing to establish a business in any of the unemployment blackspots of Britain. In the debate on the *First Report of the Commissioners for the Special Areas* in the House of Lords on 31 July 1935, the Marquis of Londonderry, speaking for the Government said:

> I have no reason to believe that any obstacle will be placed in the way of any individual, if he is likely to be of credit and assistance to this country, who may wish to introduce an industry into this country and give employment to men who are now unemployed.[17]

Refugee businesses had been set up, particularly in the London area, by those who had arrived shortly after 1933. As far as we have been able to establish there is no evidence that any found their way to south Wales until after 1938. In the following year the Home Secretary announced that three hundred factories had been started by aliens — mainly refugees — but this figure applied to the whole country.[18] We do, however, have evidence that by early 1939 forty-nine Jewish-owned companies had commenced production, or were about to commence production, in south Wales: almost all of them at the Treforest Industrial Estate.[19]

Herbert Loebl interviewed a number of refugee industrialists who settled in the north-west before the war. Many reported that they were given the impression by the British consular staff that admission to Britain was conditional on their agreement to start a business in one of the depressed areas.[20] We infer that a similar approach was made to some of the industrialists who settled in south Wales.[21] Herbert Loebl further states that the Home Office lacked the authority to make such conditions under an Aliens Order; but nevertheless, early in 1936, the Home Office had initiated discussions with the Ministry of Labour and the Board of Trade on new procedures for dealing with applications for entry by foreign industrialists. He quotes from a letter dated 11 March 1936 from the Ministry of Labour to the Aliens Branch of the Home Office referring to the *Second Report of the Commissioner for England and Wales*, and in particular to the Commissioner's intention to 'exercise persuasion' on refugee industrialists to settle in the Special Areas. The letter suggested that the needs of public policy were sufficient,

> ... to justify *any* [my italics] steps that may be practicable to induce foreign firms to establish themselves in areas of high unemployment...
>
> It is recognised that there might be objections to using the statutory powers of the Aliens orders to the length of refusing permission to a foreigner to establish himself in the U.K. solely on account of the proposed situation of the factory, but there seems no good reason why advantage should not be taken of these powers to persuade employers in the desired direction.
>
> Our suggestion is that in response to any enquiry on the part of a foreigner as to permission to come here and set up a factory, the earliest opportunity should be taken of raising doubt whether permission will be given, if the foreigner proposes to establish his factory in London or the Home Counties ...
>
> There may be a few cases in which the employer ... refuses to accept the advice given ... and it may be that in such an event you might not be able to withhold the grant of permission. The probability is, however, that the general policy will become known and foreigners will be induced to act accordingly, without any pressure or persuasion.[22]

As Loebl says, this was, by any standards, an extraordinary letter. It proposed that the Home Office should pretend to powers it did not possess: that few foreigners would dare to call its bluff. Jews in particular, being desperate to gain entry, would be unlikely to do so, even if they suspected it was a bluff. But if they did, the Home Office should give way. In the circumstances it is, perhaps, not surprising that Jewish companies formed such a high proportion of the businesses established before the last war at Treforest.

The government, if not some sections of the press and public, had come round to the view that a policy of admitting refugee industrialists, if they could be encouraged to settle in the Special Areas, would have a remedial effect on the country's level of unemployment. This would not only agree with the principle that Britain should obtain the maximum benefit from the admission of refugees — it also had political advantages. The authorities would be seen as acting humanely in at least one area of the refugee problem where, fortunately, the numbers involved would be reasonably small. Furthermore, capital would be brought to Britain, if not by the refugees themselves, then by their friends and relatives from other countries. The fall in unemployment would then enable the government to open the doors a little more widely to other refugees, particularly if the connection between the people admitted and the new employment created could be demonstrated.

Support for the notion that certain groups of refugees could actually create employment was contained in an article which appeared in the *Spectator* magazine on 20 January 1939. It stated:

> At a low estimate, each of these entrants has given employment to an average of no less than three British subjects.

This finding supported the claim made by the Home Secretary, that by 1 December 1938 15,000 jobs had been created by the refugees. Sir John Hope Simpson put the figure at 25,000.[23] The discrepancy in numbers is probably because official employment statistics ignored factories employing less than twenty-five people, and a proportion of the new ventures established by refugee industrialists, being at an early stage of development, probably employed less than twenty-five workers.

The government naturally made attempts to ascertain that refugees seeking admission had the necessary skills, experience and capital to undertake the business ventures they promised. This vetting was initially undertaken by British consular officials on the continent. Admission to Britain was not made easy. The authorities well understood that people desperate to escape would use all possible subterfuges, and would promise anything to effect that escape. The following extract from a letter written by Thomas H. Frame, an official in the Commercial Department of the British Embassy in

Berlin, to Mr Holmes of the Tyneside Industrial Development Board makes the point well.

> We often get enquiries in the Embassy from Germans, mostly Jews, who wish to explore the possibilities of manufacturing in England. We have literature about the distressed areas' efforts to attract new industries, but most of these enquiries are very vague and the enquirers are themselves not practical men ... I have given your address on one or two occasions to enquirers, but most of the applicants prefer the South of England. One or two have fixed up in the Cardiff district...[24]

It was practical men that were sought; preferably with means. However, the absence of finance, if all other elements were available, was not necessarily a bar to entry.

Efforts were made by the consular staff to sort out the potential serious industrialist from the mere desperate candidate. The first hurdle facing these applicants was to complete convincingly the *Letter and Questionnaire for Foreign Persons Desirous of Setting up Manufacture in this Country*. It was a searching document which could only be answered satisfactorily by an applicant either running his own business or who held a fairly senior post in an existing enterprise.

The letter which accompanied the questionnaire called the attention of the applicant to:

> The resolution of the House of Commons of the 12th March 1936, that His Majesty's Government should endeavour to discourage the undue concentration of modern industries in the southern counties and to encourage new industries, where practicable to establish themselves in the older industrial centres...

The question of localities would be considered, among other matters, in consultation with the Ministry of Labour and the Board of Trade on receipt of the completed form.[25]

Before 1939 it had been possible for industrialists to transfer abroad at least part of their capital. By the time the majority of refugees were seeking admission to Britain, after 1938, the situation had changed dramatically for the worse. All that mattered then was to leave, and no doubt officials such as Thomas Frame pointed out that requests to start up in the Special Areas would be treated more sympathetically than requests to start up elsewhere.

A section of the questionnaire requested information on the provision and source of capital. The applicant had to answer the following questions:
What would be the proposed capital of the undertaking and who would provide it?

(a) Where is it?
(b) Will it be possible to transfer it to this country?
(c) In what form will it be possible to transfer it to this country?

Notwithstanding the importance of the availability of finance, the authorities were prepared to make allowances if satisfied that the business proposal was sound in all other aspects and that the industrialist intended to establish his enterprise in one of the Special Areas. Indeed, the advantages offered by the areas were real enough. The availability of factories for rent coupled with the initial rent concessions and other financial inducements would, for many, be a decisive factor. A Home Office official wrote to the Commissioner for the Special Areas on 13 February 1937:

> It has occurred to us that the Commissioners ... might be in a position to inform foreign industrialists who have no definite plans, of the more desirable forms of activity which might be followed in the Areas, having regard, of course, to the previous experience of the foreign persons concerned and to the amount of capital available.

Obviously the Home Office had refugees in mind. It was prepared to be very accommodating.

> Further, it is suggested that if a foreigner is not in possession of sufficient capital to finance the enterprise, or as frequently happens in the case of Germans, is unable to realise his capital immediately from abroad, the Special Areas Reconstruction Association or the Nuffield Trust might be prepared to assist him if he were able to satisfy them that his proposals were industrially sound and that he had the necessary experience and enterprise to carry out his proposals.[26]

As it happened, the period after 1938, when the refugee industrialists experienced relative ease in gaining admission to Britain, was also a time when the government, softening its stance a little in the face of the growing crisis, opened the door more widely to other classes of refugees. The nine months before the outbreak of war saw five times as many people admitted as in the previous five and a half years. They included a large number who had been manufacturers in their former countries.

> Statistics which break down by occupation the total number of 'enemy aliens', classified by tribunals show that one third of the men examined had been manufacturers on their own account. No less than 1,040 had been in the textile trade. Eight hundred and thirty six had been engaged in the manufacture of clothing; two hundred and twenty five had been concerned with the manufacture of chemicals for industry; five hundred and two had been making leather goods.[27]

Therefore, of the 55,000 adult German and Austrian refugees in Britain at the start of the war around 9,000 had been manufacturers, of whom 2,603 were in the four industries mentioned above. The large proportion of manufacturers illustrates the degree of selection carried out under the policy of the British government. It also resulted from the undertaking given by the Co-ordinating Committee of Jewish Organizations that no refugee would become a charge on the public purse. Manufacturers and other businessmen were more likely than others to have connections willing and able to provide the necessary financial guarantees.

III

By April 1939 seventy-eight companies had taken premises on the Treforest Trading Estate. Of these forty-nine were Jewish owned. Furthermore the Jewish companies were exclusively manufacturing concerns, not warehouses or depots, and accordingly would tend to be labour-intensive. This is an important consideration when attempting to assess the impact of the new firms on the unemployment situation. In the absence of data regarding the numbers of workers employed by each firm on the estate, it can be inferred that a manufacturing unit would employ more workers than a warehouse unit, although both might occupy the same area of floor space. At least five of the non-Jewish companies in occupation by April 1939 were depots or distribution units for goods manufactured elsewhere. The variety of trades represented by the Jewish refugee business at Treforest showed a good spread across the industrial spectrum. The numbers were, of course, not large, but they do at least suggest a useful injection of variety into the occupations of the local community. At the same time they contributed to the diversification of the industrial base of south Wales.

The temptation to infer that the refugee industrialists had abandoned the traditional Jewish occupations before other Jews in Britain should be avoided. There is insufficient evidence for this and, as the statistics show, approximately 40 per cent of the refugee businesses at Treforest continued to have links with those occupations long associated with Jews — clothing, textiles, footwear and furniture.

Table 2: Types of Industry Established by Jewish Refugees at Treforest Trading Estate — April 1939

Number of firms represented in brackets	
Leather goods (esp. gloves)	(13)
Textiles and fabrics	(6)
Greetings cards and stationery	(2)
Artificial flowers etc.	(2)
Hairdressing appliances and toilet articles	(2)
Fashion footwear	(1)
Chocolates	(1)
Fibre and paper	(1)
Watch straps	(1)
Gelatine products	(1)
Chemicals	(1)
Surgical adhesive	(1)
Medical drugs	(1)
Paint and varnish	(1)
Flexible metal tubes	(1)
Aluminium containers	(1)
Abrasives	(1)
Lighter fuel	(1)
Cigarette papers	(1)
Unbreakable pencils	(1)
Musical instrument strings	(1)
Photographic apparatus	(1)
Perfume and cosmetics	(1)
Furniture polish	(1)
Zips	(1)
Industrial brushes	(1)
Toys	(1)
Mica components	(1)
Speciality filters	(1)

This can be supplemented by the table in the Appendix which gives the names of the companies and their founders, the products they manufactured and whether the firm was still in business in the 1950s. Where available the employment figures, male and female, are given for 1973 and 1983.

The success of these enterprises can be estimated by answers to the following questions:

(i) Have the refugee companies lasted; can we offer an opinion about their stability?
(ii) What type of industry and what type of employment did they introduce to the region?
(iii) How many people did the companies employ directly and indirectly?
(iv) Were the companies loyal to the region; have they remained there?

(i) Fifty-five firms were established by refugee industrialists in south Wales between 1938 and 1941.[28] Of these thirty were still successfully trading in the 1950s at Treforest and a further five in various parts of the valleys.[29] Considering the great difficulties which the founders encountered in the early years of the war; internment of those who came from Germany and Austria; severe restrictions on the movements of those not interned; the compulsory acquisition by the authorities of their factories for use by strategic war industries; then, if these additional handicaps which faced the fledgling firms are taken into account, their continuation as viable businesses into the 1950s must be considered a reasonably good record of stability.[30] Many were still in existence in the 1970s and 1980s, although a number were controlled by other organizations with which they had merged or by which they had been taken over.

(ii) The overwhelming majority of south Wales refugee firms can be classified as light industry. Most founders began with very small resources, and it is difficult to understand how they survived. Clearly there was a dependence on particular skills and special knowledge of the products and their markets coupled with outstanding sales ability. But these attributes would not have been sufficient without the tenacity and genius for improvisation displayed by the founders. Generally speaking the new industries did not make use of advanced technology. They produced ordinary products which happened not to have been manufactured before in south Wales, and which required comparatively inexpensive capital equipment to produce. The success of the company often depended on the recognition of new markets for products such as fibres, paper, gelatine products and zips.

When the trading estates were established it was expected that the new factories would produce goods for local consumption, goods which were until then imported into the region. This was seen as an essential part of the strategy for improving the economic base of the Special Areas. An analysis of the products made at Treforest, however, suggests that this only occurred in a few cases. The products manufactured were quite specialized and therefore found a national market and, when conditions allowed, in the post-war period, an international market; examples are Treforest Silk Printers (silkscreen printing of fabrics) and Leiner & Sons (initially surgical adhesives but later gelatine products for the photographic and food trades). On the other hand, goods made for the national retailers like British Home Stores and Marks & Spencers found their way back to the region when sold in the local stores. It was probably only the carton manufacturers, J. Beatus and Wilnack (a subsidiary of the General Paper and Box Manufacturing Co.), that had the definite intention of supplying mainly to the local market.

Refugee members of the small and medium-size firms, of which south Wales had far too few when compared with the national average (a legacy of its heavy industry past), introduced new skills into the region and trained local people to acquire them, thereby demonstrating the adaptability of Welsh labour. Again, the firms were significant employers of women and girls, most of whom entered industrial employment for the first time and were trained in the new skills. The refugee firms created a whole new range of managerial and technical employment.[31] It was a very desirable development. This type of employment was difficult to obtain in pre-war south Wales although it quickly developed when factories turned their attention to war work. Furthermore, as the firms were not branch factories with headquarters situated outside the region, essential activities such as research and development had to be carried on 'in house' thereby creating new technical and scientific posts. However, if certain special skills were not available in the UK but were judged essential for the factory to get off the ground, the Home Office permitted the industrialists to bring these key workers from the continent. Frequently these men, mostly Jews, had been employees of the industrialist in his former business. Sometimes little more than a perfunctory search was carried out to find suitable local labour. Then where a case could be made — which was not too difficult — relatives or friends were brought over to fill these vacancies. Without doubt this subterfuge saved the lives of these fortunate few and their families.[32]

Weighing, then, the contribution which the refugee industries made to the local economy by introducing new products, new skills and encouraging new types of employment, they can be judged a success.

(iii) The successors of the refugee firms provided direct employment on the Treforest Estate for 3,881 workers in 1973; 2,385 males and 1,496 females. (Welsh unemployment at the time was 32,000.)[33] To put this figure into perspective, the total employment for all firms on the estate was 10,484; 6,923 males and 3,561 females.[34] Refugee firms and their successors therefore accounted for 37 per cent of all employment in 1973. The following points, however, should be considered when evaluating the significance of the figures. Six companies, BOAC, Firth Cleveland, ITT Creed, GEC, Standard Telephone and Cable and Wiggins Teape, accounted for 4,526 out of the 10,484 employees. These companies are mainly in industries which require substantial investment in very expensive capital goods, often amounting to millions of pounds. Such sums were far beyond the resources available to refugee industrialists when they set up their businesses. Furthermore, Wiggins Teape apart, the companies were directed to Treforest as part of the dispersal of strategic war industries programme which operated in the early years of the war. As such they form a distinct category, and if we deduct the total employed by these six firms from the overall total of 10,484 we are left with a figure of 5,958. Now, the figure of 3,881 accounted for by the refugee firms forms a much more significant proportion of this number — 65 per cent.

Direct employment in the manufacturing enterprises was not the total employment created. The indirect employment produced by firms supplying goods and services, by the various utilities, by banks and public services to the refugee industries, was also likely to be considerable although it is impossible to quantify. The employment created elsewhere in Britain would also be very difficult to assess although it was undoubtedly a factor if one takes into account the 'knock on' effect produced by the refugee firms' trading activities.

An analysis of the 1973 labour returns reveals that more males than females were employed by the refugee industries; 2,385 to 1,496. This is surprising. We would have expected female employment to predominate in light industries — this anyway is the traditionally accepted view. The result has a further significance because of the opposition from some quarters to light industries in south Wales expressed before the war, on the grounds that such industries would not solve the area's main problem — male unemployment. Given these results the opposition, at least in south Wales, appears to have been without justification.

These conclusions are tentative since it is impossible to obtain complete employment statistics. But enough data can be found from the various sources at least to identify trends.

In his book *The Location of Industry in the Depressed Areas*, S.R. Dennison claims that in the Depressed Areas newer industries were more likely to produce 'spin off', that is create additional economic activity and accordingly more employment, than the traditional industries.[35] (If one considers the spin-off effect of a contemporary industry such as electronics or computers the claim seems obvious, but it was true also of the new industries established by the refugee industrialists.) We have, in fact, a number of examples of this phenomenon. The picture cannot be considered complete as our information is fragmentary, but the business history of Mr Ben Glaser (the writer's father) is one where, for obvious reasons, we have detailed and complete information.

Mr Glaser arrived at the Treforest Estate Factory of the London Metal and Refining Company (later Aero Zip) in 1938. He was sent there by his boss, Mr K. Koppel, from Czechoslovakia where he had worked as an engineer in a zip fastener business. His task as Technical Manager was to purchase the equipment necessary to start pilot production of zips in the new factory. He remained with the firm until 1945, at which time he joined his brother-in-law Felix Lowbury (also a refugee, from Austria) in his business Lionite Chemical and Asphalt Products which he had started, also on the Treforest Estate, in 1939. In 1946 the two partners moved the business to the docks area of Cardiff, and in the early 1950s moved it once more to a new factory which they built themselves in the Canton district of Cardiff. The company, renamed Lionite Specialities, employed over 200 people by the end of the 1950s. Their main product lines were electric shaver cases which were supplied to all the major electric shaver manufacturers — Phillips, Sunbeam, Schick etc. — and also a wide range of jewel boxes which they supplied to some of the main high street retail outlets.

In 1963 the company was sold, and one of the non-Jewish engineers, Arthur Lewis, started his own business, Compact Cases, in Caerphilly, while another, Arthur Magrath, started a metal plating company, Magrath Metal Finishing on the Penarth Road, Cardiff. Meanwhile Ben Glaser started up once more, using the proceeds of the sale. This company, Vicrem Engineering, currently employs seventy people and has been in existence for twenty-five years. In the early 1970s its director, realizing the great potential in electronics, founded a company in Bristol — Digicon Electronics. This company was sold after three years and eventually acquired by the Ferranti Group. The specialist electronic products developed by Digicon now have world-wide sales of many millions of pounds.

The spin-off process has not stopped. A number of tool-making firms have been started up in south Wales by toolmakers formerly employed by Lionite and Vicrem. The seed has produced much fruit.

It is generally accepted that small firms generate more spin-off than large ones, which may be because the leadership qualities displayed by the founders are 'catching', or at least are seen as capable of emulation. The limited means available to most refugee industrialists and the improvisation they were forced to practise in order to survive in the early days may have had an instructive role which their more perceptive and enterprising employees followed.

To summarize, considering the number of jobs, direct and indirect, created by the refugee firms, their presence in south Wales was beneficial.

(iv) While there has been an influx of light industry into the Special Areas of south Wales since the war, most of the enterprises have been branch factories of national or international companies.[36] Their record of stability has, on the whole, been good, but there always remains a doubt about their permanent location in the region, particularly in periods of economic recession, precisely when they are most needed. But even if they are stable there remain certain disadvantages.

An analysis of the refugee firms set out in the Appendix shows that only two which started their existence in south Wales transferred to other parts of the country of their own accord.[37] Thirteen firms, for a variety of reasons, moved away from the Treforest Estate to other locations in south Wales, and continued to make their contribution to the local economy. O.P. Chocolates and Gnome Photographic became, in due course, substantial employers of labour. Another quite small firm, Blossom Ltd., simply moved off the estate and into the town of Treforest, while a further three went to Merthyr, two relocated in Bridgend and two each moved to Porth and Cardiff. Pontyclun, Caerphilly and Williamstown each received one firm.[38] Eighteen companies had disappeared by the mid 1950s. Most likely they went bankrupt or simply ceased trading.

In view of the fact that by the 1960s only two of the companies after achieving maturity had left the region, although eighteen had disappeared in the normal course of commercial vicissitudes, we must conclude that the refugee firms have been loyal to the area.

Judging from our criteria the refugee enterprises have been successful from the point of view of south Wales. In all probability, few, if any, would have settled there but for government pressure. Most were virtually forced to choose between the four Special Areas of south Wales, south-west Scotland, west Cumberland and the north-east coast, undesirable despite some advantages in the shape of lower wage rates, a lower cost of living and factories for rent on advantageous terms. As Herbert Loebl has observed, refugee industries might well have grown faster and become more important in more favourable areas. But most prospered, reasonably in some cases and outstandingly in a few, in spite of their location. From the standpoint of the national economy, it might well be that reasonably successful and stable businesses located in those parts of the country where they are badly needed are of greater social importance than very successful firms in affluent areas. If this proposition is accepted we must conclude that government policies in the 1930s, inward-looking, cynical and of limited compassion, were as helpful to the British unemployed as to the few they saved from extinction.

Notes to Chapter 8

1. *Jewish Chronicle*, 13 January 1905.
2. Lloyd P. Gartner, *The Jewish Immigrant in England 1810–1914* (London, George Allen and Unwin, 1960), 49.

3. V.D. Lipman, *A Social History of the Jews in England 1850-1950* (London, Watts & Co., 1954), 85. Lipman estimated that 100,000 to 150,000 Jewish immigrants settled in Britain between 1881 and 1914.
4. Marion Berghahn, *Continental Britons* (London, Macmillan, 1984), 75.
5. H.F. Modder, *The Jew in the Literature of England* (Philadelphia, Jewish Publication Society of America, 1944), 44.
6. House of Commons Select Committee on Alien Immigration 1882, quoted by V.D. Lipman in op.cit., 136.
7. Report of the Royal Commission on Alien Immigration (HMSO, 1903), *passim*. Many of these charges seem to have been due to the influence of Major W. Evans Gordon, a leading anti-Semite who was on the Commission.
8. Israel Finestein, 'The New Community', in V.D. Lipman (ed.), *Three Centuries of Anglo-Jewish History*, Jewish Historical Society of England (W. Heffer and Sons Ltd., 1961), 114.
9. Report of the Royal Commission on Alien Immigration (HMSO, Vol. I, 1903), 10.
10. St George's Settlement run by Basil Q. Henriques.
11. A.J. Sherman, *Island Refuge: Britain and Refugees from the Third Reich, 1933-1939* (London, Paul Elek, 1973), 30.
12. Herbert Loebl, 'Government Financed Factories and the Establishment of Industries by Refugees in the Special Areas of the North of England, 1937-61', (unpublished M.Phil. thesis, University of Durham, 1978), 90. Quoted from Cabinet Minutes.
13. Ibid., quoted from House of Commons Debate.
14. 'Natural Increase and Migration from the Special Areas from 1931 to 1935', Commission for Special Areas, England and Wales, 3rd Report, Cmd 5303, HMSO 1936.
15. Sir Alexander Gibb and Partners, *Report on the South Wales Trading Estate*, June 1936, Pontypridd Public Library. This firm of consulting engineers had also undertaken an investigation of possible locations for siting trading estates in the north-east of England.
16. Ibid., 1-2.
17. Speech by Lord Privy Seal in debate on the Commission for Special Areas. House of Lords, reported by Herbert Loebl, op.cit. 160.
18. 'Refugees: their Contribution to English National Life'. Speech by the Home Secretary, Sir Samuel Hoare, to the Society for the Protection of Science and Learning, 6 February 1939, at University College, London. Quoted by Loebl, op.cit. 122.
19. Letter from South Wales and Monmouthshire Trading Estates Ltd., to the Pontypridd Trades Council and Labour Party, 24 April 1939.
20. Herbert Loebl, op.cit., 123-4.
21. Discussions with Mr B. Glaser. Mr Glaser who was sent by his employer, Mr K. Koppel, from Czechoslovakia to south Wales in 1938 to take possession of a factory at Treforest, has confirmed this.
22. Ministry of Labour, ET 1315/1936, 11 March 1936. Besso to Sir Ernest Adderness, Loebl, op.cit., 124-5.

23. Sir John Hope Simpson, 'Can Refugees be an Asset?' from *Planning* no.216 (PEP 14 January 1944), 4. Quoted Loebl, op.cit., 121.
24. See Appendix.
25. Letter and questionnaire supplied by the Home Office to foreign applicants wishing to start up factories in Great Britain.
26. Cooper to Boyd, 13 February 1937. Loebl, op.cit., 131.
27. Austin Steven, *The Dispossessed: German Refugees in Britain* (London, Barrie & Jenkins, 1975), 293. Thirteen manufacturers using leather had set up businesses on the Treforest Estate by April 1939.
28. The majority were started on the Treforest site. The exceptions are Welsh Products at Dowlais, Polikoff at Ynyswen, Flex Fasteners and Mendle Bros. at Porth.
29. I am indebted to Mr Pugsley of the Welsh Development Agency for details of tenancies and employment figures. A part of what follows in this section is based upon information which he kindly supplied from the records held by the WDA who inherited the files of the South Wales and Monmouthshire Trading Estates Ltd. and the Industrial Estates Management Corporation for Wales, which it became in 1960. In 1966 it was reconstructed as the Welsh Industrial Estates Corporation and remained as such until 1975 when it assumed its present status as the Welsh Development Agency, albeit with enhanced powers and a somewhat different role.
30. The authorities suspected the Axis Powers of planting spies in Britain masquerading as refugees. The strategic industries included BOAC, Symond Air Accessories, Standard Telephone and Cable and Helliwels. Most moved in between 1940 and 1941 when the refugee industries were still in their infancy.
31. Conversations with Mr B. Glaser. It is unfortunate that the founders have either died or moved away from the region, although efforts are being made to trace those still alive. They could have contributed valuable material for case histories of the firms.
32. In this way Aero Zip brought over six key workers and their families from Czechoslovakia. Not all were Jewish. Conversations with Mr. B Glaser.
33. Labour returns for 30 June 1973. Extracted from the records of the Welsh Development Agency.
34. Employment Records of the Welsh Development Agency. The peak employment figure for the Treforest Estate was 16,300 in April 1944. With the cessation of government contracts the figure fell to below 9,000 in December 1945. It never approached the peak again, and was below 10,000 in 1975 when Welsh unemployment was over 70,000.
35. S.R. Dennison, *The Location of Industry in the Depressed Areas* (London, OUP, 1939), 95.
36. South Wales has the highest concentration of Japanese firms in Europe.
37. Rosedale transferred to Coleford in the Forest of Dean in the 1960s. Gustav Holtzer moved to the Home Counties, also in the 1960s.

38. Conversations with Mr Windsor Roper who was Chief Engineer to the South Wales and Monmouthshire Trading Estates Company and to its successor the Industrial Estates Management Corporation for Wales.

APPENDIX. Refugee Firms starting on the Treforest Estate in the late 1930s and 1940s

Company	Founder	Products	Present in 1950s	Employment 1973			Employment 1983			Comments
				M	F	Tot	M	F	Tot	
B. Prince	B. Prince	watch straps	yes							
Treforest Chrome Leather	Ostraiker	chrome leather	yes							Moved to Caerphilly
H. Stanier	Stanier	lock knit fabrics	yes	50	52	102				
E.M. Manufacturing	E. Mergerle	hair dressing appliances	yes							Moved to Pontyclun
Treforest Silk Printers	Kurt Jellinek	silk screen printing	yes	233	59	292	69	21	90	
Treforest Chem. Co. (Leiner & Sons)	Leiner	surgical adhesives, gelatine prods	yes	488	66	554	71	6	77	
Pearl Paints	Stern Brothers	paint and varnish	yes	100	13	113	102	18	120	
Jacob Engl	Jacob Engl	flexible tubes	yes							Moved to Bridgend
Embee Abrasives	Alfred Meyer	abrasives	yes							Moved to Dowlais
Gnome Photographic	Löbstein	photographic apparatus	yes							Moved to Cardiff
O.P. Chocolates	Oscar Peschek Sneider, Kutzman	chocolates & confectionery	yes							Moved to Dowlais T/O by Avanna, T/O R.H.M.
Fashion Footwear	H. Klausner	footwear	yes							Moved to Merthyr

Company	Founder	Products	1950s	1973	1983	Comments
H. Dixon & Son Western Brush	Mayer	brushes and toolmakers	yes			
London Metal & Refining — Aero Zip	K. Koppel	zips	yes	457 724 1181		Taken over by Textron
Burlington Gloves	J. Krakauer	leather gloves	yes	246 127	24 151	T/O Stewart Hosiery (1951)
Gustav Holzer	Gustav Holzer	cotton shawls	yes			Left area
H. Labin & Co.	H. Labin, E. Greenstein	toilet articles, jewel boxes	yes	7 60 67		
J. Beatus	Jacob Beatus	cardboard cartons	yes			Moved to Porth T/O Glampack (1978)
Rudolf Gross & Co.	Rudolf Gross	leather gloves	yes			Became Western Gloves
Micalectric Manufacturing	Freedman	mica articles	yes	6 39 45		
Western Board Mills	Arthur Vogel	fibre and paper board	yes	146 5 151	64 39 103	
General Paper and Box — Rizla	R. Willheim	cigarette papers	yes	79 205 284	129 231 360	
P. Messinger	P. Messinger, Stern	musical strings	yes	35 41 76	10 20 30	Became General Music Strings
N. Weisinger	N. Weisinger	artificial flowers	yes			Became Treforest Flowers
Lionite Asphalt & Chem. Prods.	F. Lowbury	cement, chem. prods.	yes	(1963) 80 120	200	Became Lionite Spec. Moved to Cardiff
Rosedale	N. Rosedale	plastic combs	yes			Moved to Coleford

Company	Founder	Products	1950s	1973			1983			Comments
Metal Alloys	Tofler Eisker	metal refining	yes	52	4	56	39	3	42	
Plastic Engineers	Schindler	combs, spectacle frames	yes	287	89	376	95	27	122	
Metal Products	Golten family	light engineering	yes							
Trehawk	Gutig Weissmayer		yes							Moved to Williamstown Became Hawks Musical Strings
British Gelaprint		petrol capsules, bottle caps	no							
Lion Leather		leather belting	no							Moved to Porth
Perma Products	K. Posner	cigarette lighter fuels	no							Moved to Bridgend
Unbreakable Pencils	Joseph	unbreakable pencils & chalks	no							
J. Loewenstern	J. Loewenstern	filters	no							
Finetex Manufacturing	Wilhelm Jondorf	fancy ribbons	no							
Cardiff Cards		greeting cards	no							Moved to Cardiff
Treforest Belt	H. Podolsky	leather belts	no							
Guttenplan		ladies leather belts	no							
ELCO Ltd.	Paul Beck Mestiz	domestic hotplates	no							
Blossom Ltd.	H. Stern Hornung Waldeck	artificial flowers	no							Moved to Porth

Company	Founder	Products	1950s	1973	1983	Comments
B. Altschul	B. Altschul	gloves	no			Moved to Caerphilly
J. Fallenbaum	J. Fallenbaum	pharmaceuticals	no			
Magner & Saabor	Magner	paper goods	no			
Papyrus		handbags	no			
Sandringham Leather Goods			no			
H. Lippman	H. Lippman	aluminium containers	no			
Grunberger & Co.	N. Grunberger	fancy leather & metal goods	no			Moved to Rhydyfelin
J. Jacobsons	J. Jacobsons	cosmetics	no			
Polya Leather	Polya, Buda	gloves	no			
British Nova Works	Lefkowitz R. Hubsch	floor and furniture polish	no			Moved to Llantwit Fardre
Livia Leather	Weisinger	leather goods	no			

Refugee Firms Outside Treforest

Company	Founder	Products	1950s	1973	1983	Comments
Flex Fasteners	R.E. Benedict Bernstiel	zips	Porth			
Mendel Bros.	Mendel Brothers	plastic moulding	Porth			
Alfred Polikoff (Wales) Ltd.	A. Polikoff	garments	Ynyswen			T/O by G.H.S. Fashions in 1980s

Epilogue

URSULA R. Q. HENRIQUES

I

The last half century has been, by and large, a period of decline in the Jewish communities of south Wales. The process of decline, which began even before the Second World War, had occasional reversals, such as the numerically small but important influx of industrialists described in Chapter 8 and the sojourn in the valleys of wartime refugees from the German bombing of east London. But these were only temporary pauses in a very slow long-term trend. None the less there were some positive developments, especially in the community of Cardiff, a burgeoning city where prosperity was maintained and Jewish numbers did not begin to fall in all probability until the later 1960s. Here there were significant movements in the organization of religious life.

The First World War had opened with the religious life of Cardiff Jewry organized in two synagogues, the old Hebrew Congregation in its grand new synagogue in Cathedral Road and the smaller one in Edwards Place.

In 1918 the Edwards Place lease ran out, and its congregation moved to a new building based on a converted church in Windsor Place. It was still known as the Foreign Shul, although this would seem to have been something of a misnomer for a place of worship whose leading officers included two of the thoroughly anglicized Instone brothers and the lawyer Captain H.H. Roskin. However, the second congregation, which before the war had attracted Lithuanian immigrants, was now a magnet for incomers from Tredegar and other valley communities noted for their orthodoxy. According to Maurice Dennis, Cathedral Road ran a choir, but Windsor Place maintained chanting in its services and an interest in them, 'woefully lacking in the later years of Cathedral Road'.[1]

The first hint of a union between the two synagogues is found in a Windsor Place Minute Book for the years 1928–32, read by Mr Dennis in 1980.[2] There was a proposal by Roskin to write to Cathedral Road with a view to the two congregations sharing a cemetery. This resulted in long negotiations which soon turned acrimonious over sharing the costs of buying a piece of land and of burying the poor who could not afford burial fees. The matter slipped into oblivion until it was revived in January 1932 by an offer from the Marquis of Bute to sell them some land. A joint committee of both synagogues examined the offer, and decided to raise money by cutting the salaries of the minister and all the paid synagogue staff.[3] Not surprisingly acrimony again prevailed, which spilled over into the pages of the *Jewish Chronicle*. Not until 1941 were arrangements for a joint burial ground and joint *shechita* (ritual slaughter of animals for meat) agreed. Thereafter plans for a joint council and a joint constitution were discussed.

In the end two developments made a reorganization of Cardiff's synagogues inevitable. One was the approaching expiry of the lease at Windsor Place. Another, less immediate but more profound, was the movement of population. By the late 1930s many prosperous Jews were moving from Grangetown and Riverside to the new and salubrious suburb of Cyncoed overlooking the city from the top of Pen-y-lan Hill. As Lady Sherman pointed out in 1955, the place of worship had of necessity to follow the movement of the Jewish population, and a synagogue was needed in each area.[4] In this matter the development of modern transport, buses and cars, made little difference, since orthodox Jews will travel only on foot on the Sabbath.

At the time of the establishment of the Cardiff United Synagogue a plan was proposed to raise money for the new synagogue building. In the event, doubtless due to the war, the plan did not materialize until 1952 when a prime site on Pen-y-lan Hill was donated by Julius Skrek in honour of his parents' golden wedding. The foundation stone was laid with due ceremony by the Chief Rabbi, Israel Brodie, on 2 November,[5] and the new building was formally opened in January 1955.[6] Although it was well furnished and adorned with new stained-glass windows, nobody, it seems, gave thought or money to the care of the surrounding land. What could have become a pleasant garden, an ornament to the neighbourhood and a credit to its Jewish residents, remained for the next thirty years a bramble-filled wasteland.

For a time the two synagogues were run by their councils and a joint committee with representatives from each. However the constitution drafted in 1941 but amended successively up to June 1990, provides for government by a joint council elected by members of any constituent synagogue in the ratio of one representative per thirty members, and executive officers (president, vice-president and treasurer) elected by the full membership at the Annual General Meeting. Women can vote, sit on the Council, but not hold executive office. The old graduated subscriptions conferring graduated powers and privileges have disappeared. The Cardiff United Synagogue is sliding towards democracy.

The constitution and its amendments were inevitably affected by changes in the membership of the two synagogues. In 1959 Cathedral Road had 402 members, the new synagogue at Pen-y-lan had 326.[7] Thereafter Cathedral Road went into a long, slow but irreversible decline, while the numbers at Pen-y-lan increased as more of the community moved out from central Cardiff. By 1963 the balance was roughly equal, but from then on, while Pen-y-lan remained almost static, Cathedral Road continued to decline. By 1972 the chronicler Maurice Dennis was foreseeing that ultimately Cathedral Road would become unviable and would have to close.[8] Yet the final collapse was long delayed, the closure and sale of the building not being completed until 1989.

These membership figures were not the whole story, since there was now a smaller but flourishing Reform synagogue in Moira Place. None the less, a feeling of depression is detectable in the pages of CAJEX in the 1970s. 'Where are all the youth gone?' asks Phillip Kaye, and he answers himself that the parents are too apathetic to bring them to *shul*.[9] The real situation was that while the city of Cardiff was expanding its Jewish population was contracting.

II

The Reform movement came late to Cardiff. The city was noted for its orthodoxy, which had been refreshed in the 1920s and 1930s by immigration from the valley communities. Yet in England it was a hundred years old.

Reform Judaism was originally a German movement, to which the ideas of the eighteenth-century Enlightenment, the French Revolution and the Biblical criticism of the early nineteenth century had all contributed. In England it had taken the less theoretical and more practical form of a revolt against foreignness of religious practice and lack of decorum in contemporary synagogues. A small group of wealthy and anglicized London Sephardim seceded from the Bevis Marks synagogue in 1840, and joining with a smaller group of Ashkenazis founded the New West End Reform synagogue.[10] The movement was immediately denounced as assimilationist by orthodox grandees such as Sir Moses Montefiore (an enthusiastic advocate of assimilation to local custom when he travelled in Poland or Russia). It was closely associated with the struggle for Jewish emancipation (seats in Parliament) by leaders of Anglo-Jewry, 'English gentlemen of the Jewish persuasion', whose ideal of religious practice, if not doctrine, tended to approach that of English Nonconformity.

The movement produced a few offshoots in the provinces. The 1850s saw the foundation of a Reform synagogue in Manchester and a small group in Hull, and in 1875 some immigrant German woollen merchants founded a synagogue in Bradford.[11] Thereafter the movement atrophied, becoming conservative, dull and static. What enthusiasm there was could be found in its extreme wing, which broke off early in the twentieth century under the leadership of Claude Montefiore and Israel Mattuck to become the Liberal Jewish movement. The well-to-do, middle-class patrons of these movements and their English services and sermons did not appeal to refugees from east Europe flooding into Britain after 1881.[12] The new refugees from Hitler, however, came from Germany or from countries influenced by the German Reform movement. Among them were a group of rabbis educated in continental universities and continental Reform seminaries (of which there were none in Britain at this time). Under their influence Reform Judaism regained its youth and enthusiasm. Encouraged and co-ordinated by the American Harold Reinhart, rabbi at the New West End Synagogue, Reform congregations began to multiply. In the 1930s synagogues were founded in Golders Green, Edgeware and Glasgow. In the 1940s six more were started in Hendon, Wimbledon, Bournemouth, Southport, Leeds and Cardiff, and there were twelve more to come. Thus the new Reform Congregation in Cardiff was part of a much wider movement.[13]

The Cardiff Reform synagogue was started soon after the Second World War by a small group of well-educated doctors and lawyers and professional men. They were in revolt from the ritualism, formalism and lack of decorum and dignity which they perceived in the conduct of Cardiff services, the Cardiff United Synagogue seeming to have fallen under the influence of a very orthodox leadership stemming from Windsor Place. The father of a young solicitor already active in communal affairs, on holiday in Bournemouth, visited the new Reform synagogue there and came back much impressed with the cordiality of his welcome and carrying a leaflet explaining the aims and principles of the Reform movement. Further enquiries, which met with encouragement from the German Rabbi and the president of the Bournemouth congregation, were passed on to Rabbi Reinhart in London, who replied with advice on organization and further information on the aims of Reform. As he expressed it, these were the realization of the Jewish tradition expressed in dignity and earnestness and not stifled in formalism; also the reverent adaptation of ritual and the enlightened interpretation of Jewish law.[14]

If the inaugural movement of 1840 had endeavoured to harmonize Jewish tradition with the ethos of mid-nineteenth-century Britain, that of 1948 did the same for mid-twentieth-century British Jews. Reformers envisaged shorter services held in a synagogue as an act of worship rather than a social gathering. They emphasized the moral message of Judaic law rather than the minutiae of observance, they laid much emphasis on education, and most of them advocated the equal participation of women in the services and government of the synagogue. On the one hand they tended to perceive reformed Judaism as a return to a spiritual faith purged of some at least of its medieval accretions, on the other hand they thought of it as a developing religion rather than one bound by a code of practice which had ceased to develop in Talmudic times. But Alan Liss has pointed out that their rabbis represented a Western, university-educated point of view bound to bring them into collision with the yeshivah-trained rabbis of the east European tradition.[15]

The Cardiff pioneers had to consider whether they wanted to adopt Reform or the more extreme Liberal movement. But by the time

Rabbi Mattuck of the St John's Wood (London) Liberal Synagogue had declined an invitation to a public debate with a champion of Reform, the matter had already been decided. On 2 June 1948 a meeting was arranged in Cardiff Town Hall addressed by Rabbi Van der Zyl of the North West London Reform Synagogue, who was to be guide, philosopher and friend to the young congregation. And so Cardiff New Synagogue was born.

With missionary zeal the Reformers set about canvassing the Jewish community for recruits, distributing pamphlets explaining their aims and principles, and organizing services. They were faced with two big problems — they had nowhere to hold their services and they incurred the immediate hostility of the Orthodox establishment in Cardiff. The first problem was temporarily solved by hiring the United Nations Association's Temple of Peace in Cathays Park, an impressive venue and suitable except when the United Nations Association wanted to use it when the services or meetings had to move to a hired hall or restaurant. A succession of rabbis came from London and elsewhere to help on festivals and Holy Days.

By September 1949 the new organization had appointed a radical rabbi from Berlin, Gerhard Graf, and had drawn up a constitution based on a council, and executive officers (two wardens and a treasurer) all elected by the members at the Annual General Meeting. It was specified that women could hold office. A hunt was in progress for a suitable building, but due partly to difficulties with the City Hall the purchase of the old Primitive Methodist Church in Moira Place was not completed until March 1952. Repairs and conversion cost considerably more than the purchase price, and the new synagogue was officially opened on 8 February 1953.

The second problem was more painful and intractable than the first. The distinguished honorary life president of the Cardiff United Synagogue expressed his feelings by calling the Reform members 'Camouflage Jews'. The senior rabbi or 'Rav' of Cardiff was a cleric of a narrow and rigid orthodoxy whose view of the Reformers was that they were 'new assimilationists, one of whose objects it was to legalize intermarriage'.[15] The row between Cardiff Orthodox and Reform soon became public. The Cardiff United Synagogue tried to prohibit the local butcher from selling kosher meat to his Reform customers, and had to be stopped by the Chief Rabbi. The burial of Reform members in the Jewish cemetery was forbidden until the New Synagogue Council, on advice from Bournemouth, obtained from the City Council a plot of ground in the Cardiff Western Cemetery. The confrontation was in many ways reminiscent of the strife which had broken out in 1840. It seemed that orthodoxy had not advanced in tolerance since that date. Indeed it had retreated. Rabbi Graf was not invited to the ceremonial opening of the Pen-y-lan Synagogue in 1955. That such a ceremony could be chaired by the president of the New West End (Reform) Synagogue, as was the opening of Cathedral Road in 1896, was now inconceivable. Although the two wings of Cardiff Jewry gradually grew closer so that they now co-operate in many communal, social and charitable activities, the Orthodox continue to make a show of refusing to recognize the Reformers religiously as Jews. In religious toleration of other Jews they are fifty years behind the Christian churches in most of England.

In one respect the 'Rav's' denunciation had some substance. One of the founding group had married a Christian wife, and the first boy to be *barmitzvah* in the new synagogue was his son. Reform appealed not only to the new generation of foreign refugees (who made up at least one-third of the membership); it acted as a kind of long stop for religious Jews of both sexes who married non-Jewish spouses and who, under the constitution of the Orthodox synagogue, would have been driven out of the community. While the Orthodox claimed that Reform enticed Jews away from their faith towards conversion, Reformers could reply that it saved many more from being driven away by giving them an acceptable alternative. But in addition to this, Reform Judaism began to attract converts from the Christian population. Judaism is not a proselytizing religion, and far from seeking converts, the Orthodox Beth Din (Ecclesiastical Court) makes it very difficult for them to join. Yet religiously minded people, dissatisfied with the faith in which they were brought up, come battering on the doors of Judaism demanding to be let in. Reform, although extremely careful and requiring of converts a long period of training and proofs of sincerity, is a little more welcoming. How many members of the Cardiff Reform Synagogue, whether marrying in or single candidates, are converts is uncertain, but probably at least one-third. Their stories remain in the confidential files of the London Reform Beth Din. Until these files are opened the full story of Cardiff New Synagogue will not be told.

The membership of the Reform synagogue increased apace. Between 1953 and 1962 the number of children in its *cheder* grew from thirty-eight to over one hundred. Between 1949 and 1970 its affiliated membership increased from 220 to 319.[17] (These figures require some further examination. According to the present treasurer the membership peaked in the 1960s at 220 family units, subsequently declining to 190 family units and then remaining static.) However, as the membership of the Cardiff United Synagogue declined its percentage share of worshippers in the Jewish community continued to grow. It soon acquired several groups for the young, a variety of education classes organized by Rabbi Graf, including adult ones, a Chevra Kadisha or Burial Board, an annual garden party and dinner dance, and a whole galaxy of charitable and fund-raising festivities. The women did not sit in the gallery but sat with the men (without, so far as is known, any disastrous effects on their male nervous systems) and in 1986 the first woman rabbi from the Leo Baeck Training Seminary was appointed. Despite the period of comparative apathy which afflicted all the synagogues in the 1970s it would appear that Cardiff Reform has come to stay.

III

The last purpose-built or converted synagogue to be opened was probably Bridgend in 1928, and this was on the coastal plain. In the 1920s the industrial economy of the south Wales valleys collapsed. The sudden end to the requirement for guns and ammunition, the chaos which accompanied the transition from a wartime to a peacetime economy, and the competition from free German coal delivered as 'reparations' produced recession and mass unemployment in all the areas of heavy industry in Great Britain, and south Wales was probably the worst hit. By 1931 the Rhondda valleys had lost one-fifth of their 1921 population, and in the same decade south Wales as a whole lost 250,000 people by migration. Only Cardiff increased its population from 219,580 to 223,589, an addition of some 4,000.[18] The Jewish population of the valleys had grown with their industrial growth and could be expected to decline with their decline. The surprising feature of the 1920s was that, despite a good deal of movement of individual families from one valley town to another, and even of groups into Cardiff, the valley communities, on the whole, kept up their numbers so well. The reasons for this are not altogether clear. Despite the prevailing poverty there was probably still a demand for what the Jewish shops had to sell or lend on pledge. In the

1920s the local people were selling their gold and silver. Only when their valuables had been exhausted and they had no more to pledge (excepting wedding rings with which they would not part) did pawnbroking begin to decline. Even then, according to Charles Jones, many Jewish people remained, especially elderly parents or families with children at a critical stage in their school education.[19] But by the 1930s the drift of Jewish families away from the industrial valleys had begun in earnest.

Small communities were the first to evaporate. As early as 1918 Newbridge in Gwent whose small congregation included members from the neighbouring villages of Abercarn, Crumlin and Llanhilleth, gave up the attempt at independence and amalgamated with the Newport Hebrew Congregation.[20] In the mid 1930s the Ebbw Vale congregation incorporated with Brynmawr. In the 1920s Tredegar, the riots of 1911 only an evil memory, was at its peak. In the 1930s many of its families moved to Cardiff, and by 1955 its synagogue had closed. After the war the south Wales economy staged a recovery, turning to new manufactures and increasing its population. But the Jewish communities continued to dwindle, and moved into a terminal decline. By the mid 1970s the Jews of Brynmawr, Aberdare and Pontypridd had gone. In 1984 the Ark from Pontypridd synagogue was stacked against the wall of a small disused chapel near Aberystwyth, now a part of the National Museum of Wales, housing a collection of figurines of preachers and other relics of Welsh Nonconformity. Its *sefarim* (scrolls of the law) had been flown to Israel and ceremonially handed over to the congregation of Petach Tikvah. Merthyr's synagogue was finally sold in the early 1980s. Of synagogues there remain only those of Cardiff, Newport and Swansea. The valleys communities have virtually disappeared.

Why did this happen? At present the answer remains speculative, but it would seem that it lies as much in the development of the Jewish community as a whole as in the movement of the south Wales economy. The original immigrants from east Europe, desperate for a livelihood, had spread out among the growing industrial towns and villages until, at their furthest reach, there were families living miles away from their nearest Jewish neighbours. Their sons and daughters were no longer content with such isolation, nor with walking over the mountain to the nearest synagogue. Lady Sherman described how her two small brothers had had to leave school early on Friday afternoon, rush home to change and be put on an unheated train to the nearest synagogue, attend Friday night and Saturday services and *cheder* on Sunday morning and come home by train in time for Monday school. She thought parents wanted a full Jewish life for their children, but an easier life among their own kind.[21] On the economic side, while the new steel-making, car-building and electronics factories were tending to settle once more on the coastal plain of south Wales, the valleys offered few openings for businessmen and professionals. Llanelli had produced seven orthodox rabbis including a Chief Rabbi of Ireland. Small New Tredegar had produced twelve medical doctors including a professor, and a number of teachers.[22] They had to look for jobs elsewhere. Even where a business or legal career opened in south Wales, probably on one of the new trading estates, it was more agreeable to live in town and travel daily by car.

The valleys' loss should have been Cardiff's gain; and this was largely true. Its Jewish population seems to have increased strongly between the First World War and the late 1950s, but from the mid 1960s it, too, also went into decline. Maurice Dennis writing in CAJEX in March 1972 headed the sixteenth part of his 'History of the Cardiff Jewish Community', 'A Community in Decline'.[23] His population graphs showed that the membership of Cathedral Road Synagogue had, between 1959 and 1972, dwindled from 402 to 297, while the Pen-y-lan membership, having risen between 1959 and 1964 from 320 to 355, had fallen again by 1971 to 323. He did not include in his figures the membership of the Reform Synagogue which was holding fairly steady, helped no doubt by the members who travelled into services by car from the outlying parts of town and the Vale of Glamorgan. And the number of unaffiliated secular Jews was, as always, incalculable. But however speculative these population figures may be the trend was unmistakable. It was confirmed by a further review in 1978 showing that the total membership of the Cardiff United Synagogue between 1958 and 1977 had fallen from 780 to 544.[24] Cardiff Jews were leaving for London, for the New World (notably Canada) and, a significant new factor since it included many young people and families with children, for Israel. Nor does it seem that in the 1980s the trend was reversed.

The history of the Jews of south Wales is one of rise and fall. But it is largely a rise of destitute immigrants and largely a fall of well-educated, middle-class families looking for business and professional openings. There has also been some immigration into Cardiff and Swansea of students, university teachers, hospital doctors and civil servants. So is south Wales Jewry not merely a diminished community, but a community in terminal decline? So long as openings remain for ambition and talent, I think not.

Notes to the Epilogue

1. M. Dennis, 'History of the Cardiff Jewish Community', Part VII. CAJEX, 4 No.2 (June 1954), 46.
2. M. Dennis, 'History of the Cardiff Jewish Community', Part XXX no.3, CAJEX, 30 No.4 (September 1980), 32. The Minute Book was presumably lost in the flood with the others in 1981.
3. Ibid.
4. CAJEX, 5 No.1 (March 1955), 51.
5. CAJEX, 3 No.1 (January 1953), 4.
6. Ibid., 5 No.1 (March 1955), 56.
7. M. Dennis, 'History of the Cardiff Jewish Community, Part XVI; A Community in Decline', CAJEX, 22 No.1 (March 1972), 31–5.
8. Ibid., 35.
9. CAJEX, 24 No.3 (September 1974), 9.
10. Michael Leigh, 'Reform in England 1840–1933', in Dow Marmur (ed.), *Reform Judaism* (London, Reform Synagogues of Great Britain, 1973), 23 et seq.
11. Ibid., 36.
12. There may have been exceptions. Basil Henriques' synagogue, in his St George's Settlement in the East End of London, was Reform.
13. Michael Leigh, ibid., 42–4.
14. A.S. Liss, 'A Short History of Reform Judaism in South Wales, 1949–70.' (Thesis for the University of Wales relating to the Certificate of Education, March 1977) 20.
15. Ibid., 60.
16. Ibid., 27.
17. Ibid., 94.
18. Census figures, from Brinley Thomas, 'Growth of Population', in J.F. Rees (ed.), *The Cardiff Region: A Survey* (Cardiff, University of Wales Press, 1960) Chap.VII, 115.
19. Charles Jones, 'Merthyr', CAJEX, 34 No.3 (September 1984), 27.
20. H.M. Jaffa, 'The Small Communities' Seminar', CAJEX, 24 No.4 (December 1974), 29.
21. Lady Sherman's toast to the United Synagogue at the festivities for the opening of Pen-y-lan Synagogue, January 1955. CAJEX, 5 No.1 (March 1955), 51.
22. Nay Joseph, 'New Tredegar', CAJEX, 25 No.1 (March 1975), 31.
23. CAJEX, 22 No.1 (March 1972), 34.
24. Ibid., 28 No.1 (April 1978), 16.

Jewish Festivals

Sabbath	Day of Rest. Seventh day of the week, from sundown on Friday to sundown on Saturday.
Rosh Chodesh	New Moon.
Rosh Hashanah	Jewish New Year in the autumn. Commences the 10 days of awe which culminate in
Yom Kippur	The Day of Atonement. The most solemn day in the Jewish calendar.
Sukkot	Feast of Tabernacles. A week-long harvest festival, after *Yom Kippur*.
Simchat Torah	Rejoicing of the Torah. The day following the end of *Sukkot*. Marks the end of the year's reading of the Torah and the commencement of the annual cycle of reading beginning with the Book of Genesis. Two men are honoured with these readings, the *Chatan Torah* and the *Chatan Bereshit*, respectively the bridegroom of the Torah and the bridegroom of the Genesis.
Chanucah	Dedication. An eight-day celebration in midwinter which marks the re-consecration of the Temple after its desecration by the Greeks in 175 BCE. Candles are lit on successive evenings.
Purim	Marks the deliverance of Jews from the threat of extermination in Persia about twenty-five centuries ago. The main details are found in the Book of Esther.
Pesach	Passover. The spring festival. Celebrates the

	exodus of the Hebrew slaves from Egypt.
Shavuot	Feast of Weeks. Seven weeks after Pesach. Commemorates the receipt of the Ten Commandments on Mount Sinai.
Tish B'Av	The 9th day of the month of Av. A fast day of mourning which commemorates the destruction of both the first and second temples.

Glossary of Hebrew Words

Achei Brit	'Brothers of the Covenant'. A Jewish mutual aid and insurance society.
Ashkenazi	Jew from central or eastern Europe.
Baltifila	Reader of the Law in a synagogue.
Baltekea	Blower of the ram's horn or *shofar*.
Barmitzvah/Bar Mitzva	Religious ceremony for coming of age of boys at thirteen.
Beit Hamedrash/Beth Hamedrash	House of Study. Often used for a small synagogue.
bima	Platform in the synagogue where prayers are conducted, usually in front of the Ark or cupboard where the scrolls of the Law are kept.
Chatan Bereshit	'Bridegroom of the beginning'. The congregant who is honoured to recommence the annual cycle of the reading of the Jewish Bible which begins with the Book of Genesis. He is paired with the *Chatan Torah*.
Chatan Torah	'Bridegroom of the Law'. He concludes the annual cycle of the reading on the festival of Simchat Torah or Rejoicing of the Law.
chazan	cantor or prayer leader.
cheder	religion school.
chevra kadisha	'sacred society' or burial society.
Chovevei Zion	Society of the Lovers of Zion which preceded Herzl's political Zionism.

chupah	wedding canopy.
Dorshei Zion	'Demanders of Zion'. Universal Zionist Society.
diaspora	totality of Jews scattered around the world.
Haham	'The sage'. Religious leader of the British Sephardim.
Hazkarat Neshamot	memorial prayer for deceased souls.
ketubah	marriage contract.
kiddush cup	cup for drinking wine on sabbath and festivals.
matzos	unleavened biscuits eaten especially at Passover.
mikvah	ritual bath.
minyan	ten adult males required for a formal Jewish service.
mohel	qualified circumcisor.
sefer torah	scroll of the Law.
sepharim	'books'. Scrolls of the Law.
Sephardi	Jew from Spain, Portugal, Italy, the Middle East or the Orient.
shabbat	sabbath; from sundown on Friday to sundown on Saturday.
shammas	beadle.
shechita	ritual slaughter.
shochet	ritual slaughterer.
'schnorrer'	Yiddish for itinerant pauper or beggar.
Sidra	Weekly portion of the Pentateuch read on the sabbath and festivals, to which is linked the Haphtorah, the reading from the Prophets.
shul	synagogue.
stetl	small Jewish town in Poland or Russia.
semicha	ordination of a rabbi.
Talmud	corpus of rabbinical writings commentating on the Torah.
Torah	the first five books of the Bible; but often used to indicate the whole corpus of Jewish religious and moral teaching.
tsedaka	justice, realized as charity.

yeshiva	religious seminary.
Yiddishkeit	Yiddish expression meaning Jewishness; specifically observance of Jewish custom.

Select Bibliography

I

Printed Books

J. Buckman, *Immigration and the Class Struggle: The Jewish Immigrant in Leeds 1880–1914* (Manchester University Press, 1983)

Marion Berghahn, *Continental Britons: German Jewish Refugees in England: The Ambiguities of Assimilation* (London, Macmillan, 1984)

S.A. Cohen, *English Zionists and British Jews* (Princeton University Press, 1982)

M.J. Daunton, *Coal Metropolis in Cardiff 1870–1914* (Leicester University Press, 1977)

S.R. Dennison, *The Location of Industry in the Depressed Areas* (London, Oxford University Press, 1939)

L.P. Gartner, *The Jewish Immigrant in England 1810–1914* (London, George Allen and Unwin, 1960)

P. Goodman, *Zionism in England 1899–1949* (London, Zionist Federation of Great Britain and Ireland, 1949)

J. Hardaker, *A Brief History of Pawnbroking* (London, Jackson Ruston and Keeson, 1892)

Colin Holmes (ed.), *Immigrants and Minorities in British Society* (London, George Allen and Unwin, 1978)

——, *John Bull's Island: Immigration and British Society 1871–1971* (London, Macmillan Education, 1988)

Kenneth Hudson, *Pawnbroking: An Aspect of British Social History* (London, Bodley Head, 1982)

A.M. Hyamson, *Jews' College, London, 1855–1955* (London, Jews' College, 1955)

Zoe Josephs (ed.), *Birmingham Jewry*, Vols. I and II (The Birmingham History Research Group, 1980)

Ernest Krausz, *Leeds Jewry: Its History and Structure* (London, Jewish Historical Society of England, 1964)

Arnold Levy, *History of the Sunderland Jewish Community* (London, McDonald, 1956)

Bernard Lewis, *Semites and Anti-Semites* (London, Weidenfeld and Nicolson, 1986)
V.D. Lipman, *A Social History of the Jews in England 1850–1950* (London, Watts and Co., 1954)
V.D. Lipman (ed.), *Three Centuries of Anglo-Jewish History* (London, Jewish Historical Society of England, 1961)
Dow Marmur (ed.), *Reform Judaism* (London, R.S.G.B., 1973)
P.R. Mendes Flohr and J. Reinharz, *The Jew in the Modern World* (Oxford University Press, 1980)
Harold Pollins, *An Economic History of the Jews in England* (Littman Library, Associated Presses, 1982)
Evan Powell, *A History of Tredegar* (Newport, South Wales Argus Ltd., 1884, revised 1902)
William Rees, *Cardiff, A History of the City* (Corporation of the City of Cardiff, 2nd edn, 1969)
Cecil Roth, *A History of the Jews in England* (Oxford, Clarendon Press, 1941)
——, *The Rise of Provincial Jewry* (London, Jewish Monthly, 1950)
N.H. Saunders, *Swansea Hebrew Congregation, 1730–1980* (250th Anniversary Volume, 1980)
Austin Steven, *The Dispossessed: German Refugees in Britain* (London, Barrie and Jenkins, 1975)
Melanie Tebbutt, *Making Ends Meet: Pawnbroking and Working Class Credit* (London, Methuen, 1983)
Bill Williams, *The Making of Manchester Jewry* (Manchester University Press, 1976)

II

Articles

Geoffrey Alderman, 'The Anti-Jewish Riots of August 1911 in South Wales', *Welsh History Review*, 6 (1972–3), 190–200
——, 'Into the Vortex: South Wales Jewry before 1914', *Report of the Jewish Historical Society of England, Conference on Provincial Jewry in Victorian England* (6 July 1975)
——, 'The Jew as Scapegoat? The Settlement and Reception of the Jews of South Wales before 1914', *Transactions of the Jewish Historical Society of England*, XXVI (1974–8), 62–70
M. Barclay, '"The Slaves of the Lamp" — The Aberdare Miners' Strike 1910', *Llafur*, 2–3 (1978), 24–42
S.A. Cohen, 'The Reception of Political Zionism in England: Patterns of Alignment among the Clergy and Rabbinate, 1895–1904', *Jewish Journal of Sociology*, XVI (1974), 171–85
Maurice Dennis, 'History of the Cardiff Jewish Community', CAJEX Parts I–XX (1954–80)

Joanna Cayford, 'In Search of John Chinaman: Press Representations of the Chinese in Cardiff 1906–1911', *Llafur*, 5 No.4 (1991), 37–50
Neil Evans, 'The South Wales Race Riots of 1919', *Llafur*, 3 No.1 (1980), 5–18
——, 'Immigrants and Minorities in Wales, 1840–1940: A Comparative Perspective', *Llafur*, 5 No.5 (1991), 5–26
L.P. Gartner, 'A Quarter Century of Anglo-Jewish Historiography', *Jewish Social Studies*, XLVIII No.2 (1986), 105–26
——, 'Urban History and the Pattern of Provincial Jewish Settlement in Victorian England', *Jewish Journal of Sociology*, XXIII No.1 (1981), 37–55
M. Gouldston, 'The Status of the Anglo-Jewish Rabbinate 1840–1914', *Jewish Journal of Sociology*, X (1965), 55–82
Colin Holmes, 'The Tredegar Riots of 1911: Anti-Jewish Disturbances in South Wales', *Welsh History Review*, 11 (1982–3), 214–25
Paul O'Leary, 'Anti-Irish Riots in Wales, 1826–1882', *Llafur* 5 No.4 (1991), 27–36
David Smith, 'Tonypandy 1910: Definitions of Community', *Past and Present*, 87 (May 1980), 162–85
Brinley Thomas, 'The Growth of Population', in J.F. Rees (ed.), *The Cardiff Region*, Ch. VII (University of Wales Press, 1960), 111–17
——, 'The Migration of Labour into the Glamorganshire Coalfield (1861–1911)'. In W.E. Minchinton (ed.), *Industrial South Wales 1750–1914* (London, Cass, 1969), 37–56
A.M. Weiner, 'Tredegar Riots', CAJEX, 26 No.1 (April 1976), 17–31

III

Unpublished Theses

Albert Colin Hughes, 'The Italian Community in South Wales, 1870–1943', (University of Wales MA thesis 1988)
R.G. Lewis, 'The Swansea Jewish Community: A Study in Growth and Development', (University of London undergraduate dissertation for the Dept. of Geography 1967)
Alan S. Liss, 'A Short History of Reform Judaism in South Wales, 1949–70', (University of Wales thesis relating to the Certificate of Education, 1977)
Herbert Loebl, 'Government Financed Factories and the Establishment of Industries by Refugees in the Special Areas of the North, 1937–1961', (University of Durham M.Phil. thesis 1978)
Freda Maxfield, 'The Jewish Pedlar in Nineteenth Century Britain', (Keele University MA course paper in Victorian Studies, 1983)
Paul Brendan O'Leary, 'Immigration and Integration: A Study of the Irish in Wales', (University of Wales Ph.D. thesis 1989)

A.M. Williams, 'Social Change and Residential Differentiation: A Case Study of Nineteenth Century Cardiff', (University of London Ph.D. thesis, L.S.E. 1976)

IV

Sources, Printed and MS

Trade and Street Directories for Cardiff and south Wales
Census Reports for England and Wales, 1811–81
Census of England and Wales, Preliminary Report 1911
The Jewish Chronicle 1841–
The Jewish World
CAJEX (The Journal of the Cardiff Association of Jewish Ex-Servicemen) 1954–91
Alfred Einstein (ed.), *The South Wales Jewish Review*, 1904
The Jewish Year Books
Western Mail
Cardiff and Merthyr Guardian
Cardiff Times
South Wales Argus
The Freeman
The Nonconformist
Cardiff Hebrew Congregation Marriage Register
Cardiff Hebrew Congregation Burial Register 1909–1914
Merthyr Congregation Minute Book 1918–34
Merthyr Burial Register
Tredegar Marriage Register
Swansea Hebrew Congregation Minute Book 1895–1919
Swansea Hebrew Congregation Letters Book 1902–4
Swansea Hebrew Congregation Rule Book 1892
Calendar of Prisoners in Cardiff and Swansea Gaols 1861–1908, Glamorgan County Record Office, Cardiff
Cardiff Quarter Sessions Records 1890–1914, Glamorgan County Record Office, Cardiff
Monmouth Quarter Sessions Records, Gwent County Record Office, Cwmbran
Cardiff Petty Sessions Records, Glamorgan County Record Office
Oxford Assize Circuit (Monmouth Assizes) Minute Books, Public Record Office, Chancery Lane
Rate Books, parishes of St Mary and St John and Butetown, Cardiff City Hall
Letters to Dr Gaster 28 Oct. 1900, 5 May 1905, Dec. 1906; and letters to Revd Fyne 8 Nov. 1900, 8 May 1905, 30 Dec. 1906, in the Gaster Papers, Jewish Studies Library, University College London

'Zionism', a lecture delivered at the Public Library, Swansea, on Saturday, 9 December 1906 by Revd Simon Fyne
Fred Hopkins, 'The Riots in Tredegar in 1911'. Unpublished narrative
Tredegar Riot Claims. (CC9 and A350 R B1) Gwent County Record Office
Report of the Royal Commission on Alien Immigration, 1903, HMSO
Commission for Special Areas, England and Wales, 3rd Report, 1936, HMSO
Records of the Welsh Development Agency. Treforest Industrial Estate. Report on the South Wales Trading Estate — Sir Alexander Gibb & Partners June 1936. Copy in Pontypridd Public Library

Index

Abelson, Revd J. 25, 29, 31–2
Aberaman 53
Aberavon 99
Aberdare 47, 48, 49, 50, 53, 215
Abraham(s), Joseph 79, 82
Abrahams, Charles 34
Abrahams, Samuel 34
Abrahamson family 27
Abrahamson, Charles 21, 36
Abrahamson, Joe 38
Abrahamson, Joshua 21
Abrahamson, Louis 21, 37
Abrahamson, Rebecca 21
Achei Brit 39
Adler, Dr Hermann 24, 26, 50, 86, 92, 97, 101, 105, 106
Adler, Dr Nathan Marcus 56, 144
Aero Zip 196
Alderman, Dr G. 40, 152, 172–3
'Anti-Jewish Riots of August 1911 in South Wales, The' 48
Alexander II, Czar 2, 48
Alexandra Dock (Cardiff) 12
Aliens Immigration Act (1905) 4, 34, 63, 125, 151, 178, 179, 182
Allen, Mr (solicitor) 137, 138
Alliance Universelle 36
Angel, C., & Co. 18
Angel, Menasseh 18
Anglo-Jewish Association 39, 118
anti-Semitism 2, 7, 107
in Cardiff 39–40
see also riots: Tredegar (1911)
Arthur, Mrs Alice 133
Ash, Nathan 77
Ashkenazi Jews 1, 208
Asquith, Herbert 154

Atlas Furnishing Co. 17, 19

Baddiel family 102
Bakalov, Jacob 77
Baptist Association 172
Barnett, Braham 18
Barnett, Ernest 113
Barnett, Joseph 56
Barnett, Louis (landlord and pawnbroker) 14, 21, 23, 26, 82, 157
Barnett, Montague 81
Barnett, Solomon 21
Barry Dock 12
Barton, Jane (pseud. Esther Lyons) 134
Basle Programme 37
Beatus, J. and Wilnack 194
Beaumarsh 27
Beaver, Hugh 185
Benevolent Society (Swansea) 85, 94, 95
Berghahn, Marion 178
Bernstein (Cardiff landlord) 14
Bernstein Mr (Tredegar) 171
Bernstein, Mrs (Abertillery) 7
Bernstein, William 77
Beth Hamedrash (Swansea) 85, 103–4, 108, 118
Bevis Marks Synagogue (London) 1, 210
Blackburn, Mr Justice 135, 136, 141, 142
Blagdon, Miss *see* Thomas, Mrs Laura Emily Ann
Blagdon, Mrs 133, 140
Blaiberg, S. 157
Blaiberg, Solomon 14, 21, 30
Blaiberg family 14
Blatchford 159
Bloom, Revd Eli 58
Blossom Ltd. 198

Board of Deputies of British Jews 144
Bogod, Joseph 32, 77
Bomash, J.S. 27
Bomash, L. 27
Booth, General 123
BOAC 195
Bosanquet, Victor 161, 163, 165
Briggs, Bryant 80
British Home Stores 194
British Medical Association 181
Brodie, Israel 208
Brodie family 171
Brukewich family 14, 18
Bryant, William 77
Brynmawr 7, 37, 48, 55, 64, 161, 215
Burial Acts 92
Bute, Marquis of 13, 19, 29, 32, 39, 208
   Second 12
   Third 39
Bute West Dock (Cardiff) 12

Caminetsky, H. 25, 31, 32
Cardiff 3
   crime in 76
   docks 12–13
   Irish in 4
   Jews in 6, 9–41
   population 11, 12, 14–15, 48–9
   riots 5, 7, 40, 76, 155–7
   synagogues 22–33, 107, 205–7, 209-12, 214
Cardiff and Merthyr Guardian 131, 136, 142, 145
Cardiff Dorshei Zion Association 37
Cardiff Dry Dock Company 78
Cardiff Jewish Cycling Club 39
Cardiff Jewish Literary and Musical Institute 35
Cardiff Quarter Sessions 70–1, 75, 77
Cardiff Reform Synagogue 33, 209, 211–14, 216
Cardiff Times 146, 154, 167
Cardiff United Synagogue 32–3, 208, 209, 211, 212, 214, 216
Carver, Sarah (Mrs Sarah Jones) 132, 133, 134, 140
Cathedral Road Synagogue (Cardiff) 27, 30–1, 32–3, 35, 36, 118, 119, 207, 208, 209, 213, 216
Catholicism 4, 5, 52
chain immigration 3
Channell, Baron 139, 140
charity

   in Cardiff 33–8
   in Swansea 94–5
   valleys 60–2
Chinese immigrants 5
   riots against (1911) 5, 7
Chitty, Mr 139
Chovevei Zion 28, 36, 37, 63
Church of England 11
Church Times 30
Churchill, Winston 153, 155, 161, 172
Clarion 159
coalmining 183
Cohen family 18
Cohen, Aaron 173
Cohen, David 173
Cohen, Revd J.H. 24
Cohen, Joseph 77, 164–5, 170
Cohen, Lazarus 23
Cohen, Menasseh 23
Cohen, Michael 164, 173
Cohen, J.F., & Co. 18
Coleman, William 79
Compact Cases 197
Compagnie Maritime Boulonnaise 18
Cory & Co. 18
Cory family 19
Costa, John da 76
crime 69–82
Cromwell, Oliver 1
Crouch, H.B. (goldsmiths) 82

Daily Express 178, 182
Daily Mail 178, 182
Daily News 167
Dangerfield, George: *Strange Death of Liberal England, The* 172
Davidson, I. 167, 173
Davies, E.H. 162
Davies, Mrs Marie 171, 172
Davies family 19
Deggotts, Asher 88, 89, 97
Deggotts family 89
Dennis, Maurice 15, 23, 107, 207, 208, 209, 216
Dennison, S.R.: *Location of Industry in the Depressed Areas, The* 196
Diamond, Thomas, & Co. 18
Dickens, Charles: *Oliver Twist* 69
Digicon Electronics 197
Disraeli, Benjamin 7
Dixon, Arthur L. 164
Doron, E. 181
Dorshei Zion 36, 37–8

Index

Doyle, Katherine 131

East Bute Dock (Cardiff) 12
East Terrace Synagogue (Cardiff) 23–4, 25, 26, 29, 30, 40
Ebbw Vale 50, 215
Ecclesiastical Board 144
Edwards Place Synagogue (Cardiff) 26–7, 32, 108, 207, 208
Einstein, Alfred 18, 19, 32, 34
Einstein, Samuel 18, 36
Einstein, Theodore 18
Einstein family 20
Einstein, S., & Co. 19
Einstein Holmes & Co., Messrs 18
Emanuel, Charles 91
Emanuel, Joel 139, 144
Emanuel, Josiah 49
English Zionist Federation 63, 118, 120
Englishe Shul *see* Cathedral Road Synagogue (Cardiff)

Fenians 5
Ferranti Group 197
Fillo, Revd Samuel 25
Fine, Israel 171
Fine, L.L. 173
Fine, Morris 81
Fine family 171
Fineburg, Revd H. 98
Finkelbach, Myer 94
Firth Cleveland 195
Fligelstone, J. 34
Fligelstone, Louis 34
Fligelstone, M.L. 31
Follick, Coleman 82
Foreign Shul ('Furriners' Shul') *see* Edwards Place Synagogue (Cardiff)
Fosdike 40
Frame, Thomas H. 188, 189
Freedman, Abraham 21, 23, 90, 93, 98
Freedman, Hyman 76, 81
Freedman, Mr (Merthyr) 58
Freedman, Simon 78
Freeman, The 145
Freemasonry 39
Freeth, Colonel 161–2
Freydburg, Fanny 81
Friedman, Anna 14
Friedman, Solomon 14
Friendly Societies 39
Fyne, Revd Simon 50, 96, 99, 100, 107, 111–26

Gartner, Lloyd 178
Gaster, Revd Dr Moses 112, 119–20, 125
GEC 195
General Paper and Box Manufacturing Co. 194
George V, King 153
Gibb, Sir Alexander, and Partners 184–5
Giffard, Lord Justice Hardinge 139, 141, 147
Gittelshohn, Julian 53
Gladstone, William 147
Glamorgan Assizes and Quarter Sessions 69, 72, 74, 75
Glamorganshire Canal Basin 9
Glaser, Ben 196, 197
Gnome Photographic 198
Goat Street Synagogue (Swansea) 85–6, 104, 118
Gobineau 7
Goldberg, Barnett, 86, 88
Goldberg, Mrs Barnett 94, 104
Goldberg, Hyam 19, 85, 88, 89, 91, 92, 94, 96, 99, 100, 105, 106, 113
Goldberg, Simon 88–9
Goldberg family 104, 126
Goldman, Jean 76
Goldsmid, Colonel Albert Edward Williamson 27–8, 29, 30, 31, 34, 37, 39, 63, 119
Goldsmid, Sir Julian 31
Goodman, David 136
Goodman, H.L. 18
Goodman, Theodore 132
Goodman brothers 57
Goodman family 140
Gottlieb, Samuel 78
Gottwaltz, William 18
Grove, Mr 139
Graf, Rabbi Gerhard 212–14
Green, Janet 133
Griffiths, William 23
Gryham, Gerson 24
Gwent Local History 171

Halpern, M. 37
Halsbury, Lord 139
Hamburg, J. 25
Hamill, William 82
Hamilton, Benjamin 65
Hand in Hand Benevolent Society 34
Hardie, Keir 155
Harris, Ephraim 14, 23
Harris, Levi 50

Harris, Levi, jun. 50
Harris, Louis 62, 158
Harris, Solomon 47
Harris family 171
Hebrew 3
Heitzman, Albert 80
Herbert, Major 156
Herzl, Theodore 28, 63, 64
Hettich, Julius 82
Himmelstein, Benjamin 65
Hirsch, Baron de 28
Hirwaun 48
Hitler, Adolf 40, 177, 180, 182
Hollyer, J.E. 137, 139, 141
Hollyer, Mrs 134, 139, 140, 141, 142, 146
Holmes, Mr (Tyneside Industrial Development Board) 189
Home Rule 5
Homfrays 13
Hopkins, Fred 158, 159, 166, 170, 171, 172
Huet, Jean 78
Hughes, Hezekiah 77
Hunt, Mr (auctioneer) 170
Hyam, Mrs 104
Hyamson, Dr 169
Hyman, Henry 79
Hyman, Mr S. 62

immigration
 'chain' 3
 Chinese 5
 from Germany 33
 from Russia 2, 48
 into America 2
 into Britain 1–3, 177–91
 into Wales 2–7, 177–91
 Irish 4, 5, 12
 Italian 5–6
 volume of 177–8
Immigration Act (1905) *see* Aliens Immigration Act (1905)
Industrial Transference Board 183
Instone brothers 207
Instone family 19
International Arbitration Bureau 124
Irish 4, 5, 12
 in Cardiff 4, 5
 in London 4
 riots against (1848, 1882) 155–7
Irish famine 4, 12
iron industries 183
Isaac, John 49

Isaac, Kate 76
Israel, William David 77, 79
Israelstam, Revd 58–9
Italian immigration 5–6
ITT Creed 195

J.C.Gs. 7
Jacob (Cardiff landlord) 14
Jacob, Hier 18
Jacob, John 77
Jacobs, Barnett 30, 37, 157
Jacobs, Bertram 167–9, 173
Jacobs, Greenbone 81, 88
Jacobs, Hyam 80
Jacobs, Michael 88
Jacobs, Morris 78
Jacobs, Revd Nathan 24, 132
Jacobs, William 16
Jerevitch, Revd Harris 33, 40
Jewess Abduction Case (1867) 24, 40, 88, 131–47, 159
Jewish Board of Guardians 34, 118, 179
Jewish Chronicle 11, 23, 24, 28, 29, 31, 35, 38, 55, 57, 60, 117, 118, 119, 143, 144, 145, 146, 147, 160, 208
Jewish Colonization Association 61
Jewish Ladies' Benevolent Society 34
Jewish Lads' Brigade 28, 34, 39, 63
Jewish Literary and Debating Society (Cardiff) 36
Jewish Literary and Social Society (Cardiff) 36
Jewish Literary Society 107
Jewish National Fund 38
Jewish Territorial Organization 37
Jewish Workmen's Benefit Society 39
Jewish World 166, 167
Jewish Year Book 14, 64, 126
Jones, Brynmor 106
Jones, Charles 215
Joseph, Mr (Cardiff) 50
Joseph, A.H. 18
Joseph, Benjamin 50–1
Joseph, David 33
Joseph, Delissa 29
Joseph, J.W. 26
Joseph, Leo 37
Joseph, Leopold 26
Joseph, Morris 33
Joseph, Solomon 33

Kantorovich, Isaac 78
Kantorovich, Rachel 78

Index

Katz, Revd S. 32, 37
Kaye, Phillip 207
Keep, Mr 137
Keep, Mrs Ellen 134, 136, 138, 139, 140, 141, 142
Kelly's Directory (1895) 49
Kelly's Birmingham Directory 52
'Kinder Transports' 181
Kisseleff, Count 2
Koppel, K. 196
Kransky, Jacob 77
Kristallnacht 181

Ladino 3
Lamb, Charles Frederick 82
Landau, Revd J.H. 25, 35
language 3
Lazarone, Dr 136
Leiner & Sons 194
Leo Baeck Training Seminary 214
Letter and Questionnaire for Foreign Persons Desirous of Setting up Manufacture in this Country 189
Levine, Mr (Pen-y-graig) 101
Levinsohn, Benjamin 77
Levy, Abraham 88, 103, 104, 105
Levy, Henry 76
Levy, Moses 77
Levy, Rees Gershon 40
Levy, Thomas 39
Levy, Youtaff 60
Lewis, Arthur 197
Lewis, Leah 79
Lewis, M. 25
Lewis, Moses 78
Lionite Chemical and Asphalt Products 196
Lionite Specialities 196, 197
Lipman, V.D.: *Social History of the Jews in England (1850–1950) A* 178
Liss, Alan 211
Lissarman, J. 29
Llanelli 48, 216
  riots 160
Lloyd, D. 77
Lloyd, Harold 40
Lloyd, Price 77
Lloyd George, David 152
Loebl, Herbert 186–7, 198
London Carmen's Union 154
London Jews 1, 32, 48
London Jews' Hospital and Orphan Asylum 94
London Metal and Refining Company 196
London Society for Promoting Christianity among the Jews 144
Londonderry, Marquis of 186
Lowbury, Felix 196
Lubner, M. 98, 116
Lush, Justice 141
Lyons, A. 101
Lyons, Abraham 88
Lyons, Barnett 15, 88, 131, 132, 133, 134–9, 141–3, 144
Lyons, Mrs Barnett 132
Lyons, Dinah 133, 134, 140
Lyons, Esther 88, 131–47
Lyons, Henry 47
Lyons, Rachel 133
Lyons, Reuben (Esther's uncle) 137–8, 141
Lyons, Reuben (Esther's brother) 132, 133, 134, 137, 138
Lyons, Solomon 86, 88, 101
Lyons vs Thomas and Others 24, 40, 88, 131–47, 159
Lyons & Co. 170

Maccabees for Sport 39
MacDonald, Ramsay 183
Maclean, J.M., MP 29
Magrath, Arthur 197
Magrath Metal Finishing 197
Manchester Guardian 182
Marks & Co. (Watch and Nautical Instrument Maker) 11
Marks & Spencers 194
Marks, Anne 11
Marks, B.S. 30, 31
Marks, Barnett 12
Marks, Julia 17
Marks, Julian 17
Marks, Levi 11
Marks, Levi (son of Barnett) 12
Marks, Louise 17
Marks, M.L. 113
Marks, Mark 11, 17, 23
Marks, Mary Ann 12
Marks, Michael 11
Marks, Nelson 12
Marks, Nelson (watchmaker) 80
Marks, Samuel (dyer) 11, 12, 16
Marks, Samuel (publican) 16
Marks, Samuel (tobacconist) 78, 80
Marks, Solomon 11–12, 17, 23, 24

Marks family 18, 19, 20, 40, 142
Mattuck, Rabbi Israel 210, 212
Melcher, Abraham 27
Mellor, Justice 141
Merthyr District Jewish Literary and Social Society 62–3
Merthyr Tydfil 3, 48
  Jews in 47
  population 49
  riots (1831) 11
  synagogues 55, 56, 57, 59, 60, 62, 215
Merthyr Guardian 47
Michael, Mr 139
Minski, Revd Louis 25, 27
Miron, Mrs 98
Miron, Revd Israel 91, 98, 112, 115–16
Mocatta, F.D. 30, 31
Moira Place Synagogue 207
Monmouth Quarter Sessions and Assizes 72, 73, 74, 75
Monmouthshire Welsh Baptist Association 159
Montefiore, Claude 210
Montefiore, J.M. 144
Montefiore, Sir Moses 2, 35, 52, 144, 146, 210
Morgan, Sir Charles 155
Mortara, Edgar 146
Mortara case 146
Municipal Corporations Act (1835) 11
Myers, Lennie 7
Myers, Revd J.C. 25

Naturalization Society 34
Neft, Mr 97
New Tredegar 50, 216
New West End Reform Synagogue (London) 210
Newland, Davies and Hunt (auctioneers) 170
News Chronicle 182
Nonconformist, The 145
Norris and Allen, Messrs 137
North East Trading Estate Company 185

O.P. Chocolates 198
occupations, Jewish 6
  in Cardiff 15–22
  in valleys 51–2, 54–5
  see also pawnbroking
Old Congregation *see* Cathedral Road Synagogue (Cardiff)
Oppenheim, Mr (counsel) 135, 136

Osborne Case (1908) 152
Owen's *Cardiff Directory* 18
Owens, T.D. 88

Pale of Settlement 2, 178
Parker, Captain 156
Parnell, Charles Stuart 156
Pawnbrokers' Act (1872) 53, 81
pawnbroking
  in Cardiff 6, 19–22
  crime and 81–2
  in valleys 52–5
Pen-y-lan Synagogue 208–9
  see also Cardiff United Synagogue
Penberthy family 171
Perryman, Mary 81
Phillips (manufacturers) 197
Phillips, David 76
Phillips, G.A. 82
Phillips, Henry 77
Phillips, Jehiel 23
Phoenix Park murders 5
Pigot's *Trade Directory* 47
Pius IX, Pope 146
Plaskowsky, Revd Elias 27, 36
Polish Jews 62
Pollins, Harold: *Economic History of the Jews in England* 51
Pontypool 47, 184
Pontypridd 47, 48, 159, 184, 215
  synagogue 56, 57, 215
Poor Jews' Temporary Shelter 51, 179
Poor Law 95
population, Jewish
  in Cardiff 14–15
  declining 214–17
Powell, Evan 155
Prince of Wales Road Minyan 101–3, 108
Provincial Ministers' Fund 58

Rabbinowitz, Revd 103
rack renting 163, 173
Raffalovich, Revd I. 60
Rapport family 18
Redford, Mr (New Theatre proprietor) 34
Reform Judaism 209–14
Reinhart, Rabbi Harold 210, 211
Report on the South Wales Trading Estate 184
Rice, Elizabeth 76
Riot Act 162
riots
  Cardiff 76
    anti-Chinese (1911) 5, 7

anti-coloured seamen (1919) 7, 40
anti-Irish (1848, 1882) 155-7
Jew Bill (1753) 151
Llanelli (1911) 160
London (1753) 1
Merthyr (1831) 11
Tonypandy 153-4
Tredegar anti-Jewish (1911) 7, 40, 55, 65, 106, 147, 151-74, 215
Rittenberg, Revd B.J. 26
Roath Dock (Cardiff) 12
Rosenbaum, Gershwin 159
Rosenbaum, Lionel 158
Rosenberg, J.D. 100
Rosenthal, Hyman 78
Roskin, Captain H.H. 207, 208
Roskin, Leo 65
Rothschild, Baron Lionel de 56-7
Rothschild, Lord 169, 173
Rothschild family 56
Royal Commission on Alien Immigration (1902) 151, 179, 182
Royal Commission on Labour (1892) 17
Rubenstein, Revd L. 25
Rubinstein, S. 105
Russell, Revd A.G. 30
Russian Jewry 2, 122, 124
Russian pogroms 2, 14, 34, 38, 106, 180
Rutter, David 101, 103, 104

Sampson Samuel and Emanuel, Messrs 135, 137
Samuel, Albert 19
Samuel, Henry 19
Samuel, Herbert 19
Samuel, Isaac 17, 19, 25, 26, 28, 30, 31, 32, 35-6, 37, 39, 40
Samuel, Mrs Isaac 36
Samuel, Louis 19, 30, 34
Samuel, Moses 19
Samuel, Sampson 137
Samuel, Stuart 167
Samuel, Wilfred 19
Samuel brothers 26, 31, 39
Samuel family 19
Samuel & Co. (clothiers) 17
Samuel, I., & Co. Ltd. 19
Samuels, Revd H.J. *see* Sandheim, Revd H.J.
Sandheim, Revd H.J. 90, 93, 96-7, 98, 107
Sandler, B. 115, 116
Saunders, Dr 85, 98

Schick (manufacturers) 197
schools, Jewish
  Cardiff 24-5, 32
  Swansea 92-4, 95-6
Schwartz, Dr 136, 138, 141, 144, 146
Selig (sailmaker) 14
Seline, David 88, 104, 105
Seline, Mrs 104
Sephardi Jews 1
Shatz, B. 37
Shepherd, A. 101, 113
Sherman, Lady 208, 215
Shibko, Abraham 81, 82
Shibko family 18
Sidle, Simon 170
Simon Goldberg fund 93
Simpson, Sir John Hope 188
Singer, Henry 79
Skrek, Julius 208
Sleeman, Mrs 134, 140, 142
Sleeman, Revd 136
Slivensky, Louis 77
Smith, David 153, 158
Snipper, Louis 98, 104
Society for Propagating the Gospel among the Jews 144
Solomon, David 78
Solomon, Mr (*shammas*) 93
Solomon, Mrs (Merthyr) 62
Solomons, Samuel 18
South Wales Argus 160, 165, 167, 168
South Wales Daily Post 106, 120
South Wales Jewish Review 34, 39, 50, 61, 63, 64
South Wales Zionist Federation 64
Special Areas Acts 183
Spectator 188
Spiro, Rabbi Abraham 40
Standard 145, 147
Standard Telephone and Cable 195
steel industries 183
Stott, Mr 136
strikes 152-3, 154-5, 160
  mining (1899) 31, 38
Stuart, Colonel 147
Sun Alliance 52
Sunbeam 197
Sunday Trading Acts 17
Swansea 3
  Jews 23, 85-108
  synagogues 85-108, 118
Symonds, W.T. 19
synagogues
  Cardiff 22-33, 107, 207-14

closure of 215–17
Merthyr 55, 56, 57, 59, 60, 62, 215
Swansea (1895–1914) 85–108, 118, 215
Tredegar 56, 57, 215
valleys 55–60, 215

Taff Vale railway 12
Taff Vale Railway Company 77
Tallis, A.S. 162, 163
Tanchan, Jacob 78, 79, 80
Tanchan, Nathan 78, 79, 80
Thomas, Brinley 14
Thomas, Ebenezer 172
Thomas, Mrs Laura Emily Ann 131, 134–6, 139–40, 143, 145–6
Thomas, Revd Nathaniel 131, 133, 134, 136, 137, 142, 143, 145–7
Thomas and Evans (Porth) 77, 165
Times, The 125, 147
Tonypandy Riots 153–4
Tredegar, Lord 13, 29, 159
Tredegar 47, 48, 50, 63
  Riots (1911) 7, 40, 55, 65, 106, 147, 151–74, 215
  synagogue 56, 57, 215
Tredegar and New Tredegar Zionist Society 64
Tredegar Men's Literary and Library Society 158
Treforest Silk Printers 194
Treforest Trading Estate (Industrial Estate) 184, 186, 187, 191–8, 202–5
Troed-y-rhiw 48
Truman, Jane 47
Tumpowsky, Isaac 27, 36

Uganda Proposal 120
unemployment 182
Union of Jewish Literary Societies 63

Van der Zyl, Rabbi 212
Vicrem Engineering 197

Wasserzug, Revd D. 25, 29
Weichert (landlord) 14
Weichert, William 17, 18
Weiner, Abraham M. 158, 159, 165
Western Mail 30, 40, 53, 71, 78, 155–6, 157, 167
Widows' Institution 94
Wiggins Teape 195
Williams, Benjamin 70
Windsor, Lord 29
Windsor Place Synagogue (Cardiff) 207–8
Winstone, Councillor Jim 170
Wolf, Lucien 37
Wolfers, Revd Philip 32, 37, 96
Wolfson, S. 158
Woolfe, Raymond 131
Wood, Elizabeth (pseud, Sarah Carver) 134
Workmen's Benefit Society 34, 36
Workmen's Literary Institute 158
Worrall's *Cardiff Directory* 16

Yiddish 3
Young Men's Jewish Association 34, 39
Ystalyfera 99

Zangwill, Israel 37, 159
Zionism 6
  in Cardiff 36–8
  in Swansea 118–25
  in valleys 63–4
Zussen, Jan Dirk 20